Love and Marriage

Love and Marriage

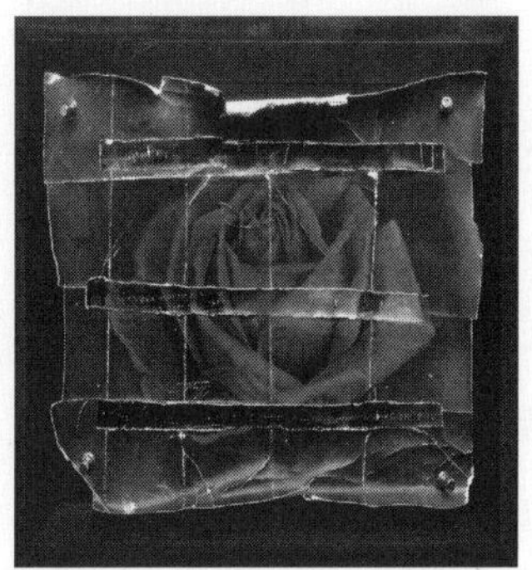

The Great Books Foundation
A nonprofit educational organization

ISBN 1-880323-75-3

First Printing
9 8 7 6 5 4 3 2 1 0

Published and distributed by

 **The Great Books Foundation**
A nonprofit educational organization

35 East Wacker Drive, Suite 2300
Chicago, IL 60601-2298

CONTENTS

PREFACE

"So that's what Kierkegaard meant by cultivating the art of remembering and forgetting!" "Is there an element of deception in every happy marriage?" "Is the search for truth an expression of our erotic natures?"

Anyone who has been in a book discussion group has experienced the joy of new insight. Sometimes an idea or question occurs to us during the group meeting. Often, it is afterward—sometimes much later—that an idea we had overlooked unexpectedly strikes us with new force. A good group becomes a community of minds. We share perspectives, questions, insights, and surprises. Our fellow readers challenge and broaden our thinking as we probe deeply into characters and ideas. They help us resolve questions, and raise new ones, in a creative process that connects literature with life.

It is this kind of experience that makes book discussion groups worthwhile, and that the Great Books Foundation fosters for thousands of readers around the world.

The Great Books Foundation is a pioneer of book discussion groups that bring together dedicated readers who wish to continue to learn throughout their lives. The literature anthologies published by the Foundation have been the focus of many enlightening discussions among people of all educational backgrounds and walks of life. And the *shared inquiry* method practiced by Great Books groups has proven to be a powerful approach to literature that solves many practical concerns of new discussion groups: How can we maintain a flow of ideas? What kinds of questions should we discuss? How can we keep the discussion focused on the reading so that we use our time together to really get at the heart of a work—to learn from it and each other?

With the publication of its 50th Anniversary Series, the Great Books Foundation continues and expands upon its tradition of helping all readers engage in a meaningful exchange of ideas about outstanding works of literature.

About *Love and Marriage*

The reading selections in *Love and Marriage* have been chosen to stimulate lively shared inquiry discussions. This collection brings together works from around the world that speak to each other on a theme of universal human significance. In this volume you will find classic works by Plato and Kierkegaard; modern fiction by Nobel Prize winner Isaac Bashevis Singer, the Japanese author Yukio Mishima, and the lesser-known Czech expatriate Josef Škvorecký; and two traditional folktales that we have found generate enthusiastic discussions among adults. In addition to the prose selections, you will discuss a sonnet by Shakespeare alongside classics of beat and feminist poetry.

These are carefully crafted works that readers will interpret in different ways. They portray characters whose lives and motivations are complex, embody concepts that go beyond simple analysis, and raise many questions to inspire extended reflection.

As an aid to reading and discussion, open-ended *interpretive questions* are included with each selection in the volume, and also for the recommended novels *To the Lighthouse* by Virginia Woolf and *Lolita* by Vladimir Nabokov. A fundamental or *basic* interpretive question about the meaning of the selection is printed in boldface, followed by a list of related questions that will help you fully discuss the issue raised by the basic question. Passages for *textual analysis* that you may want to look at closely during discussion are suggested for each set of questions. Questions under the heading "For Further Reflection" can be used at the end of discussion to help your group consider the reading selection in a broader context.

About Shared Inquiry

The success of Great Books discussions depends not only on thought-provoking literature, but also on the *shared inquiry* method of discussion. A shared inquiry discussion begins with a basic interpretive question—a genuine question about the meaning of the selection that continues to be puzzling even after careful reading. As participants offer different possible answers to this question, the discussion leader or members of the group follow up on the ideas that are voiced, asking questions about how responses relate to the original question or to new ideas, and probing what specifically in the text prompted the response.

In shared inquiry discussion, readers think for themselves about the selection, and do not rely on critical or biographical sources outside the text for ideas about its meaning. Discussion remains focused on the text. Evidence for opinions is found in the selection. Because interpretive questions have no single "correct answer," participants are encouraged to entertain a range of ideas. The exchange of ideas is open and spontaneous, a common search for understanding that leads to closer, more illuminating reading.

Shared inquiry fosters a habit of critical questioning and thinking. It encourages patience in the face of complexity, and a respect for the opinions of others. As participants explore the work in depth, they try out ideas, reconsider simple answers, and synthesize interpretations. Over time, shared inquiry engenders a profound experience of intellectual intimacy as your group searches together for meaning in literature.

Improving Your Discussions

The selections in *Love and Marriage* will support seven meetings of your discussion group, with each prose selection and the poetry group being the focus of a single meeting. Discussions usually last about two hours, and are guided by a member of the group who acts as leader. Since the leader has no special knowledge or qualification beyond a genuine curiosity about the text, any member of the group may lead discussion. The leader carefully prepares the interpretive questions that he or she wants to explore with the group, and is primarily responsible for continuing the process of questioning that maintains the flow of ideas.

To ensure a successful discussion, we encourage you to make it a policy to read the selection twice. A first reading will familiarize you with the plot and ideas of a selection; on a second reading you will read more reflectively and discover many aspects of the work that deepen your thinking about it. Allowing a few days to pass between your readings will also help you approach a second reading with deeper insight.

Read the selection actively. Make marginal comments that you might want to refer to in discussion. While our interpretive questions can help you think about different aspects of the work, jotting down your own questions as you read is the best way to engage with the selection and bring a wealth of ideas and meaningful questions to discussion.

During discussion, expect a variety of answers to the basic question. Follow up carefully on these different ideas. Refer to and read from the text often—by way of explaining your answer, and to see if the rest of the group understands the author's words the same way you do. (You will often be surprised!) As your group looks closely at the text, many new ideas will arise.

While leaders in shared inquiry discussion strive to keep comments focused on the text and on the basic interpretive question the group is discussing, the entire group can share responsibility for politely refocusing comments that wander from the text into personal anecdotes or issues that begin to sidetrack discussion.

Remember that during shared inquiry discussion you are investigating differing perspectives on the reading, not social issues. Talk should be about characters in the story, not about participants' own lives. By maintaining this focus, each discussion will be new and interesting, with each participant bringing a different perspective to bear on the text. After the work has been explored thoroughly on its own terms, your thinking about important issues of the day or in your own life will be enhanced. We have found that it is best to formally set aside a time—perhaps the last half-hour of discussion, or perhaps over coffee afterward—for members of the group to share personal experiences and opinions that go beyond a discussion of the selection.

Discussing the Poetry Selections

Many book groups shy away from the challenge of discussing poetry, but the shared inquiry method will enable you to make poetry a very satisfying part of your discussion group. Poetry, by its very nature, communicates ideas through suggestion, allusion, and resonance. Because meaning in poetry resides in the interaction between author and reader, and is brought to light through the pooling of different perspectives and readers' responses, poems are ideal for shared inquiry discussion.

We suggest that you discuss the four poems in *Love and Marriage* in turn, rather than all together as a group. The accompanying interpretive questions will help you focus on each poem individually, and the questions marked "For Further Reflection" will help you consider common and differing elements of the poems.

It is helpful to read each poem aloud before beginning discussion. Because poetry is usually more densely constructed than prose and highly selective in detail, it often lends itself to what we call *textual analysis*—looking closely at particular lines, words, and images as an entryway to discussing the whole work. Having readers share their different associations with a word or image can often help broaden interpretations.

Discussing the Novels

Of course, many novels come to mind that relate to the theme of love and marriage. We have recommended *To the Lighthouse* and *Lolita* as particularly enriching novels on this theme, and have provided interpretive questions that can be a significant aid to the reader. Even readers familiar with these novels will find a shared inquiry discussion of them a new and rewarding experience.

Most shared inquiry groups discuss a novel at a single discussion; some prefer to spread the discussion over more than one session, especially for longer novels. Since it is usually not realistic to expect participants to read a novel twice in full before discussion, we recommend that you at least reread parts of the novel that seemed especially important to you or that raised a number of questions in your mind. Our passages for textual analysis suggest parts of the novel where reading twice might be most valuable. You might even begin your discussion, after posing a basic question, by looking closely at one or two short passages to get people talking about central ideas and offering a variety of opinions that can be probed and expanded into a discussion of the whole work.

How the Great Books Foundation Can Help You

The Great Books Foundation can be a significant resource for you and your discussion group. Our staff conducts shared inquiry workshops throughout the country that will help you or your entire group conduct better discussions. Thousands of people—from elementary school teachers and college professors to those who just love books and ideas—have found our workshops to be an enjoyable experience that changes forever how they approach literature.

The Foundation publishes a variety of reading series that might interest you. We invite you to call us at 1-800-222-5870 or visit our Web site at http://www.greatbooks.org. We can help you start a book group, put you in touch with established Great Books groups in your area, or give you information about many special events—such as poetry weekends or week-long discussion institutes—sponsored by Great Books groups around the country.

Finally, we invite you to inquire about Junior Great Books for students in kindergarten through high school, to learn how you can help develop the next generation of book lovers and shared inquiry participants.

We hope you enjoy *Love and Marriage* and that it inaugurates many years of exciting discussions for your group. Great Books programs—for children as well as adults—are founded on the idea that readers discussing together can achieve insight and great pleasure from literature. We look forward, with you, to cultivating this idea through the next century.

Footnotes by the author are not bracketed; footnotes by the Great Books Foundation, an editor, or a translator are [bracketed].

The Spinoza of Market Street

Isaac Bashevis Singer

Isaac Bashevis Singer (1904–1991) is widely regarded as the greatest Yiddish writer of his time. Born in Poland, Singer emigrated to the United States in 1935, where he joined his older brother in New York City as a journalist for the Yiddish newspaper the *Jewish Daily Forward*. The descendant of rabbis on both sides of his family, Singer wrote of his fascination "both with my brother's rationalism and with my parents' mysticism." Singer was the author of numerous short stories and novels, as well as several highly acclaimed works for children. He won the Nobel Prize for literature in 1978.

1

DR. NAHUM FISCHELSON paced back and forth in his garret room in Market Street, Warsaw. Dr. Fischelson was a short, hunched man with a grayish beard, and was quite bald except for a few wisps of hair remaining at the nape of the neck. His nose was as crooked as a beak and his eyes were large, dark, and fluttering like those of some huge bird. It was a hot summer evening, but Dr. Fischelson wore a black coat which reached to his knees, and he had on a stiff collar and a bow tie. From the door he paced slowly to the dormer window set high in the slanting room and back again. One had to mount several steps to look out. A candle in a brass holder was burning on the table and a variety of insects buzzed around the flame. Now and again one of the creatures would fly too close to the fire and sear its wings, or one would ignite and glow on the wick for an instant. At such moments Dr. Fischelson grimaced. His wrinkled face would twitch and beneath his disheveled mustache he would bite his lips. Finally he took a handkerchief from his pocket and waved it at the insects.

"Away from there, fools and imbeciles," he scolded. "You won't get warm here; you'll only burn yourself."

The insects scattered but a second later returned and once more circled the trembling flame. Dr. Fischelson wiped the sweat from his wrinkled forehead and sighed, "Like men they desire nothing but the pleasure of the moment." On the table lay an open book written in Latin, and on its broad-margined pages were notes and comments printed in small letters by Dr. Fischelson. The book was Spinoza's *Ethics* and Dr. Fischelson had been studying it for the last thirty years. He knew every proposition, every proof, every corollary, every note by heart. When he wanted to find a particular passage, he generally opened to the place immediately without having to search for it. But, nevertheless, he continued to study the *Ethics* for hours every day with a magnifying glass in his bony hand, murmuring and nodding his head in agreement. The truth was that the more Dr. Fischelson studied, the more puzzling sentences, unclear passages, and cryptic remarks he found. Each sentence contained hints unfathomed by any of the students of Spinoza. Actually the philosopher had anticipated all of the criticisms of pure reason made by Kant and his followers. Dr. Fischelson was writing a commentary on the *Ethics*. He had drawers full of notes and drafts, but it didn't seem that he would ever be able to complete his work. The stomach ailment which had plagued him for years was growing worse from day to day. Now he would get pains in his stomach after only a few mouthfuls of oatmeal. "God in Heaven, it's difficult, very difficult," he would say to himself using the same intonation as had his father, the late Rabbi of Tishvitz. "It's very, very hard."

Dr. Fischelson was not afraid of dying. To begin with, he was no longer a young man. Secondly, it is stated in the fourth part of the *Ethics* that "a free man thinks of nothing less than of death and his wisdom is a meditation not of death, but of life." Thirdly, it is also said that "the human mind cannot be absolutely destroyed with the human body but there is some part of it that remains eternal." And yet Dr. Fischelson's ulcer (or perhaps it was a cancer) continued to bother him. His tongue was always coated. He belched frequently and emitted a different foul-smelling gas each time. He suffered from heartburn and cramps. At times he felt like vomiting and at other times he was hungry for garlic, onions, and fried foods. He had long ago discarded the medicines prescribed for him by the doctors and had sought his own remedies. He found it beneficial to take grated radish after meals and lie on his bed, belly down, with his head hanging over the side. But these home remedies offered only temporary relief. Some of the doctors he consulted insisted there was nothing the matter with him. "It's just nerves," they told him. "You could live to be a hundred."

But on this particular hot summer night, Dr. Fischelson felt his strength ebbing. His knees were shaky, his pulse weak. He sat down to read and his vision blurred. The letters on the page turned from green to gold. The lines became waved and jumped over each other, leaving white gaps as if the text had disappeared in some mysterious way. The heat was unbearable, flowing down directly from the tin roof; Dr. Fischelson felt he was inside of an oven. Several times he climbed the four steps to the window and thrust his head out into the cool of the evening breeze. He would remain in that position for so long his knees would become wobbly. "Oh it's a fine breeze," he would murmur, "really delightful," and he would recall that, according to Spinoza, morality and happiness were identical, and that the most moral deed a man could perform was to indulge in some pleasure which was not contrary to reason.

2

Dr. Fischelson, standing on the top step at the window and looking out, could see into two worlds. Above him were the heavens, thickly strewn with stars. Dr. Fischelson had never seriously studied astronomy but he could differentiate between the planets, those bodies which, like the earth, revolve around the sun, and the fixed stars, themselves distant suns, whose light reaches us a hundred or even a thousand years later. He recognized the constellations which mark the path of the earth in space and that nebulous sash, the Milky Way. Dr. Fischelson owned a small telescope he had bought in Switzerland where he had studied and he particularly enjoyed looking at the moon through it. He could clearly make out on the moon's surface the volcanoes bathed in sunlight and the dark, shadowy craters. He never wearied of gazing at these cracks and crevasses. To him they seemed both near and distant, both substantial and insubstantial. Now and then he would see a shooting star trace a wide arc across the sky and disappear, leaving a fiery trail behind it. Dr. Fischelson would know then that a meteorite had reached our atmosphere, and perhaps some unburned fragment of it had fallen into the ocean or had landed in the desert or perhaps even in some inhabited region. Slowly the stars which had appeared from behind Dr. Fischelson's roof rose until they were shining above the house across the street. Yes, when Dr. Fischelson looked up into the heavens, he became aware of that infinite extension which is, according to Spinoza, one of God's attributes. It comforted Dr. Fischelson to think that although he was only a weak, puny man, a changing mode of the absolutely infinite Substance, he was nevertheless a part of the cosmos, made of the same matter as the celestial bodies; to the extent that he was a part of the Godhead, he knew he could not be destroyed. In such moments, Dr. Fischelson experienced the *Amor Dei Intellectualis*[1] which is, according to the philosopher of Amsterdam, the highest perfection of the mind. Dr. Fischelson breathed deeply, lifted his head as high as his stiff collar permitted, and actually felt he was whirling in company with the earth, the sun, the stars of the Milky Way, and the infinite host of galaxies known only to infinite thought. His legs became light and weightless and he grasped the window frame with both hands as if afraid he would lose his footing and fly out into eternity.

1. [The intellectual love of God.]

When Dr. Fischelson tired of observing the sky, his glance dropped to Market Street below. He could see a long strip extending from Yanash's market to Iron Street with the gas lamps lining it merged into a string of fiery dots. Smoke was issuing from the chimneys on the black, tin roofs; the bakers were heating their ovens, and here and there sparks mingled with the black smoke. The street never looked so noisy and crowded as on a summer evening. Thieves, prostitutes, gamblers, and fences loafed in the square which looked from above like a pretzel covered with poppy seeds. The young men laughed coarsely and the girls shrieked. A peddler with a keg of lemonade on his back pierced the general din with his intermittent cries. A watermelon vendor shouted in a savage voice, and the long knife which he used for cutting the fruit dripped with the bloodlike juice. Now and again the street became even more agitated. Fire engines, their heavy wheels clanging, sped by; they were drawn by sturdy black horses which had to be tightly curbed to prevent them from running wild. Next came an ambulance, its siren screaming. Then some thugs had a fight among themselves and the police had to be called. A passerby was robbed and ran about shouting for help. Some wagons loaded with firewood sought to get through into the courtyards where the bakeries were located but the horses could not lift the wheels over the steep curbs and the drivers berated the animals and lashed them with their whips. Sparks rose from the clanging hoofs. It was now long after seven, which was the prescribed closing time for stores, but actually business had only begun. Customers were led in stealthily through back doors. The Russian policemen on the street, having been paid off, noticed nothing of this. Merchants continued to hawk their wares, each seeking to outshout the others.

"Gold, gold, gold," a woman who dealt in rotten oranges shrieked.

"Sugar, sugar, sugar," croaked a dealer of overripe plums.

"Heads, heads, heads," a boy who sold fishheads roared.

Through the window of a Chassidic study house across the

way, Dr. Fischelson could see boys with long sidelocks swaying over holy volumes, grimacing and studying aloud in singsong voices. Butchers, porters, and fruit dealers were drinking beer in the tavern below. Vapor drifted from the tavern's open door like steam from a bathhouse, and there was the sound of loud music. Outside of the tavern, streetwalkers snatched at drunken soldiers and at workers on their way home from the factories. Some of the men carried bundles of wood on their shoulders, reminding Dr. Fischelson of the wicked who are condemned to kindle their own fires in hell. Husky record players poured out their raspings through open windows. The liturgy of the High Holidays alternated with vulgar vaudeville songs.

Dr. Fischelson peered into the half-lit bedlam and cocked his ears. He knew that the behavior of this rabble was the very antithesis of reason. These people were immersed in the vainest of passions, were drunk with emotions, and, according to Spinoza, emotion was never good. Instead of the pleasure they ran after, all they succeeded in obtaining was disease and prison, shame and the suffering that resulted from ignorance. Even the cats which loitered on the roofs here seemed more savage and passionate than those in other parts of the town. They caterwauled with the voices of women in labor, and like demons scampered up walls and leaped onto eaves and balconies. One of the toms paused at Dr. Fischelson's window and let out a howl which made Dr. Fischelson shudder. The doctor stepped from the window and, picking up a broom, brandished it in front of the black beast's glowing, green eyes. "Scat, begone, you ignorant savage!"—and he rapped the broom handle against the roof until the tom ran off.

3

When Dr. Fischelson had returned to Warsaw from Zurich, where he had studied philosophy, a great future had been predicted for him. His friends had known that he was writing an important book on Spinoza. A Jewish Polish journal had invited him to be a contributor; he had been a frequent guest at several wealthy households and he had been made head librarian at the Warsaw synagogue. Although even then he had been considered an old bachelor, the matchmakers had proposed several rich girls for him. But Dr. Fischelson had not taken advantage of these opportunities. He had wanted to be as independent as Spinoza himself. And he had been. But because of his heretical ideas he had come into conflict with the rabbi and had had to resign his post as librarian. For years after that, he had supported himself by giving private lessons in Hebrew and German. Then, when he had become sick, the Berlin Jewish community had voted him a subsidy of five hundred marks a year. This had been made possible through the intervention of the famous Dr. Hildesheimer, with whom he corresponded about philosophy. In order to get by on so small a pension, Dr. Fischelson had moved into the attic room and had begun cooking his own meals on a kerosene stove. He had a cupboard which had many drawers, and each drawer was labeled with the food it contained—buckwheat, rice, barley, onions, carrots, potatoes, mushrooms. Once a week Dr. Fischelson put on his widebrimmed black hat, took a basket in one hand and Spinoza's *Ethics* in the other, and went off to the market for his provisions. While he was waiting to be served, he would open the *Ethics*. The merchants knew him and would motion him to their stalls.

"A fine piece of cheese, Doctor—just melts in your mouth."

"Fresh mushrooms, Doctor, straight from the woods."

"Make way for the Doctor, ladies," the butcher would shout. "Please don't block the entrance."

During the early years of his sickness, Dr. Fischelson had still gone in the evening to a café which was frequented by Hebrew teachers and other intellectuals. It had been his habit to sit there and play chess while drinking a half a glass of black coffee. Sometimes he would stop at the bookstores on Holy Cross Street where all sorts of old books and magazines could be purchased cheap. On one occasion a former pupil of his had arranged to meet him at a restaurant one evening. When Dr.

Fischelson arrived, he had been surprised to find a group of friends and admirers who forced him to sit at the head of the table while they made speeches about him. But these were things that had happened long ago. Now people were no longer interested in him. He had isolated himself completely and had become a forgotten man. The events of 1905 when the boys of Market Street had begun to organize strikes, throw bombs at police stations, and shoot strike breakers so that the stores were closed even on weekdays had greatly increased his isolation. He began to despise everything associated with the modern Jew—Zionism, socialism, anarchism. The young men in question seemed to him nothing but an ignorant rabble intent on destroying society, society without which no reasonable existence was possible. He still read a Hebrew magazine occasionally, but he felt contempt for modern Hebrew, which had no roots in the Bible or the Mishnah. The spelling of Polish words had changed also. Dr. Fischelson concluded that even the so-called spiritual men had abandoned reason and were doing their utmost to pander to the mob. Now and again he still visited a library and browsed through some of the modern histories of philosophy, but he found that the professors did not understand Spinoza, quoted him incorrectly, attributed their own muddled ideas to the philosopher. Although Dr. Fischelson was well aware that anger was an emotion unworthy of those who walk the path of reason, he would become furious, and would quickly close the book and push it from him. "Idiots," he would mutter, "asses, upstarts." And he would vow never again to look at modern philosophy.

4

Every three months a special mailman who only delivered money orders brought Dr. Fischelson eighty rubles. He expected his quarterly allotment at the beginning of July but as day after day passed and the tall man with the blond mustache and the shiny buttons did not appear, the doctor grew anxious. He had scarcely a groschen left. Who knows—possibly the Berlin

Community had rescinded his subsidy; perhaps Dr. Hildesheimer had died, God forbid; the post office might have made a mistake. Every event has its cause, Dr. Fischelson knew. All was determined, all necessary, and a man of reason had no right to worry. Nevertheless, worry invaded his brain, and buzzed about like the flies. If the worst came to the worst, it occurred to him, he could commit suicide, but then he remembered that Spinoza did not approve of suicide and compared those who took their own lives to the insane.

One day when Dr. Fischelson went out to a store to purchase a composition book, he heard people talking about war. In Serbia somewhere, an Austrian prince had been shot and the Austrians had delivered an ultimatum to the Serbs. The owner of the store, a young man with a yellow beard and shifty yellow eyes, announced, "We are about to have a small war," and he advised Dr. Fischelson to store up food because in the near future there was likely to be a shortage.

Everything happened so quickly. Dr. Fischelson had not even decided whether it was worthwhile to spend four groschen on a newspaper, and already posters had been hung up announcing mobilization. Men were to be seen walking on the street with round, metal tags on their lapels, a sign that they were being drafted. They were followed by their crying wives. One Monday when Dr. Fischelson descended to the street to buy some food with his last kopecks, he found the stores closed. The owners and their wives stood outside and explained that merchandise was unobtainable. But certain special customers were pulled to one side and let in through back doors. On the street all was confusion. Policemen with swords unsheathed could be seen riding on horseback. A large crowd had gathered around the tavern where, at the command of the tsar, the tavern's stock of whiskey was being poured into the gutter.

Dr. Fischelson went to his old café. Perhaps he would find some acquaintances there who would advise him. But he did not come across a single person he knew. He decided, then, to visit the rabbi of the synagogue where he had once been librarian, but the sexton with the six-sided skullcap informed him that the rabbi and his family had gone off to the spas. Dr. Fischelson had other old friends in town but he found no one at home. His feet ached from so much walking; black and green spots appeared before his eyes and he felt faint. He stopped and waited for the giddiness to pass. The passersby jostled him. A dark-eyed high school girl tried to give him a coin. Although the war had just started, soldiers eight abreast were marching in full battle dress—the men were covered with dust and were sunburnt. Canteens were strapped to their sides and they wore rows of bullets across their chests. The bayonets on their rifles gleamed with a cold, green light. They sang with mournful voices. Along with the men came cannons, each pulled by eight horses; their blind muzzles breathed gloomy terror. Dr. Fischelson felt nauseous. His stomach ached; his intestines seemed about to turn themselves inside out. Cold sweat appeared on his face.

"I'm dying," he thought. "This is the end." Nevertheless, he did manage to drag himself home, where he lay down on the iron cot and remained, panting and gasping. He must have dozed off because he imagined that he was in his hometown, Tishvitz. He had a sore throat and his mother was busy wrapping a stocking stuffed with hot salt around his neck. He could hear talk going on in the house; something about a candle and about how a frog had bitten him. He wanted to go out into the street but they wouldn't let him because a Catholic procession was passing by. Men in long robes, holding double-edged axes in their hands, were intoning in Latin as they sprinkled holy water. Crosses gleamed; sacred pictures waved in the air. There was an odor of incense and corpses. Suddenly the sky turned a burning red and the whole world started to burn. Bells were ringing; people rushed madly about. Flocks of birds flew overhead, screeching. Dr. Fischelson awoke with a start. His body was covered with sweat and his throat was now actually sore. He tried to meditate about his extraordinary dream, to find its rational connection with what was happening to him and to comprehend it *sub specie eternitatis,* but none of it made sense.

"Alas, the brain is a receptacle for nonsense," Dr. Fischelson thought. "This earth belongs to the mad."

And he once more closed his eyes; once more he dozed; once more he dreamed.

5

The eternal laws, apparently, had not yet ordained Dr. Fischelson's end.

There was a door to the left of Dr. Fischelson's attic room which opened off a dark corridor, cluttered with boxes and baskets, in which the odor of fried onions and laundry soap was always present. Behind this door lived a spinster whom the neighbors called Black Dobbe. Dobbe was tall and lean, and as black as a baker's shovel. She had a broken nose and there was a mustache on her upper lip. She spoke with the hoarse voice of a man and she wore men's shoes. For years Black Dobbe had sold breads, rolls, and bagels which she had bought from the baker at the gate of the house. But one day she and the baker had quarreled and she had moved her business to the marketplace and now she dealt in what were called "wrinklers," which was a synonym for cracked eggs. Black Dobbe had no luck with men. Twice she had been engaged to baker's apprentices but in both instances they had returned the engagement contract to her. Some time afterwards she had received an engagement contract from an old man, a glazier who claimed that he was divorced, but it had later come to light that he still had a wife. Black Dobbe had a cousin in America, a shoemaker, and repeatedly she boasted that this cousin was sending her passage, but she remained in Warsaw. She was constantly being teased by the women who would say, "There's no hope for you, Dobbe. You're fated to die an old maid." Dobbe always answered, "I don't intend to be a slave for any man. Let them all rot."

That afternoon Dobbe received a letter from America. Generally she would go to Leizer the Tailor and have him read it to her. However, that day Leizer was out and so Dobbe thought of Dr. Fischelson, whom the other tenants considered a convert since he never went to prayer. She knocked on the door of the doctor's room but there was no answer. "The heretic is probably out," Dobbe thought, but, nevertheless, she knocked once more, and this time the door moved slightly. She pushed her way in and stood there frightened. Dr. Fischelson lay fully clothed on his bed; his face was as yellow as wax; his Adam's apple stuck out prominently; his beard pointed upward. Dobbe screamed; she was certain that he was dead, but—no—his body moved. Dobbe picked up a glass which stood on the table, ran into the corridor, filled the glass with water from the faucet, hurried back, and threw the water into the face of the unconscious man. Dr. Fischelson shook his head and opened his eyes.

"What's wrong with you?" Dobbe asked. "Are you sick?"

"Thank you very much. No."

"Have you a family? I'll call them."

"No family," Dr. Fischelson said.

Dobbe wanted to fetch the barber from across the street but Dr. Fischelson signified that he didn't wish the barber's assistance. Since Dobbe was not going to the market that day, no "wrinklers" being available, she decided to do a good deed. She assisted the sick man to get off the bed and smoothed down the blanket. Then she undressed Dr. Fischelson and prepared some soup for him on the kerosene stove. The sun never entered Dobbe's room, but here squares of sunlight shimmered on the faded walls. The floor was painted red. Over the bed hung a picture of a man who was wearing a broad frill around his neck and had long hair. "Such an old fellow and yet he keeps his place so nice and clean," Dobbe thought approvingly. Dr. Fischelson asked for the *Ethics,* and she gave it to him disapprovingly. She was certain it was a gentile prayer book. Then she began bustling about, brought in a pail of water, swept the floor. Dr. Fischelson ate; after he had finished, he was much stronger and Dobbe asked him to read her the letter.

He read it slowly, the paper trembling in his hands. It came from New York, from Dobbe's cousin. Once more he wrote that he was about to send her a "really important letter" and a ticket to America. By now, Dobbe knew the story by heart and she helped the old man decipher her cousin's scrawl. "He's lying," Dobbe said. "He forgot about me a long time ago." In the evening, Dobbe came again. A candle in a brass holder was burning on the chair next to the bed. Reddish shadows trembled on the walls and ceiling. Dr. Fischelson sat propped up in bed, reading a book. The candle threw a golden light on his forehead which seemed as if cleft in two. A bird had flown in through the window and was perched on the table. For a moment Dobbe was frightened. This man made her think of witches, of black mirrors and corpses wandering around at night and terrifying women. Nevertheless, she took a few steps toward him and inquired, "How are you? Any better?"

"A little, thank you."

"Are you really a convert?" she asked although she wasn't quite sure what the word meant.

"Me, a convert? No, I'm a Jew like any other Jew," Dr. Fischelson answered.

The doctor's assurances made Dobbe feel more at home. She found the bottle of kerosene and lit the stove, and after that she fetched a glass of milk from her room and began cooking kasha. Dr. Fischelson continued to study the *Ethics,* but that evening he could make no sense of the theorems and proofs with their many references to axioms and definitions and other theorems. With trembling hand he raised the book to his eyes and read, "The idea of each modification of the human body does not involve adequate knowledge of the human body itself. . . . The idea of the idea of each modification of the human mind does not involve adequate knowledge of the human mind."

6

Dr. Fischelson was certain he would die any day now. He made out his will, leaving all of his books and manuscripts to the synagogue library. His clothing and furniture would go to Dobbe since she had taken care of him. But death did not come. Rather his health improved. Dobbe returned to her business in the market, but she visited the old man several times a day, prepared soup for him, left him a glass of tea, and told him news of the war. The Germans had occupied Kalish, Bendin, and Cestechow, and they were marching on Warsaw. People said that on a quiet morning one could hear the rumblings of the cannon. Dobbe reported that the casualties were heavy. "They're falling like flies," she said. "What a terrible misfortune for the women."

She couldn't explain why, but the old man's attic room attracted her. She liked to remove the gold-rimmed books from the bookcase, dust them, and then air them on the window sill. She would climb the few steps to the window and look out through the telescope. She also enjoyed talking to Dr. Fischelson. He told her about Switzerland, where he had studied, of the great cities he had passed through, of the high mountains that were covered with snow even in the summer. His father had been a rabbi, he said, and before he, Dr. Fischelson, had become a student, he had attended a yeshiva. She asked him how many languages he knew and it turned out that he could speak and write Hebrew, Russian, German, and French, in addition to Yiddish. He also knew Latin. Dobbe was astonished that such an educated man should live in an attic room on Market Street. But what amazed her most of all was that although he had the title "Doctor," he couldn't write prescriptions. "Why don't you become a real doctor?" she would ask him. "I am a doctor," he would answer. "I'm just not a physician." "What kind of a doctor?" "A doctor of philosophy." Although she had no idea of what this meant, she felt it must be very important. "Oh my blessed mother," she would say, "where did you get such a brain?"

Then one evening after Dobbe had given him his crackers and his glass of tea with milk, he began questioning her about where she came from, who her parents were, and why she had not married. Dobbe was surprised. No one had ever asked her such questions. She told him her story in a quiet voice and stayed until eleven o'clock. Her father had been a porter at the kosher butcher shops. Her mother had plucked chickens in the slaughterhouse. The family had lived in a cellar at No. 19 Market Street. When she had been ten, she had become a maid. The man she had worked for had been a fence who bought stolen goods from thieves on the square. Dobbe had had a brother who had gone into the Russian army and had never returned. Her sister had married a coachman in Praga and had died in childbirth. Dobbe told of the battles between the underworld and the revolutionaries in 1905, of blind Itche and his gang and how they collected protection money from the stores, of the thugs who attacked young boys and girls out on Saturday afternoon strolls if they were not paid money for security. She also spoke of the pimps who drove about in carriages and abducted women to be sold in Buenos Aires. Dobbe swore that some men had even sought to inveigle her into a brothel, but that she had run away. She complained of a thousand evils done to her. She had been robbed; her boyfriend had been stolen; a competitor had once poured a pint of kerosene into her basket of bagels; her own cousin, the shoemaker, had cheated her out of a hundred rubles before he had left for America. Dr. Fischelson listened to her attentively. He asked her questions, shook his head, and grunted.

"Well, do you believe in God?" he finally asked her.

"I don't know," she answered. "Do you?"

"Yes, I believe."

"Then why don't you go to synagogue?" she asked.

"God is everywhere," he replied. "In the synagogue. In the marketplace. In this very room. We ourselves are parts of God."

"Don't say such things," Dobbe said. "You frighten me."

She left the room and Dr. Fischelson was certain she had gone to bed. But he wondered why she had not said "good night." "I probably drove her away with my philosophy," he thought. The very next moment he heard her footsteps. She came in carrying a pile of clothing like a peddler.

"I wanted to show you these," she said. "They're my trousseau." And she began to spread out, on the chair, dresses—

woolen, silk, velvet. Taking each dress up in turn, she held it to her body. She gave him an account of every item in her trousseau—underwear, shoes, stockings.

"I'm not wasteful," she said. "I'm a saver. I have enough money to go to America."

Then she was silent and her face turned brick-red. She looked at Dr. Fischelson out of the corner of her eyes, timidly, inquisitively. Dr. Fischelson's body suddenly began to shake as if he had the chills. He said, "Very nice, beautiful things." His brow furrowed and he pulled at his beard with two fingers. A sad smile appeared on his toothless mouth and his large fluttering eyes, gazing into the distance through the attic window, also smiled sadly.

7

The day that Black Dobbe came to the rabbi's chambers and announced that she was to marry Dr. Fischelson, the rabbi's wife thought she had gone mad. But the news had already reached Leizer the Tailor, and had spread to the bakery, as well as to other shops. There were those who thought that the "old maid" was very lucky; the doctor, they said, had a vast hoard of money. But there were others who took the view that he was a run-down degenerate who would give her syphilis. Although Dr. Fischelson had insisted that the wedding be a small, quiet one, a host of guests assembled in the rabbi's rooms. The baker's apprentices, who generally went about barefoot, and in their underwear, with paper bags on the tops of their heads, now put on light-colored suits, straw hats, yellow shoes, gaudy ties, and they brought with them huge cakes and pans filled with cookies. They had even managed to find a bottle of vodka although liquor was forbidden in wartime. When the bride and groom entered the rabbi's chamber, a murmur arose from the crowd. The women could not believe their eyes. The woman that they saw was not the one they had known. Dobbe wore a wide-brimmed hat which was amply adorned with cherries, grapes, and plumes, and the dress that she had on was of white silk and was equipped with a train; on her feet were high-heeled shoes, gold in color, and from her thin neck hung a string of imitation pearls. Nor was this all: her fingers sparkled with rings and glittering stones. Her face was veiled. She looked almost like one of those rich brides who were married in the Vienna Hall. The baker's apprentices whistled mockingly. As for Dr. Fischelson, he was wearing his black coat and broad-toed shoes. He was scarcely able to walk; he was leaning on Dobbe. When he saw the crowd from the doorway, he became frightened and began to retreat, but Dobbe's former employer approached him saying, "Come in, come in, bridegroom. Don't be bashful. We are all brethren now."

The ceremony proceeded according to the law. The rabbi, in a worn satin gabardine, wrote the marriage contract and then had the bride and groom touch his handkerchief as a token of agreement; the rabbi wiped the point of the pen on his skullcap. Several porters who had been called from the street to make up the quorum supported the canopy. Dr. Fischelson put on a white robe as a reminder of the day of his death and Dobbe walked around him seven times as custom required. The light from the braided candles flickered on the walls. The shadows wavered. Having poured wine into a goblet, the rabbi chanted the benedictions in a sad melody. Dobbe uttered only a single cry. As for the other women, they took out their lace handkerchiefs and stood with them in their hands, grimacing. When the baker's boys began to whisper wisecracks to each other, the rabbi put a finger to his lips and murmured, *"Eh nu oh,"* as a sign that talking was forbidden. The moment came to slip the wedding ring on the bride's finger, but the bridegroom's hand started to tremble and he had trouble locating Dobbe's index finger. The next thing, according to custom, was the smashing of the glass, but though Dr. Fischelson kicked the goblet several times, it remained unbroken. The girls lowered their heads, pinched each other gleefully, and giggled. Finally one of the apprentices struck the goblet with his heel and it shattered. Even the rabbi could not restrain a smile. After the ceremony the guests drank vodka and ate cookies. Dobbe's former employer came up to Dr. Fischelson and said, "*Mazel tov,* bridegroom. Your luck should be as good as your wife." "Thank you, thank you," Dr. Fischelson murmured, "but I don't look forward to any luck." He was anxious to return as quickly as possible to his attic room. He felt a pressure in his stomach and his chest ached. His face had become greenish. Dobbe had suddenly become angry. She pulled back her veil and called out to the crowd, "What are you laughing at? This isn't a show." And without picking up the cushion-cover in which the gifts were wrapped, she returned with her husband to their rooms on the fifth floor.

Dr. Fischelson lay down on the freshly made bed in his room and began reading the *Ethics*. Dobbe had gone back to her own room. The doctor had explained to her that he was an old man, that he was sick and without strength. He had promised her nothing. Nevertheless she returned wearing a silk nightgown, slippers with pompoms, and with her hair hanging down over her shoulders. There was a smile on her face, and she was bashful and hesitant. Dr. Fischelson trembled and the *Ethics* dropped from his hands. The candle went out. Dobbe groped for Dr. Fischelson in the dark and kissed his mouth. "My dear husband," she whispered to him, "*Mazel tov.*"

What happened that night could be called a miracle. If Dr. Fischelson hadn't been convinced that every occurrence is in accordance with the laws of nature, he would have thought that Black Dobbe had bewitched him. Powers long dormant awakened in him. Although he had had only a sip of the benediction wine, he was as if intoxicated. He kissed Dobbe and spoke to her of love. Long-forgotten quotations from Klopstock, Lessing, Goethe, rose to his lips. The pressures and aches stopped. He embraced Dobbe, pressed her to himself, was again a man as in his youth. Dobbe was faint with delight; crying, she murmured things to him in a Warsaw slang which he did not understand. Later, Dr. Fischelson slipped off into the deep sleep young men know. He dreamed that he was in Switzerland and that he was climbing mountains—running, falling, flying. At dawn he opened his eyes; it seemed to him that someone had blown into his ears. Dobbe was snoring. Dr. Fischelson quietly got out of bed. In his long nightshirt he approached the window, walked up the steps, and looked out in wonder. Market Street was asleep, breathing with a deep stillness. The gas lamps were flickering. The black shutters on the stores were fastened with iron bars. A cool breeze was blowing. Dr. Fischelson looked up at the sky. The black arch was thickly sown with stars—there were green, red, yellow, blue stars; there were large ones and small ones, winking and steady ones. There were those that were clustered in dense groups and those that were alone. In the higher sphere, apparently, little notice was taken of the fact that a certain Dr. Fischelson had in his declining days married someone called Black Dobbe. Seen from above, even the Great War was nothing but a temporary play of the modes. The myriads of fixed stars continued to travel their destined courses in unbounded space. The comets, planets, satellites, asteroids kept circling these shining centers. Worlds were born and died in cosmic upheavals. In the chaos of nebulae, primeval matter was being formed. Now and again a star tore loose and swept across the sky, leaving behind it a fiery streak. It was the month of August when there are showers of meteors. Yes, the divine substance was extended and had neither beginning nor end; it was absolute, indivisible, eternal, without duration, infinite in its attributes. Its waves and bubbles danced in the universal cauldron, seething with change, following the unbroken chain of causes and effects, and he, Dr. Fischelson, with his unavoidable fate, was part of this. The doctor closed his eyelids and allowed the breeze to cool the sweat on his forehead and stir the hair of his beard. He breathed deeply of the midnight air, supported his shaky hands on the window sill and murmured, "Divine Spinoza, forgive me. I have become a fool."

Interpretive Questions for Discussion

Why does his study of Spinoza cause Dr. Fischelson to withdraw from the Jewish community?

1. Why does Dr. Fischelson feel superior to the rabble of Market Street even though he is living a painful, isolated life?

2. Why does Dr. Fischelson compare men to the insects who immolate themselves in the candle flame, saying that "they desire nothing but the pleasure of the moment"? (4)

3. Why does Dr. Fischelson study Spinoza for hours every day and carry the *Ethics* with him everywhere, even though the result of his study is more confusion?

4. Why is Dr. Fischelson fascinated by the "two worlds" he sees from his garret window—a world of infinite extension above and a world of degradation below? (5)

5. Why does Dr. Fischelson investigate the heavens with a telescope? Why do the cracks and crevasses of the moon hold particular fascination for Dr. Fischelson?

6. Why does Dr. Fischelson take pleasure in the sensation that he is "whirling in company with the earth, the sun, the stars of the Milky Way, and the infinite host of galaxies known only to infinite thought"? Why does Dr. Fischelson experience the *Amor Dei Intellectualis* when he is looking up at the sky outside his window? (6)

7. Why does Dr. Fischelson admire Spinoza's teaching that "morality and happiness were identical, and that the most moral deed a man could perform was to indulge in some pleasure which was not contrary to reason"? (5)

8. Why is Dr. Fischelson plagued by ill health, although some doctors insist there is nothing wrong with him?

9. Are we meant to admire Dr. Fischelson's dedication to Spinoza, and to the *Amor Dei Intellectualis,* even though it has ruined his promising career and made him a bachelor and an outcast?

Suggested textual analysis
Pages 5–8: beginning, "Dr. Fischelson, standing on the top step at the window and looking out," and ending, "and he rapped the broom handle against the roof until the tom ran off."

Why does Dr. Fischelson accept Dobbe's unspoken offer of marriage?

1. Why does the mobilization for war have such a profound effect on Dr. Fischelson, sending him to lie on his bed expecting death?

2. Why is Dr. Fischelson plagued by nightmares? Why does he dream of being comforted by his mother?

3. Why is Dr. Fischelson unable to make sense of the theorems and proofs of the *Ethics* the evening following his collapse?

4. Why does Dr. Fischelson's health begin to improve once Dobbe begins to take care of him? (14)

5. Why is Dobbe attracted to Dr. Fischelson's attic room?

6. Why is the heretical Dr. Fischelson more certain of his belief in God than Dobbe is? Why is Dobbe frightened when Dr. Fischelson tells her, "God is everywhere. . . . We ourselves are parts of God"? (17)

7. Why does Dobbe show Dr. Fischelson her trousseau as a way of hinting that they marry? Why does she own such a variety of feminine and even extravagant items, when she is a "saver" who lives very simply? (18)

8. Why does Dr. Fischelson's body "shake as if he had the chills" when Dobbe presents him with her trousseau? Why does he smile sadly in response to her gesture? (18)

9. Why does the intellectually refined Dr. Fischelson end up marrying an ignorant, coarse woman who wears men's shoes and has endured a difficult life on Market Street?

Suggested textual analysis
Pages 16–18: beginning, "She couldn't explain why, but the old man's attic room attracted her," and ending, "also smiled sadly."

In the end, does Dr. Fischelson feel that he has betrayed his life of philosophy, or that he has finally achieved the enlightenment he has been searching for?

1. Why does love come to Dr. Fischelson only late in life?

2. Why is Dr. Fischelson unable to complete his commentary on the *Ethics?* Why does Spinoza become more puzzling and unclear the more Dr. Fischelson studies him? (4)

3. Why does Dr. Fischelson become "again a man as in his youth" on his wedding night? Why is Dobbe able to awaken in him "powers long dormant"? (20)

4. Why does Dr. Fischelson go quietly to the window to gaze with wonder on a sleeping Market Street and the star-filled night sky—where "little notice was taken of the fact that a certain Dr. Fischelson had in his declining days married someone called Black Dobbe"? (21)

5. Is Dr. Fischelson comforted by the fact that "seen from above, even the Great War was nothing but a temporary play of the modes," or does he think that such an unemotional, rationalistic view of human events is absurd? (21)

6. Why does Dr. Fischelson, reflecting on the "chaos of nebulae," on eternal, primeval forces, and on "the universal cauldron, seething with change," feel "part of this"? What is his "unavoidable fate" that he seems to be accepting? (21)

7. In marrying Dobbe, has Dr. Fischelson reconciled his two realities—the low, earthly Market Street and the divine, eternal heavens?

8. Why does Dr. Fischelson murmur, "Divine Spinoza, forgive me. I have become a fool"? (21)

Suggested textual analysis
Pages 20–21: from "What happened that night could be called a miracle," to the end of the story.

For Further Reflection

1. Can a human being be happy and fulfilled living alone?

2. What contribution do intellectuals make to the moral improvement of humanity?

3. Do older people marry for different reasons than younger people?

4. Do you agree that morality and happiness are identical?

5. Do you think Dr. Fischelson was right to view marriage as an impediment to "the highest perfection of the mind"?

Either/Or

(selection)

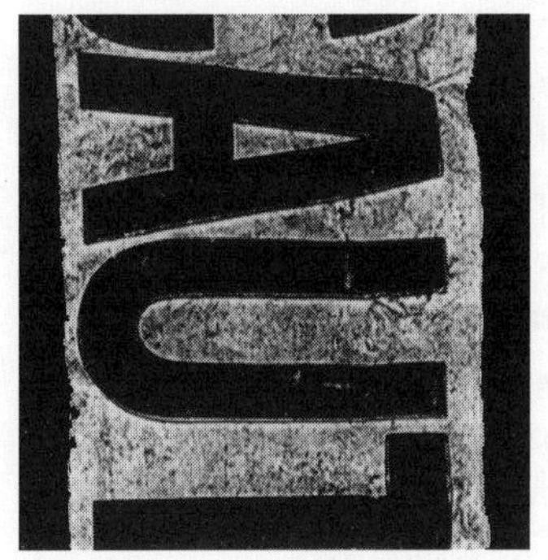

Søren Kierkegaard

Søren Kierkegaard (1813–1855), Danish theologian and critic of rationalism, is generally considered to be the founder of existentialist philosophy. At the age of twenty-eight, after making a painful decision to withdraw a marriage proposal, Kierkegaard retreated to Berlin for six months, then returned to Copenhagen with the manuscript of *Either/Or* (from which the present selection is taken). Subtitled *A Fragment of Life,* this first book—like most of Kierkegaard's others—was published under a pseudonym. Victor Eremita, whose name can be translated as "hermit conqueror," is a fictional editor of a correspondence between two other unnamed writers: Author A ("The Rotation Method") and Author B ("Equilibrium"), who present the "either" and the "or," respectively.

Either/Or
A Fragment of Life

Edited by
Victor Eremita

PREFACE

DEAR READER: I wonder if you may not sometimes have felt inclined to doubt a little the correctness of the familiar philosophic maxim that the external is the internal, and the internal the external.[1] Perhaps you have cherished in your heart a secret which you felt in all its joy or pain was too precious for you to share with another. Perhaps your life has brought you in contact with some person of whom you suspected something of the kind was true, although you were never able to wrest his secret from him either by force or cunning. Perhaps neither of these presuppositions applies to you and your life, and yet you are not a stranger to this doubt; it flits across your mind now and then like a passing shadow. Such a doubt comes and goes, and no one knows whence it comes, nor whither it goes. For my part I have always been heretically-minded on this point in philosophy, and have therefore early accustomed myself, as far as possible, to institute observations and inquiries concerning it. I

1. [A familiar maxim of Hegelian philosophy.]

have sought guidance from those authors whose views I shared on this matter; in short, I have done everything in my power to remedy the deficiency in the philosophical works.

Gradually the sense of hearing came to be my favorite sense; for just as the voice is the revelation of an inwardness incommensurable with the outer, so the ear is the instrument by which this inwardness is apprehended, hearing the sense by which it is appropriated. Whenever, then, I found a contradiction between what I saw and what I heard, then I found my doubt confirmed, and my enthusiasm for the investigation stimulated. In the confessional the priest is separated from the penitent by a screen; he does not see, he only hears. Gradually as he listens, he constructs an outward appearance which corresponds to the voice he hears. Consequently, he experiences no contradiction. It is otherwise, however, when you hear and see at the same time, and yet perceive a screen between yourself and the speaker. My researches in this direction have met with varying degrees of success. Sometimes I have been favored by fortune, sometimes not, and one needs good fortune to win results along this road. However, I have never lost my desire to continue my investigations. Whenever I have been at the point of regretting my perseverance, an unexpected success has crowned my efforts. It was such an unexpected bit of luck which in a very curious manner put me in possession of the papers which I now have the honor of offering to the reading public. These papers have afforded me an insight into the lives of two men, which has confirmed my hunch that the external is not the internal. This was especially true about one of them. His external mode of life has been in complete contradiction to his inner life. The same was true to a certain extent with the other also, inasmuch as he concealed a more significant inwardness under a somewhat commonplace exterior.

Still, I had best proceed in order and explain how I came into possession of these papers. It is now about seven years since I first noticed at a merchant's shop here in town a secretary which from the very first moment I saw it attracted my attention. It was not of modern workmanship, had been used a good deal, and yet it fascinated me. It is impossible for me to explain the reason for this impression, but most people in the course of their lives have had some similar experience. My daily path took me by this shop, and I never failed a single day to pause and feast my eyes upon it. I gradually made up a history about it; it became a daily necessity for me to see it, and so I did not hesitate to go out of my way for the sake of seeing it, when an unaccustomed route made this necessary. And the more I looked at it, the more I wanted to own it. I realized very well that it was a peculiar desire, since I had no use for such a piece of furniture, and it would be an extravagance for me to buy it. But desire is a very sophisticated passion. I made an excuse for going into the shop, asked about other things, and as I was leaving, I casually made the shopkeeper a very low offer for the secretary. I thought possibly he might accept it; then chance would have played into my hands. It was certainly not for the sake of the money I behaved thus, but to salve my conscience. The plan miscarried, the dealer was uncommonly firm. I continued to pass the place daily, and to look at the secretary with loving eyes. "You must make up your mind," I thought, "for suppose it is sold, then it will be too late. Even if you were lucky enough to get hold of it again, you would never have the same feeling about it." My heart beat violently; then I went into the shop. I bought it and paid for it. "This must be the last time," thought I, "that you are so extravagant; it is really lucky that you bought it, for now every time you look at it, you will reflect on how extravagant you were; a new period of your life must begin with the acquisition of the secretary." Alas, desire is very eloquent, and good resolutions are always at hand.

The secretary was duly set up in my apartment, and as in the first period of my enamorment I had taken pleasure in gazing at it from the street, so now I walked back and forth in front of it at home. Little by little I familiarized myself with its rich economy, its many drawers and recesses, and I was thoroughly pleased with my secretary. Still, things could not continue thus.

In the summer of 1836 I arranged my affairs so that I could take a week's trip to the country. The postilion was engaged for five o'clock in the morning. The necessary baggage had been packed the evening before, and everything was in readiness. I awakened at four, but the vision of the beautiful country I was to visit so enchanted me that I again fell asleep, or into a dream. My servant evidently thought he would let me sleep as long as possible, for he did not call me until half-past six. The postilion was already blowing his horn, and although I am not usually inclined to obey the mandates of others, I have always made an exception in the case of the postboy and his musical theme. I was speedily dressed and already at the door, when it occurred to me, Have you enough money in your pocket? There was not much there. I opened the secretary to get at the money drawer to take what money there was. Of course the drawer would not move. Every attempt to open it failed. It was all as bad as it could possibly be. Just at this moment, while my ears were ringing with the postboy's alluring notes, to meet such difficulties! The blood rushed to my head, I became angry. As Xerxes ordered the sea to be lashed, so I resolved to take a terrible revenge. A hatchet was fetched. With it I dealt the secretary a shattering blow, shocking to see. Whether in my anger I struck the wrong place, or the drawer was as stubborn as myself, the result of the blow was not as anticipated. The drawer was closed, and the drawer remained closed. But something else happened. Whether my blow had struck exactly the right spot, or whether the shock to the whole framework of the secretary was responsible, I do not know, but I do know that a secret door sprang open, one which I had never before noticed. This opened a pigeonhole that I naturally had never discovered. Here to my great surprise I found a mass of papers, the papers which form the content of the present work. My intention as to the journey remained unchanged. At the first station we came to I would negotiate a loan. A mahogany case in which I usually kept a pair of pistols was hastily emptied and the papers were placed in it. Pleasure had triumphed, and had become even greater. In my heart I begged the secretary for forgiveness for the harsh treatment, while my mind found its doubt strengthened, that the external is not the internal, as well as my empirical generalization confirmed, that luck is necessary to make such discoveries possible.

I reached Hillerød in the middle of the forenoon, set my finances in order, and got a general impression of the magnificent scenery. The following morning I at once began my excursions, which now took on a very different character from that which I had originally intended. My servant followed me with the mahogany case. I sought out a romantic spot in the forest where I should be as free as possible from surprise, and then took out the documents. My host, who noticed these frequent excursions in company with the mahogany case, ventured the remark that I must be trying to improve my marksmanship. For this conjecture I was duly grateful, and left him undisturbed in his belief.

A hasty glance at the papers showed me that they were made up of two collections whose external differences were strongly marked. One of them was written on a kind of vellum in quarto, with a fairly wide margin. The handwriting was legible, sometimes even a little elegant, in a single place, careless. The other was written on full sheets of foolscap with ruled columns, such as is ordinarily used for legal documents and the like. The handwriting was clear, somewhat spreading, uniform and even, apparently that of a businessman. The contents also proved to be very dissimilar. One part consisted of a number of aesthetic essays of varying length, the other was composed of two long inquiries and one shorter one, all with an ethical content, as it seemed, and in the form of letters. This dissimilarity was completely confirmed by a closer examination. The second series consists of letters written to the author of the first series.

But I must try to find some briefer designation to identify the two authors. I have examined the letters very carefully, but I have found little or nothing to the purpose. Concerning the first author, the aesthete, the papers yield absolutely nothing. As for the second, the letter writer, it appears that his name was William, and that he was a magistrate, but of what court is not stated. If I were to confine myself strictly to this data, and decide to call him William, I should lack a corresponding designation for the first author, and should have to give him an arbitrary name. Hence I have preferred to call the first author A, the second B. . . .

The Editor
November 1842

The Rotation Method

An Essay in the Theory of Social Prudence
by Author A

CHREMYLOS: You get too much at last of everything.
Of love,
KARION: of bread,
CHREMYLOS: of music,
KARION: and of sweetmeats.
CHREMYLOS: Of honor,
KARION: cakes,
CHREMYLOS: of courage,
KARION: and of figs.
CHREMYLOS: Ambition,
KARION: barley-cakes,
CHREMYLOS: high office,
KARION: lentils.
(Aristophanes' *Plutus,* v. 189 *ff.*)

Starting from a principle is affirmed by people of experience to be a very reasonable procedure; I am willing to humor them, and so begin with the principle that all men are bores. Surely no one will prove himself so great a bore as to contradict me in this. This principle possesses the quality of being in the highest degree repellent, an essential requirement in the case of negative principles, which are in the last analysis the principles of all motion. It is not merely repellent, but infinitely forbidding; and whoever has this principle back of him cannot but receive an infinite impetus forward, to help him make new discoveries. For if my principle is true, one need only consider how ruinous boredom is for humanity, and by properly adjusting the intensity of one's concentration upon this fundamental truth, attain any desired degree of momentum. Should one wish to attain the maximum momentum, even to the point of almost endangering the driving power, one need only say to oneself: Boredom is the root of all evil. Strange that boredom, in itself so staid and stolid, should have such power to set in motion. The influence it exerts is altogether magical, except that it is not the influence of attraction, but of repulsion.

In the case of children, the ruinous character of boredom is universally acknowledged. Children are always well behaved as long as they are enjoying themselves. This is true in the strictest sense; for if they sometimes become unruly in their play, it is because they are already beginning to be bored—boredom is already approaching, though from a different direction. In choosing a governess, one therefore takes into account not only her sobriety, her faithfulness, and her competence, but also her aesthetic qualifications for amusing the children; and there would be no hesitancy in dismissing a governess who was lacking in this respect, even if she had all the other desirable virtues. Here, then, the principle is clearly acknowledged; but so strange is the way of the world, so pervasive the influence of habit and boredom, that this is practically the only case in which the science of aesthetics receives its just dues. If one were to ask for a divorce because his wife was tiresome, or demand the abdication of a king because he was boring to look at, or the banishment of a preacher because he was tiresome to listen to, or the dismissal of a prime minister, or the execution of a journalist, because he was terribly tiresome, one would find it impossible to force it through. What wonder, then, that the world goes from bad to worse, and that its evils increase more and more, as boredom increases, and boredom is the root of all evil.

The history of this can be traced from the very beginning of the world. The gods were bored, and so they created man. Adam was bored because he was alone, and so Eve was created. Thus boredom entered the world, and increased in proportion to the increase of population. Adam was bored alone; then Adam and Eve were bored together; then Adam and Eve and Cain and Abel were bored *en famille;* then the population of the world increased, and the peoples were bored *en masse*. To divert themselves they conceived the idea of constructing a tower high enough to reach the heavens. This idea is itself as boring as the tower was high, and constitutes a terrible proof of how boredom gained the upper hand. The nations were scattered over the earth, just as people now travel abroad, but they continued to be bored. Consider the consequences of this boredom. Humanity fell from its lofty height, first because of Eve, and then from the Tower of Babel. What was it, on the other hand, that delayed the fall of Rome, was it not *panis* and *circenses*?[2] And is anything being done now? Is anyone concerned about planning some means of diversion? Quite the contrary, the impending ruin is being accelerated. It is proposed to call a constitutional assembly. Can anything more tiresome be imagined, both for the participants themselves, and for those who have to hear and read about it? It is proposed to improve the financial condition of the state by practicing economy. What could be more tiresome? Instead of increasing the national debt, it is proposed to pay it off. As I understand the political situation, it would be an easy matter for Denmark to negotiate a loan of fifteen million dollars. Why not consider this plan? Every once in a while we hear of a man who is a genius, and therefore neglects to pay his debts—why should not a nation do the same, if we were all agreed? Let us then borrow fifteen millions, and let us use the proceeds, not to pay our debts, but for public entertainment. Let us celebrate the millennium in a riot of merriment. Let us place boxes everywhere, not, as at present, for the deposit of money, but for the free distribution of money. Everything would become gratis; theaters gratis, women of easy virtue gratis, one would drive to the park gratis, be buried gratis, one's eulogy would be gratis; I say gratis, for when one always has money at hand, everything is in a certain sense free. No one should be permitted to own any property. Only in my own case would there be an exception. I reserve to myself securities in the Bank of London to the value of one hundred dollars a day, partly because I cannot do with less, partly because the

2. [Bread and circuses.]

idea is mine, and finally because I may not be able to hit upon a new idea when the fifteen millions are gone.

What would be the consequences of all this prosperity? Everything great would gravitate toward Copenhagen, the greatest artists, the greatest dancers, the greatest actors. Copenhagen would become a second Athens. What then? All rich men would establish their homes in this city. Among others would come the shah of Persia, and the king of England would also come. Here is my second idea. Let us kidnap the shah of Persia. Perhaps you say an insurrection might take place in Persia and a new ruler be placed on the throne, as has often happened before, the consequence being a fall in price for the old shah. Very well then, I propose that we sell him to the Turks; they will doubtless know how to turn him into money. Then there is another circumstance which our politicians seem entirely to have overlooked. Denmark holds the balance of power in Europe. It is impossible to imagine a more fortunate lot. I know that from my own experience; I once held the balance of power in a family and could do as I pleased; the blame never fell on me, but always on the others. O that my words might reach your ears, all you who sit in high places to advise and rule, you king's men and men of the people, wise and understanding citizens of all classes! Consider the crisis! Old Denmark is on the brink of ruin; what a calamity! It will be destroyed by boredom. Of all calamities the most calamitous! In ancient times they made him king who extolled most beautifully the praises of the deceased king; in our times we ought to make him king who utters the best witticism, and make him crown prince who gives occasion for the utterance of the best witticism.

O beautiful, emotional sentimentality, how you carry me away! Should I trouble to speak to my contemporaries, to initiate them into my wisdom? By no means. My wisdom is not exactly *zum Gebrauch für Jedermann,*[3] and it is always more prudent to keep one's maxims of prudence to oneself. I desire no

3. [For the use of everyone.]

disciples; but if there happened to be someone present at my deathbed, and I was sure that the end had come, then I might in an attack of philanthropic delirium, whisper my theory in his ear, uncertain whether I had done him a service or not. People talk so much about man being a social animal; at bottom, he is a beast of prey, and the evidence for this is not confined to the shape of his teeth. All this talk about society and the social is partly inherited hypocrisy, partly calculated cunning.

All men are bores. The word itself suggests the possibility of a subdivision. It may just as well indicate a man who bores others as one who bores himself. Those who bore others are the mob, the crowd, the infinite multitude of men in general. Those who bore themselves are the elect, the aristocracy; and it is a curious fact that those who do not bore themselves usually bore others, while those who bore themselves entertain others. Those who do not bore themselves are generally people who, in one way or another, keep themselves extremely busy; these people are precisely on this account the most tiresome, the most utterly unendurable. This species of animal life is surely not the fruit of man's desire and woman's lust. Like all lower forms of life, it is marked by a high degree of fertility, and multiplies endlessly. It is inconceivable that nature should require nine months to produce such beings; they ought rather to be turned out by the score. The second class, the aristocrats, are those who bore themselves. As noted above, they generally entertain others—in a certain external sense sometimes the mob, in a deeper sense only their fellow initiates. The more profoundly they bore themselves, the more powerfully do they serve to divert these latter, even when their boredom reaches its zenith, as when they either die of boredom (the passive form) or shoot themselves out of curiosity (the active form).

It is usual to say that idleness is a root of all evil. To prevent this evil one is advised to work. However, it is easy to see, both from the nature of the evil that is feared and the remedy proposed, that this entire view is of a very plebeian extraction. Idleness is by no means as such a root of evil; on the contrary, it is a truly divine life, provided one is not himself bored. Idleness may indeed cause the loss of one's fortune; and so on, but the high-minded man does not fear such dangers; he fears only boredom. The Olympian gods were not bored, they lived happily in happy idleness. A beautiful woman, who neither sews nor spins nor bakes nor reads nor plays the piano, is happy in her idleness, for she is not bored. So far from idleness being the root of all evil, it is rather the only true good. Boredom is the root of all evil, and it is this which must be kept at a distance. Idleness is not an evil; indeed one may say that every human being who lacks a sense for idleness proves that his consciousness has not yet been elevated to the level of the humane. There is a restless activity which excludes a man from the world of the spirit, setting him in a class with the brutes, whose instincts impel them always to be on the move. There are men who have an extraordinary talent for transforming everything into a matter of business, whose whole life is business, who fall in love, marry, listen to a joke, and admire a picture with the same industrious zeal with which they labor during business hours. The Latin proverb, *otium est pulvinar diaboli,*[4] is true enough, but the devil gets no time to lay his head on this pillow when one is not bored. But since some people believe that the end and aim of life is work, the disjunction, idleness-work, is quite correct. I assume that it is the end and aim of every man to enjoy himself, and hence my disjunction is no less correct.

Boredom is the daemonic side of pantheism. If we remain in boredom as such, it becomes the evil principle; if we annul it, we posit it in its truth; but we can only annul boredom by enjoying ourselves—ergo, it is our duty to enjoy ourselves. To say that boredom is annulled by work betrays a confusion of thought; for idleness can certainly be annulled by work, since it is its opposite, but not boredom, and experience shows that the busiest workers, whose constant buzzing most resembles an insect's hum, are the most tiresome of creatures; if they do not

4. ["Idleness is the devil's pillow."]

bore themselves, it is because they have no true conception of what boredom is; but then it can scarcely be said that they have overcome boredom.

Boredom is partly an inborn talent, partly an acquired immediacy. The English are in general the paradigmatic nation. A true talent for indolence is very rare; it is never met with in nature, but belongs to the world of the spirit. Occasionally, however, you meet a traveling Englishman who is, as it were, the incarnation of this talent—a heavy, immovable animal, whose entire language exhausts its riches in a single word of one syllable, an interjection by which he signifies his deepest admiration and his supreme indifference, admiration and indifference having been neutralized in the unity of boredom. No other nation produces such miracles of nature; every other national will always show himself a little more vivacious, not so absolutely stillborn. The only analogy I know of is the apostle of the empty enthusiasm, who also makes his way through life on an interjection. This is the man who everywhere makes a profession of enthusiasm, who cries Ah! or Oh! whether the event be significant or insignificant, the difference having been lost for him in the emptiness of a blind and noisy enthusiasm. The second form of boredom is usually the result of a mistaken effort to find diversion. The fact that the remedy against boredom may also serve to produce boredom might appear to be a suspicious circumstance; but it has this effect only insofar as it is incorrectly employed. A misdirected search for diversion, one which is eccentric in its direction, conceals boredom within its own depths and gradually works it out toward the surface, thus revealing itself as that which it immediately is. In the case of horses, we distinguish between blind staggers and sleepy staggers, but call both staggers; and so we can also make a distinction between two kinds of boredom, though uniting both under the common designation of being tiresome.

Pantheism is, in general, characterized by fullness; in the case of boredom we find the precise opposite, since it is characterized by emptiness; but it is just this which makes boredom a pantheistic conception. Boredom depends on the nothingness which pervades reality; it causes a dizziness like that produced by looking down into a yawning chasm, and this dizziness is infinite. The eccentric form of diversion noted above sounds forth without producing an echo, which proves it to be based on boredom; for in nothingness not even an echo can be produced.

Now since boredom as shown above is the root of all evil, what can be more natural than the effort to overcome it? Here, as everywhere, however, it is necessary to give the problem calm consideration; otherwise one may find oneself driven by the daemonic spirit of boredom deeper and deeper into the mire in the very effort to escape. Everyone who feels bored cries out for change. With this demand I am in complete sympathy, but it is necessary to act in accordance with some settled principle.

My own dissent from the ordinary view is sufficiently expressed in the use I make of the word "rotation." This word might seem to conceal an ambiguity, and if I wished to use it so as to find room in it for the ordinary method, I should have to define it as a change of field. But the farmer does not use the word in this sense. I shall, however, adopt this meaning for a moment, in order to speak of the rotation which depends on change in its boundless infinity, its extensive dimension, so to speak.

This is the vulgar and inartistic method, and needs to be supported by illusion. One tires of living in the country, and moves to the city; one tires of one's native land, and travels abroad; one is *europamüde,* and goes to America, and so on; finally one indulges in a sentimental hope of endless journeyings from star to star. Or the movement is different but still extensive. One tires of porcelain dishes and eats on silver; one tires of silver and turns to gold; one burns half of Rome to get an idea of the burning of Troy. This method defeats itself; it is plain endlessness. And what did Nero gain by it? Antonine was wiser; he says, "It is in your power to review your life, to look at things you saw before, from another point of view."

My method does not consist in change of field, but resembles the true rotation method in changing the crop and the mode of cultivation. Here we have at once the principle of limitation, the only saving principle in the world. The more you limit yourself, the more fertile you become in invention. A prisoner in solitary confinement for life becomes very inventive, and a spider may furnish him with much entertainment. One need only hark back to one's schooldays. We were at an age when aesthetic considerations were ignored in the choice of one's instructors, most of whom were for that reason very tiresome; how fertile in invention one then proved to be! How entertaining to catch a fly and hold it imprisoned under a nut shell and to watch how it pushed the shell around; what pleasure from cutting a hole in the desk, putting a fly in it, and then peeping down at it through a piece of paper! How entertaining sometimes to listen to the monotonous drip of water from the roof! How close an observer one becomes under such circumstances, when not the least noise nor movement escapes one's attention! Here we have the extreme application of the method which seeks to achieve results intensively, not extensively.

The more resourceful in changing the mode of cultivation one can be, the better; but every particular change will always come under the general categories of *remembering* and *forgetting*. Life in its entirety moves in these two currents, and hence it is essential to have them under control. It is impossible to live artistically before one has made up one's mind to abandon hope; for hope precludes self-limitation. It is a very beautiful sight to see a man put out to sea with the fair wind of hope, and one may even use the opportunity to be taken in tow; but one should never permit hope to be taken aboard one's own ship, least of all as a pilot; for hope is a faithless shipmaster. Hope was one of the dubious gifts of Prometheus; instead of giving men the foreknowledge of the immortals, he gave them hope.

To forget—all men wish to forget, and when something unpleasant happens, they always say: Oh, that one might forget!

But forgetting is an art that must be practiced beforehand. The ability to forget is conditioned upon the method of remembering, but this again depends upon the mode of experiencing reality. Whoever plunges into his experiences with the momentum of hope will remember in such wise that he is unable to forget. *Nil admirari*[5] is therefore the real philosophy. No moment must be permitted so great a significance that it cannot be forgotten when convenient; each moment ought, however, to have so much significance that it can be recollected at will. Childhood, which is the age which remembers best, is at the same time most forgetful. The more poetically one remembers, the more easily one forgets; for remembering poetically is really only another expression for forgetting. In a poetic memory the experience has undergone a transformation, by which it has lost all its painful aspects. To remember in this manner, one must be careful how one lives, how one enjoys. Enjoying an experience to its full intensity to the last minute will make it impossible either to remember or to forget. For there is then nothing to remember except a certain satiety, which one desires to forget, but which now comes back to plague the mind with an involuntary remembrance. Hence, when you begin to notice that a certain pleasure or experience is acquiring too strong a hold upon the mind, you stop a moment for the purpose of remembering. No other method can better create a distaste for continuing the experience too long. From the beginning one should keep the enjoyment under control, never spreading every sail to the wind in any resolve; one ought to devote oneself to pleasure with a certain suspicion, a certain wariness, if one desires to give the lie to the proverb which says that no one can have his cake and eat it too. The carrying of concealed weapons is usually forbidden, but no weapon is so dangerous as the art of remembering. It gives one a very peculiar feeling in the midst of one's enjoyment to look back upon it for the purpose of remembering it.

5. [To wonder at nothing.]

One who has perfected himself in the twin arts of remembering and forgetting is in a position to play at battledore and shuttlecock with the whole of existence.

The extent of one's power to forget is the final measure of one's elasticity of spirit. If a man cannot forget he will never amount to much. Whether there be somewhere a Lethe gushing forth, I do not know; but this I know, that the art of forgetting can be developed. However, this art does not consist in permitting the impressions to vanish completely; forgetfulness is one thing, and the art of forgetting is something quite different. It is easy to see that most people have a very meager understanding of this art, for they ordinarily wish to forget only what is unpleasant, not what is pleasant. This betrays a complete one-sidedness. Forgetting is the true expression for an ideal process of assimilation by which the experience is reduced to a sounding board for the soul's own music. Nature is great because it has forgotten that it was chaos; but this thought is subject to revival at any time. As a result of attempting to forget only what is unpleasant, most people have a conception of oblivion as an untamable force which drowns out the past. But forgetting is really a tranquil and quiet occupation, and one which should be exercised quite as much in connection with the pleasant as with the unpleasant. A pleasant experience has as past something unpleasant about it, by which it stirs a sense of privation; this unpleasantness is taken away by an act of forgetfulness. The unpleasant has a sting, as all admit. This, too, can be removed by the art of forgetting. But if one attempts to dismiss the unpleasant absolutely from mind, as many do who dabble in the art of forgetting, one soon learns how little that helps. In an unguarded moment it pays a surprise visit, and it is then invested with all the forcibleness of the unexpected. This is absolutely contrary to every orderly arrangement in a reasonable mind. No misfortune or difficulty is so devoid of affability, so deaf to all appeals, but that it may be flattered a little; even Cerberus accepted bribes of honey-cakes, and it is not only the lassies who are beguiled. The art in dealing with such experiences consists in talking them over, thereby depriving them of their bitterness; not forgetting them absolutely, but forgetting them for the sake of remembering them. Even in the case of memories such that one might suppose an eternal oblivion to be the only safeguard, one need permit oneself only a little trickery, and the deception will succeed for the skillful. Forgetting is the shears with which you cut away what you cannot use, doing it under the supreme direction of memory. Forgetting and remembering are thus identical arts, and the artistic achievement of this identity is the Archimedean point from which one lifts the whole world. When we say that we *consign* something to oblivion, we suggest simultaneously that it is to be forgotten and yet also remembered.

The art of remembering and forgetting will also insure against sticking fast in some relationship of life, and make possible the realization of a complete freedom.

One must guard against *friendship*. How is a friend defined? He is not what philosophy calls the necessary other, but the superfluous third. What are friendship's ceremonies? You drink each other's health, you open an artery and mingle your blood with that of the friend. It is difficult to say when the proper moment for this arrives, but it announces itself mysteriously; you feel some way that you can no longer address one another formally. When once you have had this feeling, then it can never appear that you have made a mistake, like Geert Vestphaler, who discovered that he had been drinking to friendship with the public hangman. What are the infallible marks of friendship? Let antiquity answer: *idem velle, idem nolle, ea demum firma amicitia,*[6] and also extremely tiresome. What are the infallible marks of friendship? Mutual assistance in word and deed. Two friends form a close association in order to be everything to one another, and that although it is impossible for one human being to be anything to another human being except to be in his way. To be sure one may help him with money, assist him in and out of his coat, be his humble servant, and tender him congratula-

6. [To will the same and not to will the same makes for a firm friendship.]

tions on New Year's Day, on the day of his wedding, on the birth of a child, on the occasion of a funeral.

But because you abstain from friendship it does not follow that you abstain from social contacts. On the contrary, these social relationships may at times be permitted to take on a deeper character, provided you always have so much more momentum in yourself that you can sheer off at will, in spite of sharing for a time in the momentum of the common movement. It is believed that such conduct leaves unpleasant memories, the unpleasantness being due to the fact that a relationship which has meant something now vanishes and becomes as nothing. But this is a misunderstanding. The unpleasant is merely a piquant ingredient in the sullenness of life. Besides, it is possible for the same relationship again to play a significant role, though in another manner. The essential thing is never to stick fast, and for this it is necessary to have oblivion back of one. The experienced farmer lets his land lie fallow now and then, and the theory of social prudence recommends the same. Everything will doubtless return, though in a different form; that which has once been present in the rotation will remain in it, but the mode of cultivation will be varied. You therefore quite consistently hope to meet your friends and acquaintances in a better world, but you do not share the fear of the crowd that they will be altered so that you cannot recognize them; your fear is rather lest they be wholly unaltered. It is remarkable how much significance even the most insignificant person can gain from a rational mode of cultivation.

One must never enter into the relation of *marriage*. Husband and wife promise to love one another for eternity. This is all very fine, but it does not mean very much; for if their love comes to an end in time, it will surely be ended in eternity. If, instead of promising forever, the parties would say until Easter, or until May Day comes, there might be some meaning in what they say; for then they would have said something definite, and also something that they might be able to keep. And how does a marriage usually work out? In a little while one party begins to perceive that there is something wrong, then the other party complains, and cries to heaven: faithless! faithless! A little later the second party reaches the same standpoint, and a neutrality is established in which the mutual faithlessness is mutually canceled, to the satisfaction and contentment of both parties. But it is now too late, for there are great difficulties connected with divorce.

Such being the case with marriage, it is not surprising that the attempt should be made in so many ways to bolster it up with moral supports. When a man seeks separation from his wife, the cry is at once raised that he is depraved, a scoundrel, etc. How silly, and what an indirect attack upon marriage! If marriage has reality, then he is sufficiently punished by forfeiting this happiness; if it has no reality, it is absurd to abuse him because he is wiser than the rest. When a man grows tired of his money and throws it out of the window, we do not call him a scoundrel; for either money has reality, and so he is sufficiently punished by depriving himself of it, or it has none, and then he is, of course, a wise man.

One must always take care not to enter into any relationship in which there is a possibility of many members. For this reason friendship is dangerous, to say nothing of marriage. Husband and wife are indeed said to become one, but this is a very dark and mystic saying. When you are one of several, then you have lost your freedom; you cannot send for your traveling boots whenever you wish, you cannot move aimlessly about in the world. If you have a wife, it is difficult; if you have a wife and perhaps a child, it is troublesome; if you have a wife and children, it is impossible. True, it has happened that a gypsy woman has carried her husband through life on her back, but for one thing this is very rare, and for another, it is likely to be tiresome in the long run—for the husband. Marriage brings one into fatal connection with custom and tradition, and traditions and customs are like the wind and weather, altogether incalculable. In Japan, I have been told, it is the custom for husbands to lie in childbed. Who knows but the time will come when the customs of foreign countries will obtain a foothold in Europe?

Friendship is dangerous, marriage still more so; for woman is and ever will be the ruin of a man, as soon as he contracts a permanent relation with her. Take a young man who is fiery as an Arabian courser, let him marry, he is lost. Woman is first proud, then is she weak, then she swoons, then he swoons, then the whole family swoons. A woman's love is nothing but dissimulation and weakness.

But because a man does not marry, it does not follow that his life need be wholly deprived of the erotic element. And the erotic ought also to have infinitude, but poetic infinitude, which can just as well be limited to an hour as to a month. When two beings fall in love with one another and begin to suspect that they were made for each other, it is time to have the courage to break it off; for by going on they have everything to lose and nothing to gain. This seems a paradox, and it is so for the feeling, but not for the understanding. In this sphere it is particularly necessary that one should make use of one's moods; through them one may realize an inexhaustible variety of combinations.

One should never accept appointment to an official position. If you do, you will become a mere Richard Roe, a tiny little cog in the machinery of the body politic; you even cease to be master of your own conduct, and in that case your theories are of little help. You receive a title, and this brings in its train every sin and evil. The law under which you have become a slave is equally tiresome, whether your advancement is fast or slow. A title can never be got rid of except by the commission of some crime which draws down on you a public whipping; even then you are not certain, for you may have it restored to you by royal pardon.

Even if one abstains from involvement in official business, one ought not to be inactive, but should pursue such occupations as are compatible with a sort of leisure; one should engage in all sorts of breadless arts. In this connection the self-development should be intensive rather than extensive, and one should, in spite of mature years, be able to prove the truth of the proverb that children are pleased with a rattle and tickled with a straw.

If one now, according to the theory of social jurisprudence, varies the soil—for if he had contact with one person only, the rotation method would fail as badly as if a farmer had only one acre of land, which would make it impossible for him to fallow, something which is of extreme importance—then one must also constantly vary himself, and this is the essential secret. For this purpose one must necessarily have control over one's moods. To control them in the sense of producing them at will is impossible, but prudence teaches how to utilize the moment. As an experienced sailor always looks out over the water and sees a squall coming from far away, so one ought always to see the mood a little in advance. One should know how the mood affects one's own mind and the mind of others, before putting it on. You first strike a note or two to evoke pure tones, and see what there is in a man; the intermediate tones follow later. The more experience you have, the more readily you will be convinced that there is often much in a man which is not suspected. When sentimental people, who as such are extremely tiresome, become angry, they are often very entertaining. Badgering a man is a particularly effective method of exploration.

The whole secret lies in arbitrariness. People usually think it easy to be arbitrary, but it requires much study to succeed in being arbitrary so as not to lose oneself in it, but so as to derive satisfaction from it. One does not enjoy the immediate but something quite different which he arbitrarily imports into it. You go to see the middle of a play, you read the third part of a book. By this means you insure yourself a very different kind of enjoyment from that which the author has been so kind as to plan for you. You enjoy something entirely accidental; you consider the whole of existence from this standpoint; let its reality be stranded thereon. I will cite an example. There was a man whose chatter certain circumstances made it necessary for me to listen to. At every opportunity he was ready with a little philosophical lecture, a very tiresome harangue. Almost in despair, I suddenly discovered that he perspired copiously when talking. I saw the pearls of sweat gather on his brow, unite to form a stream, glide down his nose, and hang at the extreme point of his nose in a drop-shaped body. From the moment of making this discovery, all was changed. I even took pleasure in inciting him to begin his philosophical instruction, merely to observe the perspiration on his brow and at the end of his nose.

The poet Baggesen says somewhere of someone that he was doubtless a good man, but that there was one insuperable objection against him, that there was no word that rhymed with his name. It is extremely wholesome thus to let the realities of life split upon an arbitrary interest. You transform something accidental into the absolute, and, as such, into the object of your admiration. This has an excellent effect, especially when one is excited. This method is an excellent stimulus for many persons. You look at everything in life from the standpoint of a wager, and so forth. The more rigidly consistent you are in holding fast to your arbitrariness, the more amusing the ensuing combinations will be. The degree of consistency shows whether you are an artist or a bungler; for to a certain extent all men do the same. The eye with which you look at reality must constantly be changed. The Neo-Platonists assumed that human beings who had been less perfect on earth became after death more or less perfect animals, all according to their deserts. For example, those who had exercised the civic virtues on a lower scale (retail dealers) were transformed into busy animals, like bees. Such a view of life, which here in this world sees all men transformed into animals or plants (Plotinus also thought that some would become plants), suggests rich and varied possibilities. The painter Tischbein sought to idealize every human being into an animal. His method has the fault of being too serious, in that it endeavors to discover a real resemblance.

The arbitrariness in oneself corresponds to the accidental in the external world. One should therefore always have an eye open for the accidental, always be *expeditus,*[7] if anything should offer. The so-called social pleasures for which we prepare a

7. [Ready to march.]

week or two in advance amount to so little; on the other hand, even the most insignificant thing may accidentally offer rich material for amusement. It is impossible here to go into detail, for no theory can adequately embrace the concrete. Even the most completely developed theory is poverty-stricken compared with the fullness which the man of genius easily discovers in his ubiquity.

Equilibrium Between the Aesthetical and the Ethical in the Composition of Personality

by Author B

My Friend,

What I have so often said to you I say now once again, or rather I shout it: Either/or, *aut/aut*. For a single *aut* adjoined as a rectification does not make the situation clear, since the question here at issue is so important that one cannot rest satisfied with a part of it, and in itself it is too coherent to be possessed partially. There are situations in life where it would be ridiculous or a species of madness to apply an either/or; but also, there are men whose souls are too dissolute (in the etymological sense of the word) to grasp what is implied in such a dilemma, whose personalities lack the energy to say with pathos, Either/or. Upon me these words have always made a deep impression, and they still do, especially when I pronounce them absolutely and without specific reference to any objects, for this use of them suggests the possibility of starting the most dreadful contrasts into action. They affect me like a magic formula of incantation, and my soul becomes exceeding serious, sometimes almost harrowed. I think of my early youth, when without clearly comprehending what it is to make a choice I listened with childish trust to the talk of my elders and the instant of choice was solemn and venerable, although in choosing I was only following the instructions of another person. I think of the occasions in my later life when I stood at the crossways, when my soul was matured in the hour of decision. I think of the many occasions in life less important but by no means indifferent to me, when it was a question of making a choice. For although there is only one situation in which either/or has absolute significance, namely, when truth, righteousness, and holiness are lined up on one side, and lust and base propensities and obscure passions and perdition on the other; yet, it is always important to choose rightly, even as between things which one may innocently choose; it is important to test oneself, lest some day one might have to beat a painful retreat to the point from which one started, and might have reason to thank God if one had to reproach oneself for nothing worse than a waste of time. In common parlance I use these words as others use them, and it would indeed be a foolish pedantry to give up using them. But sometimes it occurs, nevertheless, that I become aware of using them with regard to things entirely indifferent. Then they lay aside their humble dress, I forget the insignificant thoughts they discriminated, and they advance to meet me with all their dignity, in their official robes. As a magistrate in common life may appear in plain clothes and mingle without distinction in the crowd, so do these words mingle in common speech; when, however, the magistrate steps forward with authority, he distinguishes himself from all. Like such a magistrate whom I am accustomed to see only on solemn occasions, these words appear before me, and my soul always becomes serious. And although my life now has to a certain degree its either/or behind it, yet I know well that it may still encounter many a situation where the either/or will have its full significance. I hope, however, that these words may find me in a worthy state of mind when they check me on my path, and I hope that I may be successful in choosing the right course; at all events, I shall endeavor to make the choice with real earnestness, and with that I venture, at least, to hope that I shall the sooner get out of the wrong path.

And now as for you—this phrase is only too often on your lips, it has almost become a byword with you. What significance has it for you? None at all. You, according to your own expression, regard it as a wink of the eye, a snap of the fingers, a *coup de main,* an abracadabra. At every opportunity you know how to introduce it, nor is it without effect; for it affects you as strong drink affects a neurasthenic, you become completely intoxicated by what you call the higher madness. "It is the compendium," you say, "of all practical wisdom, but no one has ever inculcated it so pithily (like a god in the form of a puppet talking to suffering humanity) as that great thinker and true practical philosopher who said to a man who had insulted him by pulling off his hat and throwing it on the floor, 'If you pick it up, you'll get a thrashing; if you don't pick it up, you'll also get a thrashing; now you can choose.' " You take great delight in "comforting" people when they have recourse to you in critical situations. You listen to their exposition of the case and then say, "Yes, I perceive perfectly that there are two possibilities, one can either do this or that. My sincere opinion and my friendly counsel is as follows: Do it/or don't do it—you will regret both." But he who mocks others mocks himself, and your rejoinder is not a mere nothing but a profound mockery of yourself, a sorry proof how limp your soul is, that your whole philosophy of life is concentrated in one single proposition, "I say merely either/or." In case this really were your serious meaning, there would be nothing one could do with you, one must simply put up with you as you are and deplore the fact that melancholy [literally, heavy-mindedness] or light-mindedness had enfeebled your spirit. Now on the contrary, since one knows very well that such is not the case, one is not tempted to pity you but rather to wish that some day the circumstances of your life may tighten upon you the screws in its rack and compel you to come out with what really dwells in you, may begin the sharper inquisition of the rack which cannot be beguiled by nonsense and witticisms. Life is a masquerade, you explain, and for you this is inexhaustible material for amusement; and so far, no one has succeeded in knowing you; for every revelation you make is always an illusion—it is only in this way you are able to breathe and prevent people from pressing importunately upon you and obstructing your respiration. Your occupation consists in preserving your hiding place, and that you succeed in doing, for your mask is the most enigmatical of all. In fact you are nothing; you are merely a relation to others, and what you are you are by virtue of this relation. To a fond shepherdess you hold out a languishing hand, and instantly you are masked in all possible bucolic sentimentality. A reverend spiritual father you deceive with a brotherly kiss, etc. You yourself are nothing, an enigmatic figure on whose brow is inscribed Either/or—"For this," you say, "is my motto, and these words are not, as the grammarians believe, disjunctive conjunctions; no, they belong inseparably together and therefore ought to be written as one word, inasmuch as in their union they constitute an interjection which I shout at mankind, just as boys shout 'Hep' after a Jew."

Now although nothing you say in that style has the slightest effect upon me, or, if it has any effect, it is at the utmost the effect of arousing a righteous indignation, nevertheless, for your own sake I will reply to you. Do you not know that there comes a midnight hour when everyone has to throw off his mask? Do you believe that life will always let itself be mocked? Do you think you can slip away a little before midnight in order to avoid this? Or are you not terrified by it? I have seen men in real life who so long deceived others that at last their true nature could not reveal itself; I have seen men who played hide and seek so long that at last madness through them obtruded disgustingly upon others their secret thoughts which hitherto they had proudly concealed. Or can you think of anything more frightful than that it might end with your nature being resolved into a multiplicity, that you really might become many, become, like those unhappy demoniacs, a legion, and you thus would have lost the inmost and holiest thing of all in a man, the unifying power of personality? Truly, you should not jest with that which is not only serious but dreadful. In every man there is something which to a certain degree prevents him from becoming perfectly transparent to himself; and this may be the case in so high a degree, he may be so inexplicably woven into relationships of life which extend far beyond himself that he almost cannot reveal himself. But he who cannot reveal himself cannot love, and he who cannot love is the most unhappy man of all. Your own tactic is to train yourself in the art of being enigmatic to everybody. My young friend, suppose there was no one who troubled himself to guess your riddle—what joy, then, would you have in it? But above all, for your own sake, for the sake of your salvation—for I am acquainted with no condition of soul which can better be described as perdition—stop this wild flight, this passion of annihilation which rages in you; for this is what you desire, you would annihilate everything, you would satiate the hunger of doubt at the expense of existence. To this end you cultivate yourself, to this end you harden your temper; for you are willing to admit that you are good for nothing, the only thing that gives you pleasure is to march seven times around existence and blow the trumpet and thereupon let the whole thing collapse, that your soul may be tranquilized, yea, attuned to sadness, that you may summon Echo forth—for Echo is heard only in emptiness.

However, I am not likely to get further with you along this path; moreover, my head is too weak, if you would put it that way, to be able to hold out, or, as I prefer to say, too strong to take pleasure in seeing everything grow dizzy before my eyes. I will therefore take up the matter from another side. Imagine a young man at the age when life really begins to have significance for him; he is wholesome, pure, joyful, intellectually gifted, himself rich in hope, the hope of everyone who knows him; imagine (yea, it is hard that I have to say this) that he was mistaken in you, that he believed you were a serious, tried, and experienced man from whom one could confidently expect enlightenment upon life's riddles; imagine that he turned to you with the charming confidence which is the adornment of youth, with the claim not to be gained which is youth's privilege—what would you answer him? Would you answer, "I say merely either/or"? That you would hardly do. Would you (as you are wont to express it when you would indicate your aversion to having other people vex you with their affairs of the heart), would you stick your head out of the window and say, "Try the next house"? Or would you treat him as you do others who ask your advice or seek information from you, whom you dismiss as you do the collector of tithes by saying that you are only a lodger in life, not a householder and paterfamilias? No, you would not do this either. A young man with intellectual gifts is the sort of thing you prize only too highly. But in the case I suppose, your relation to the youth is not just what you would have wished, it was not an accidental encounter which brought you in contact with him, your irony was not tempted. Although he was the younger, you the older man, it was he, nevertheless, who by the noble quality of his youth made the instant serious. It is true, is it not, that you yourself would like to be young, would feel that there was something beautiful in being young but also something very serious, that it is by no means a matter of indifference how one employs one's youth, but that before one there lies a choice, a real either/or. You would feel that, after all, the important thing is not to cultivate one's mind but to mature one's personality. Your good nature, your sympathy, would be set in motion, in that spirit you would talk to him; you would fortify his soul, confirm him in the confidence he has in the world, you would assure him that there is a power in a man which is able to defy the whole world, you would insist that he take to heart the importance of employing time well. All this you can do, and when you will, you can do it handsomely.

But now mark well what I would say to you, young man—for though you are not young, one is always compelled to address you as such. Now what did you do in this case? You acknowledged, as ordinarily you are not willing to do, the importance of an either/or. And why? Because your soul was moved by love for the young man. And yet in a way you deceived him, for he will, perhaps, encounter you at another time when it by no means suits your convenience to acknowledge this importance. Here you see one of the sorry consequences of the fact that a man's nature cannot harmoniously reveal itself. You thought you were doing the best for him, and yet perhaps you have harmed him; perhaps he would have been better able to maintain himself over against your distrust of life than to find repose in the subjective, deceitful trust you conveyed to him. Imagine that after the lapse of several years you again encountered him; he was lively, witty, intellectual, daring in his thought, bold in his expression, but your ear easily detected doubt in his soul, you conceived a suspicion that he had acquired the questionable wisdom: I say merely either/or. It is true, is it not, that you would be sorry for him, would feel that he had lost something, and something very essential. But for yourself you will not sorrow, you are content with your ambiguous wisdom, yea, proud of it, so proud that you will not suffer another to share it, since you wish to be alone with it. And yet you find it deplorable in another connection, and it is your sincere opinion that it was deplorable for the young man to have reached the same wisdom. What a monstrous contradiction! Your whole nature contradicts itself. But you can only get out of this contradiction by an either/or, and I, who love you more sincerely than you loved this young man, I, who in my life have experienced the significance of choice, I congratulate you upon the fact that you are still so young, that even though you always will be sensible of some loss, yet, if you have, or rather if you will to have the requisite energy, you can win what is the chief thing in life, win yourself, acquire your own self.

Now in case a man were able to maintain himself upon the pinnacle of the instant of choice, in case he could cease to be a man, in case he were in his inmost nature only an airy thought, in case personality meant nothing more than to be a kobold, which takes part, indeed, in the movements but nevertheless remains unchanged; in case such were the situation, it would be foolish to say that it might ever be too late for a man to choose, for in a deeper sense there could be no question of a choice. The choice itself is decisive for the content of the personality, through the choice the personality immerses itself in the thing chosen, and when it does not choose it withers away in consumption. For an instant it is so, for an instant it may seem as if the things between which a choice is to be made lie outside of the chooser, that he stands in no relationship to it, that he can preserve a state of indifference over against it. This is the instant of deliberation, but this, like the Platonic instant, has no existence, least of all in the abstract sense in which you would hold it fast, and the longer one stares at it the less it exists. That which has to be chosen stands in the deepest relationship to the chooser, and when it is a question of a choice involving a life problem the individual must naturally be living in the meantime, and hence, it comes about that the longer he postpones the choice the easier it is for him to alter its character, notwithstanding that he is constantly deliberating and deliberating and believes that thereby he is holding the alternatives distinctly apart. When life's either/or is regarded in this way one is not easily tempted to jest with it. One sees, then, that the inner drift of the personality leaves no time for thought experiments, that it constantly hastens onward and in one way or another posits this alternative or that, making the choice more difficult the next instant because what has thus been posited must be revoked. Think of the captain on his ship at the instant when it has to come about. He will perhaps be able to say, "I can either do this or that"; but in case he is not a pretty poor navigator, he will be aware at the same time that the ship is all the while making its usual headway, and that therefore it is only an instant when it is indifferent whether he does this or that. So it is with a man. If he forgets to take account of the headway, there comes at last an instant when there no longer is any question of an either/or, not because he has chosen but because he has neglected to choose, which is equivalent to saying because others have chosen for him, because he has lost his self.

You will perceive also in what I have just been saying how essentially my view of choice differs from yours (if you can properly be said to have any view), for yours differs precisely in the fact that it prevents you from choosing. For me the instant of choice is very serious, not so much on account of the rigorous cogitation involved in weighing the alternatives, not on account of the multiplicity of thoughts which attach themselves to every link in the chain, but rather because there is danger afoot, danger that the next instant it may not be equally in my power to choose, that something already has been lived which must be lived over again. For to think that for an instant one can keep one's personality a blank, or that strictly speaking one can break off and bring to a halt the course of the personal life, is a delusion. The personality is already interested in the choice before one chooses, and when the choice is postponed the personality chooses unconsciously, or the choice is made by obscure powers within it. So when at last the choice is made one discovers (unless, as I remarked before, the personality has been completely volatilized) that there is something which must be done over again, something which must be revoked, and this is often very difficult. We read in fairy tales about human beings whom mermaids and mermen enticed into their power by means of demoniac music. In order to break the enchantment it was necessary in the fairy tale for the person who was under the spell to play the same piece of music backwards without making a single mistake. This is very profound, but very difficult to perform, and yet so it is: the errors one has taken into oneself one must eradicate in this way, and every time one makes a mistake one must begin all over. Therefore, it is important to choose and to choose in time. You, on the contrary, have another method—for I know very well that the polemical side you turn towards the world is not your true nature. Yea, if to deliberate were the proper task for a human life, you would be pretty close to perfection. I will adduce an example. To fit your case the contrasts must be bold: either a parson/or an actor. Here is the dilemma. Now all your passionate energy is awakened, reflection with its hundred arms lays hold of the thought of being a parson. You find no repose, day and night you think about it, you read all the books you can lay your hands on, you go to church three times every Sunday, pick up acquaintance with parsons, write sermons yourself, deliver them to yourself; for half a year you are dead to the whole world. You can now talk of the clerical calling with more insight and apparently with more experience than many who have been parsons for twenty years. When you encounter such men it arouses your indignation that they do not know how to get the thing off their chests with more eloquence. "Is this enthusiasm?" you say. "Why I who am not a parson, who have not consecrated myself to this calling, speak with the voice of angels as compared with them." That, perhaps, is true enough, but nevertheless, you have not become a parson. Then you act in the same way with respect to the other task, and your enthusiasm for art almost surpasses your clerical eloquence. Then you are ready to choose. However, one may be sure that in the prodigious thought-production you were engaged in there must have been lots of waste products, many incidental reflections and observations. Hence, the instant you have to choose, life and animation enter into this waste mass, a new either/or presents itself—jurist, perhaps advocate, this has something in common with both the other alternatives. Now you are lost. For that same moment you are at once advocate enough to be able to prove the reasonableness of taking the third possibility into account. So your life drifts on.

After you have wasted a year and a half on such deliberations, after you have with admirable energy exerted to the utmost the powers of your soul, you have not got one step further. You break the thread of thought, you become impatient, passionate, scolding, and storming, and then you continue: "Either hairdresser/or bank teller; I say merely either/or." What wonder, then, that this saying has become for you an offense and foolishness, that it seems, as you say, as if it were like the arms attached to the iron maiden whose embrace was the death penalty. You treat people superciliously, you make sport of them, and what you have become is what you most abhor: a critic, a universal critic in all faculties. Sometimes I cannot help smiling at you, and yet it is pitiful to see how your really excellent intellectual gifts are thus dissipated. But here again there is the same contradiction in your nature; for you see the ludicrous very clearly, and God help him who falls into your hands if his case is similar to yours. And yet the whole difference is that he perhaps becomes downcast and broken, while you on the contrary become light and erect and merrier than ever, making yourself and others blissful with the gospel: *vanitas vanitatum vanitas,* hurrah! But this is no choice, it is what we call in Danish letting it go, or it is mediation like letting five count as an even number. Now you feel yourself free, you say to the world, farewell.

So zieh' ich hin in alle Ferne,
Ueber meiner Mütze nur die Sterne.[8]

Therewith you have chosen . . . not to be sure, as you yourself will admit, the better part. But in reality you have not chosen at all, or it is in an improper sense of the word you have chosen. Your choice is an aesthetic choice, but an aesthetic choice is no choice. The act of choosing is essentially a proper and stringent expression of the ethical. Whenever in a stricter sense there is question of an either/or, one can always be sure that the ethical is involved. The only absolute either/or is the choice between good and evil, but that is also absolutely ethical. The aesthetic choice is either entirely immediate and to that extent no choice, or it loses itself in the multifarious. Thus, when a young girl follows the choice of her heart, this choice, however beautiful it may be, is in the strictest sense no choice, since it is entirely immediate. When a man deliberates aesthetically upon a multitude of life's problems, as you did in the foregoing, he does not easily get one either/or, but a whole multiplicity, because the self-determining factor in the choice is not ethically accentuated, and because when one does not choose absolutely one chooses only for the moment, and therefore can choose something different the next moment. The ethical choice is therefore in a certain sense much easier, much simpler, but in another sense it is infinitely harder. He who would define his life task ethically has ordinarily not so considerable a selection to choose from; on the other hand, the act of choice has far more importance for him. If you will understand me aright, I should like to say that in making a choice it is not so much a question

8. ["I travel to all distant places,/Over my cap only the stars"—Goethe.]

of choosing the right as of the energy, the earnestness, the pathos with which one chooses. Thereby the personality announces its inner infinity, and thereby, in turn, the personality is consolidated. Therefore, even if a man were to choose the wrong, he will nevertheless discover, precisely by reason of the energy with which he chose, that he had chosen the wrong. For the choice being made with the whole inwardness of his personality, his nature is purified and he himself brought into immediate relation to the eternal Power whose omnipresence interpenetrates the whole of existence. This transfiguration, this higher consecration, is never attained by that man who chooses merely aesthetically. The rhythm in that man's soul, in spite of all its passion, is only a *spiritus lenis*.[9]

So, like a Cato[10] I shout at you my either/or, and yet not like a Cato, for my soul has not yet acquired the resigned coldness which he possessed. But I know that only this incantation, if I have the strength for it, will be capable of rousing you, not to an activity of thought, for of that you have no lack, but to earnestness of spirit. Perhaps you will succeed without that in accomplishing much, perhaps even in astonishing the world (for I am not niggardly), and yet you will miss the highest thing, the only thing which truly gives meaning to life; perhaps you will gain the whole world and lose your own self.

What is it, then, that I distinguish in my either/or? Is it good and evil? No, I would only bring you up to the point where the choice between the evil and the good acquires significance for you. Everything hinges upon this. As soon as one can get a man to stand at the crossways in such a position that there is no recourse but to choose, he will choose the right. Hence, if it should chance that, while you are in the course of reading this somewhat lengthy dissertation, which again I send you in the form of a letter, you were to feel that the instant for choice had

9. ["Light breathing"—distinguished by grammarians from a more definite aspiration of a Greek vowel.]

10. [Cato persistently insisted to the Roman senate that "Carthage must be destroyed."]

come, then throw the rest of this away, never concern yourself about it, you have lost nothing—but choose, and you shall see what validity there is in this act, yea, no young girl can be so happy with the choice of her heart as is a man who knows how to choose. So then, one either has to live aesthetically or one has to live ethically. In this alternative, as I have said, there is not yet in the strictest sense any question of a choice; for he who lives aesthetically does not choose, and he who after the ethical has manifested itself to him chooses the aesthetical is not living aesthetically, for he is sinning and is subject to ethical determinant even though his life may be described as unethical. Lo, this is, as it were, a *character indelebilis* impressed upon the ethical, that though it modestly places itself on a level with the aesthetical, it is nevertheless that which makes the choice a choice. And this is the pitiful thing to one who contemplates human life, that so many live on in a quiet state of perdition; they outlive themselves, not in the sense that the content of life is successively unfolding and now is possessed in this expanded state, but they live their lives, as it were, outside of themselves, they vanish like shadows, their immortal soul is blown away, and they are not alarmed by the problem of its immortality, for they are already in a state of dissolution before they die. They do not live aesthetically, but neither has the ethical manifested itself in its entirety, so they have not exactly rejected it either, they therefore are not sinning, except insofar as it is sin not to be either one thing or the other; neither are they ever in doubt about their immortality, for he who deeply and sincerely is in doubt of it on his own behalf will surely find the right. *On his own behalf,* I say, and surely it is high time to utter a warning against the great-hearted, heroic objectivity with which many thinkers think on behalf of others and not on their own behalf. If one would call this which I here require selfishness, I would reply that this comes from the fact that people have no conception of what this "self" is, and that it would be of very little use to a man if he were to gain the whole world and lose himself, and that it must necessarily be a poor proof which does not first of all convince the man who presents it.

My either/or does not in the first instance denote the choice between good and evil; it denotes the choice whereby one chooses good *and* evil/or excludes them. Here the question is under what determinants one would contemplate the whole of existence and would himself live. That the man who chooses good and evil chooses the good is indeed true, but this becomes evident only afterwards; for the aesthetical is not the evil but neutrality, and that is the reason why I affirmed that it is the ethical which constitutes the choice. It is, therefore, not so much a question of choosing between willing the good or the evil, as of choosing to will, but by this in turn the good and the evil are posited. He who chooses the ethical chooses the good, but here the good is entirely abstract, only its being is posited, and hence it does not follow by any means that the chooser cannot in turn choose the evil, in spite of the fact that he chose the good. Here you see again how important it is that a choice be made, and that the crucial thing is not deliberation but the baptism of the will which lifts up the choice into the ethical. The longer the time that elapses, the more difficult it is to choose, for the soul is constantly attached to one side of the dilemma, and it becomes more and more difficult, therefore, to tear oneself loose. And yet this is necessary if one is to choose and is therefore of the utmost importance if a choice signifies something. . . .

Behold, my young friend, this life of yours is despair. Hide this if you will from others, from yourself you cannot hide it, it is despair. . . .

What then must you do? Another perhaps would say, "Get married. Then you will have something else to think about." Yes, that you will, but the question remains whether this will be any advantage to you, and whatever you may think of the other sex, you think at all events too chivalrously to wish to marry for that reason; and moreover, if you are unable to sustain yourself, you will hardly get another person who is capable of sustaining you. Or one might say, "Look for a job, throw yourself into the life of affairs, that is a distraction, and you will forget your melancholy.[11] Get to work. That's the best thing." Perhaps you will succeed in getting to the point where your melancholy seems as if it were forgotten, but forgotten it is not; occasionally it will break out and will be more dreadful than ever, it will then perhaps be capable of doing what it could never do before, it may take you off your guard. Furthermore, however you may think of life and its affairs, you will nevertheless think too chivalrously of yourself to choose a profession for that reason, for that, after all, is a kind of falsehood, like marrying for the same reason. What then must you do? I have only one answer: despair.

I am a married man, my soul clings firmly and wisely to my wife, to my children, to this life which I shall always extol for its beauty. So when I counsel you to despair, it is not a fantastical youth who would whirl you away in the maelstrom of the passions, nor a mocking demon who shouts this comfort to the shipwrecked, but I shout it to you, not as a comfort, not as a condition in which you are to remain, but as a deed which requires all the power and seriousness and concentration of the soul, just as surely as it is my conviction, my victory over the world, that every man who has not tasted the bitterness of despair has missed the significance of life, however beautiful and joyous his life might be. By despairing you do not defraud the world in which you live, you are not lost to it because you have overcome it, as surely as I can affirm of myself that I am a proper married man, in spite of the fact that I, too, have despaired.

When in this way I look upon your life, I declare you fortunate, for at the instant of despair it is truly of the utmost importance for a man not to be mistaken about life; this is just as dangerous for him as for a woman in travail to go amiss. He who despairs over one particular thing incurs the danger that his despair may not be genuine and profound, that it may be a delusion, a sorrow only for a particular loss. It is not thus you

11. [Melancholy was prized in the Romantic Age as the expression of a deep and sensitive spirit.]

are to despair, for no particular thing has been taken from you, you still possess everything you had. If the despairing man makes a mistake, if he believes that the misfortune lies in his multifarious surroundings, then his despair is not genuine and it will lead him to hate the world and not to love it, for true as it is that the world is a burden to you because it is as if it would be to you something else than it can be, it is also just as true that when in despair you have found yourself you will love the world because it is what it is. If it is a fault or guilt or a troubled conscience which brings a man to despair, he will perhaps have difficulty in regaining his joyfulness. So, then, despair with all your soul and with all your mind; the longer you put it off, the harder the conditions become, and the demand remains the same. I shout this to you, like the woman who offered to sell to Tarquin a collection of books and when he would not give the sum she demanded burned one-third of them and demanded the same sum, and when again he would not give the sum she demanded burned another third of them and demanded the same sum, until finally he gave the original sum for the last third. . . .

So then choose despair, for despair itself is a choice; for one can doubt without choosing to, but one cannot despair without choosing. And when a man despairs he chooses again—and what is it he chooses? He chooses himself, not in his immediacy, not as this fortuitous individual, but he chooses himself in his eternal validity. ~

INTERPRETIVE QUESTIONS FOR DISCUSSION

Why is Author A unable to find fulfillment in friendship and marriage?

1. Why does A "begin with the principle that all men are bores"? Why does he regard boredom as the root of all evil? (35)

2. Why does A say that "all this talk about society and the social is partly inherited hypocrisy, partly calculated cunning"? Are we meant to think that A's antisocial attitude is due to his belief that man is "at bottom" a "beast of prey"? (39)

3. Why does A look down on the people we usually admire—those who keep themselves busy and are useful?

4. Why does A propose "rotation" as the best solution to boredom? (42) Why does every change in mode of cultivation come under "the general categories of *remembering* and *forgetting*"? (43)

5. Why does the philosophy "that it is the end and aim of every man to enjoy himself" lead to "the principle of limitation, the only saving principle in the world"? (40, 43)

6. How is the "art" of forgetting different from forgetfulness? What does it mean to reduce an experience to "a sounding board for the soul's own music"? (45)

7. Why does A maintain that "the essential thing is never to stick fast" and that "the whole secret lies in arbitrariness"? (47, 50)

8. Why does A consider the thought that husband and wife "become one" a "dark and mystic saying"? (48)

9. Why does A's "aesthetics" lead to change for its own sake—an appreciation of the trivial and arbitrary rather than of the beautiful and sublime?

10. Why does A put forth a philosophy that recommends abandoning hope and forsaking all meaningful human relationships?

Suggested textual analyses
Pages 43–46: beginning, "The more resourceful in changing the mode of cultivation one can be," and ending, "and make possible the realization of a complete freedom."

Pages 50–52: beginning, "The whole secret lies in arbitrariness," and ending, "which the man of genius easily discovers in his ubiquity."

Why does Author B counsel Author A to "choose despair"?

1. Why does B shout at A, "Either/or"?

2. Why do the words *either/or* affect B "like a magic formula of incantation?" Why does he think it important to choose rightly, even when good and evil are not at stake? (53)

3. Why does B accuse A of using the statement "I say merely either/or" as a mask, and warn that he might end up with his nature being "resolved into a multiplicity"? Why does B say, "In fact you are nothing; you are merely a relation to others"? (55–56)

4. Why does B "take up the matter from another side" and imagine a young man who trusts A and comes to him for advice? Why is B so confident that A would rise to the occasion and take it seriously? (57–58)

5. Why does B think that A can, through an either/or, "win what is the chief thing in life"—his "own self"? Why does B think that "the choice itself is decisive for the content of the personality"? (59)

6. Why, according to B, can A master the knowledge of a parson, but not choose to become a parson? Does B think A takes choice *too* seriously? (61–62)

7. Why is an aesthetic choice no choice? Why is the act of choosing "essentially a proper and stringent expression of the ethical"? (63)

8. Why does B want only to bring A "up to the point where the choice between the evil and the good acquires significance" for him? (64) Why does B insist that "the crucial thing is not deliberation but the baptism of the will which lifts up the choice into the ethical"? (66)

9. Why does B believe that whoever has not tasted the bitterness of despair has missed the significance of life? Why does true despair lead to love of the world rather than hatred for it? (67–68)

10. Why has B found beauty and happiness in marriage, despite having known despair? (67)

11. What is the "equilibrium between the aesthetical and the ethical" that B thinks he has acquired?

12. What is A hiding from, according to B?

Suggested textual analyses

Pages 53–57: beginning, "My Friend," and ending, "for Echo is heard only in emptiness."

Pages 64–66: beginning, "What is it, then, that I distinguish in my either/or?" and ending, "if a choice signifies something. . . ."

Why does Kierkegaard use the fiction of an editor, Victor Eremita, who has accidentally discovered a correspondence between other people?

1. Why does Kierkegaard present two authors, one a romantic aesthete arguing that choice is essentially arbitrary, the other a man of conventional morality insisting that choice is the key to the self?
2. Why does Victor say that the insight he gained into the lives of two men from their papers has confirmed his hunch "that the external is not the internal"? (30)
3. Why are we told that A's exterior was hiding a contradiction, while B's was hiding his true significance? (30)
4. Why does Victor think that the reader might share his doubt about whether the internal is the same as the external? Why does such a doubt come and go "like a passing shadow"? (29)
5. Why does Victor become obsessed with the secretary?
6. Why does Victor rationalize the purchase of the secretary as an extravagance that will mark the beginning of a new period in his life?
7. Why does Kierkegaard have the papers come to light when Victor angrily attacks his beloved secretary with a hatchet? Why is luck "necessary to make such discoveries possible"? (33)
8. Is Kierkegaard trying to convince us to adopt the viewpoint of B? Is A putting forth a serious philosophy or only expressing Kierkegaard's cynicism?

Suggested textual analysis
Pages 29–33: beginning, "Dear Reader:" and ending, "and left him undisturbed in his belief."

For Further Reflection

1. Is boredom the root of all evil? Has boredom gained the upper hand in the world today?

2. Does a lack of commitment to people and principles lead to a splintering of the personality?

3. Do you find more joy in work or in idleness?

4. Is love the cure for despair?

5. Do you want to live aesthetically or ethically? Must one choose, or is it possible to do both?

6. Do you agree that whoever has not tasted the bitterness of despair has missed the significance of life?

7. Is A's philosophy of life widespread?

Emöke

Josef Škvorecký

JOSEF ŠKVORECKÝ (1924–) is a professor emeritus of English at the University of Toronto. Born in Czechoslovakia, Škvorecký emigrated to Canada after the 1968 Soviet invasion of his homeland. In Canada, he and his wife, novelist Zdena Salivarova, founded a publishing house—Sixty-Eight Publishers—devoted to preserving Czech-language literature. Škvorecký is the author of seven collections of short stories, two plays, and twelve novels, including *The Cowards, Miss Silver's Past,* and *The Engineer of Human Souls.* His awards include the 1980 Neustadt International Prize for Literature and the 1984 Governor General's Award for Fiction. Škvorecký served as an adviser to Czech President Václav Havel in 1990, and was appointed a member of the Order of Canada in 1992.

A STORY HAPPENS *and fades and no one tells it. And yet somewhere, someone lives on, afternoons are hot and idle and Christmases come, that person dies and there is a new slab with a name on it in the graveyard. Two or three people, a husband, a brother, a mother, still bear the light, the legend, in their heads for a few more years and then they die too. For the children it remains only like an old film, the out-of-focus aura of a vague face. The grandchildren know nothing. And other people forget. Neither a name nor a memory nor even an empty space is left. Nothing.*

But a certain building, a recreation center—once a hotel maybe, a rural inn or a boarding house—still hides the story of two people and their folly, and perhaps the shades of its characters may still be glimpsed in the social hall or in the Ping-Pong room, like the materialized images of werewolves in deserted old houses, trapped in the dead thoughts of human beings, unable to leave for a hundred, five hundred, a thousand years, perhaps forever.

The room's ceiling slanted downward. It was a garret, the window high off the floor—you couldn't see out unless you pushed the table over to the wall and climbed up on it. And the very first night there (it was a hot night, August, the susurrus of ash and linden under the window like the distant rush of diluvial seas, the window open to let in the night's sounds and fragrances of grass and grasshoppers and crickets and cicadas and linden blossoms and cigarettes and from the nearby town the music of a Gypsy band playing Glenn Miller's old "In the Mood," but in an undulating Gypsy rhythm, and then "Dinah," and then "St. Louis Blues," but they were Gypsies—two fiddles, a bass, a dulcimer—and the beat wasn't boogie but rather the weaving pulse of the Gypsy, the leader embellishing on the blue tones in a swaying Gypsy rhythm), the schoolteacher began to talk about women. He talked in the dark, in bed, in a hoarse voice trying to get me to tell him how it was with me and women. What I told him was that I was getting married before Christmas, that I was marrying a widow called Irene, but all the while I was thinking about Margit and about her husband who had let it be known that he would beat me senseless if ever I showed my face in the district of Libeň again, and about the carnival in Libeň and about Margit with her nose red from crying, red like the nose of the painted clay dwarf down in the desolate, funereal garden behind the hotel, the inn, that recreation center or whatever it was. Then he began to talk about women himself; words full of salacious images, vulgar, raunchy, came pouring from his craw, from his rabbit brain, evoking in me a profound depression. It was as if the hand of Death were reaching out to me from the barren life of that country schoolteacher, fifty years old with a wife and three children, teaching at a five-grade school and shooting off his mouth here about women, about sex with young teachers whose work placement card had forced them to leave their mothers and move, with just a couple of worn suitcases, far away to God knows where in the Sudeten mountains, to a village near the border, where there wasn't even a movie house, just a tavern, just a few lumberjacks, a few Gypsies, a few locals transplanted here by all sorts of plans and desires and dreams and bad consciences, and just a deserted manse and the chairman of the local National Committee—before the revolution a day-laborer on the estate of the lords of Schwarzenberg, in his blood the congenital defiance of forefathers who had sweated over soil they never owned, he had been driven here afterward by that very defiance, that hunger for land; now he had his land, and he sweated over it like all his sinewy and unshaven forefathers had done except that now the soil was his—and then the teacher, the only one in the whole village who knew how to play the violin and who could drop words like Karel Čapek, Bedřich Smetana, Antonín Dvořák, words that embodied the magic of virginal patriotic ideals and the spirit of the Teachers College where young women were prepared for that most beautiful of professions; and when he first arrived there at the age of forty he already had a wife and (at that time) two children, but he told the young teacher he loved her, in heavy calligraphy he wrote love letters and poems that seemed almost familiar to her (he had an old handbook of love letters and love poems by anonymous poets that he would adapt to his particular needs), and of a morning she would find a bunch of primroses on her desk, or a sprig of edelweiss or a bachelor's button or a spray of lily of the valley, and she used to listen to him, go to meet him beyond the village in the shrubbery, in the underbrush of the pine woods where the wind of late summer blew over the bald hills and the town stood below, cold with the church spire pointing up to heaven, dingy, yellowish, half-deserted under the steel-gray moss of autumn clouds, and then she said Yes and took him to her room and now he was telling me about it ". . . she said the light was too bright, that she was embarrassed, but all she had was a lightbulb hanging on a cord from the ceiling, no lampshade, nothing, so I pulled the panties off her, blue jersey flimsies they were, and hung 'em over the lightbulb, and right away it was like it used to be in the streetcars during the war, in the blackouts, and then I did it to her. . . ." He was a man entirely in the sway of death, and I swayed under the bleakness of that life of his, more desolate than the life of a mouse or a sparrow, or the caged armadillo at the zoo that just stamps its feet on the steel floor and snorts greedily and rhythmically and then eats and then copulates and snorts and stamps and runs around and sleeps because it's an armadillo, a comical beast that lives an optimum life according to armadillo law; but he was a human being, until recently principal of a five-grade school and member of the local National Committee although he had now been downgraded to the two-room school on the frontier ("The inspector had it in for me, a Party man, you know, he was jealous because he couldn't make time with a young teacher like I could"), heir to that ancient tradition of schoolmasters who in days of old brought books and music and beauty and philosophy into mountain cottages and to little villages like that village, husband to a wife who had to stay behind alone and was receiving a bonus for having to maintain a separate household, father by this time to three children, and here he was, living according to the laws of white mice and armadillos.

The girl (not the young teacher, but the one that sat next to us that first evening in the dining room listening to the social director, who called himself our Cultural Guide, unfolding an extensive and substantial program of organized activity for our group) was built like a dancer, slender as a street lantern, with boyish hips and delicate sloping shoulders, and breasts like the breasts of stylized statues, that did not disturb the slender young symmetry of the jersey-clad body. And almond eyes, gazelle's eyes, dark as the charred core of a charcoal pile, and hair like a Gypsy's but brushed to the flat sheen of black marble. We had walked beside her the whole day on an excursion to Mariatal, a place of pilgrimage to which believers used to come from all over the Austro-Hungarian Empire and perhaps from all over Europe (now it was a deserted and desolate forest valley) and I felt timid by her side, and most conversation topics seemed trivial and irrelevant. It was impossible to talk with her about the usual things, to have the sort of conversation where the words mean nothing or no more than the crowing of a rooster or the hooting of an owl calling to his mate from the crown of a pine tree. It seemed to me that with her one could only talk about ideas. She wasn't the kind of girl you approach at a dance and say, May I have this dance, miss? and then something about how good the band is and that's a pretty dress she has on and what's her phone number, and then you call that number and she either comes or she doesn't, and if she comes you go dancing again, and then you don't have to say much of anything anymore, it's just a matter of whether you have an apartment or a studio or even just a furnished room with a close-mouthed landlady, or if you have none of these, at least enough money for two rooms in a hotel. No, this girl was profound, a philosophy of life rested somewhere in the depth of her soul, and you had to talk about that philosophy—it was the only way you could get to her, there was no other way. Of course, the schoolteacher didn't see that and he persisted with his noises, his vulgar expressions, crude conversational lines from common dance halls, the smart remarks of village Don Juans and small-town wolves; he trotted out the old tricks and clichés that call for an exact phrase, a precise response from a girl—like the Latin dialogue between priest and altar boy—in the eternal sexual ritual of establishing acquaintance, but she didn't come back with those petrified responses, she was silent and just said Yes (she was Hungarian, she spoke a strange combination of Slovak and Hungarian and some Gypsy or Carpathian dialect) or No, and the schoolteacher soon exhausted his stock of tricks and ploys and fell silent, plucked a blade of grass from the roadside, stuck it in his mouth and walked along chewing on it, defeated and mute with the grass sticking straight out of his mouth. Just then a huge dragonfly flew across the path and I asked the girl whether she knew that there were once dragonflies with a wingspan of two and a half feet. She voiced surprise and wonder that such a thing was possible, and I began to talk about the Mesozoic Age and the Cenozoic Age and about Darwin, about the world's evolving, the blind and inevitable course of nature where the strong devour the weak and animals are born to seek food, procreate, and die, how there's no significance to it, significance being a human term and nature a bare causal nexus, not a colorful, meaningful, mystical teleology. And that was when she told me I was mistaken, that nature does have significance, and life too. What significance? I asked, and she said, God. "All right, knock it off now," said the schoolteacher. "Say, miss, don't you feel like a beer? It's hotter than hell today." But she shook her head and I said, You believe in God? I do, she replied, and I said, There is no God. It would be nice if there were, but there isn't. You haven't come that far yet, she explained. You're still a physical person, you're still imperfect. But some day you'll find Him. I, I said, am an atheist. I used to be an atheist too, she replied, until my eyes were opened. I discovered Truth. How did it happen? I asked sarcastically, because she was slender like a dancer, and I knew dancers do go to church a lot and kneel and make the sign of the cross but they don't believe in God, they don't really think about God, they retain God as a superstition, the way they get someone to spit on them before they go on stage, before they don their professional smile and run out into the glow of the spotlights with their tiny little steps. When I got married, she said, and the schoolteacher, who had been walking alongside in silence chewing on a fresh piece of grass, awoke from his dumb stupor and said, "You're married?" No, she replied. I'm a widow. But when

I was married, I learned to believe. Your husband was religious? I asked. She shook her head. No, she said, he was very physical, he had nothing in him of spiritual man. "That makes you a young widow, eh?" said the teacher. "And would you like to get married again?" No, said Emöke (her name was Emöke, she was Hungarian, her father, a postal clerk, had made a career for himself in Slovakia when part of that country was annexed by Hungary before the war: he had been sent there as postmaster and had begun to live like a lord, with a piano, a salon, and a daughter at the lyceum who received private French lessons), I'll never marry again. Why are you so determined? I asked. Because I have discovered that there can be more elevated aims in life, she replied. For instance, you said that the eternal changing of shapes has no significance, that it's all just cause and effect. That is the way it appears to you. But I see a significance in it that you don't see yet. What sort of significance? I asked. It is all aimed toward God, she said. Toward becoming one with Him. That is the significance, the meaning of all life.

Between believers and nonbelievers there is no communication, there is a wall, a steel barrier against which understanding shatters. I did what I could to explain to her that significance and meaning, and the sense of design which people attribute to the blind activity of nature, are merely human concepts, that that was what I'd been trying to say, that meaning is an anthropomorphic idea born of the awareness that every human activity has "meaning" of one sort or another: we cook so that we may eat, go on vacation to relax, brush our teeth so they won't decay—and then we carry over this idea of purpose to nature where we feel that it is lacking; but she just smiled at all my logic and my rationale and my helpless fury (it wasn't an angry fury, just a desperate fury at the fact that I couldn't convince her of such obvious truths, that there was something in her, an ability or an inability, something beyond logic, that proudly resisted reason) and she replied to it all with a mild, calm, almost sublime smile and the words, You are simply a physical person. You are still imperfect. So I asked her whether she didn't feel hatred for me or contempt that I was an atheist, and she shook her head and said, I pity you. Why? Because you may have to live many lives before you become perfect. And before you find the truth. Many lives? I asked. Yes, replied Emöke. Because you must become a spiritual person before you see the truth. "You mean you believe in reincarnation, miss?" asked the schoolteacher. It doesn't matter what it is called, she said. You needn't even use the name God. Words don't matter. But you must know the Truth.

We entered the forest valley of Mariatal where the little white pilgrims' church stood deserted, the broad lane of deserted booths leading up to it, smelling of rotting wood. The plank-top counters where gingerbread hearts were once stacked in piles beside holy pictures and mirrors with pictures of the shrine, and the decaying beams from which black, white, and pink rosaries had hung alongside silver and gold madonnas on chains, miniature fonts for holy water with pictures of the Mother of God, tin crucifixes, wooden ones with tin Christs, carved ones and plain ones, blessings for cottage parlor walls, pictures of the Virgin of Mariatal, pictures of saints and wax figurines, and beside them a booth where a fellow in a white apron with a fez on his head would chop slabs of Turkish honey-nougat into sticky sweet flakes, and a little farther on, a stand with chenille scarves, cotton stockings, and glass jewelry, and a stand for sausages and another booth with holy pictures; and peasants in black suits and black hats wiping their sweaty faces with red bandannas, their black, laced boots dusty from the long trek, and little old ladies in white Sunday kerchiefs, and tired children, and weary couples who had come here to say a prayer for the success of their young marriage or the conception that was long in coming, and old people for a happy final hour, the sound of organ music coming from the church, and the sound of singing, the path curving up the hillside through the woods, bordered by little white chapels with wooden altars displaying hand-painted scenes from the lives of the saints, now long faded and peeling, aged by many rains and the hard heat of summer;

and the Cultural Guide, his hairy, spindly legs protruding from his shorts, climbed up on to the steps of one of the chapel pavilions (that first evening he would expound on his plans for our recreation, but the second night he got drunk and the third day he was sleeping it off and the last evening at the farewell party he drank himself speechless and rolled under the platform where the musicians tipped the spit out of their saxophones onto him) and began to lecture us about the pilgrimages that used to come here—it was immediately apparent that he was totally ignorant not only of the Catholic Church, its dogma, liturgy, tradition, and catechism, and of Biblical history, but of everything in general; he made a joke about sterile women and impotent men coming here to Mariatal to pray for the restoration of their juices, and then he waxed serious and launched into an exposé of religion, a splendid mishmash of the most desperate vulgarization of Engels, science premasticated for narrow minds—presented to us to salve his own conscience for the twelve-hundred-crown salary he was paid each month—not science popularized for the unschooled though spontaneously intelligent mind of the workingman, but rather cheap half-truths and quarter-truths for parasitical leeches who don't give a damn about truth, not science but pseudoscience, cut-rate science, a derision and an insult to science, not truth but stupidity, a lack of sensitivity, a lack of feeling, a thick-skinned denseness impervious to the arrows of that tragically desperate poetry of a desperate dream that is to come to pass only in the hereafter of the utopian world of future wisdom (in the absence of drunken bums who feel a revulsion for manual labor and make a living by spouting ill-learned phrases memorized from tour-guides to ancient castles), the poetry of sunny pilgrimages with the voice of the organ underscored by the wail of paper whistles, and the smell of evergreens and pine needles mingling with the sweet smell of incense, and little altar boys in red and green collars, their lace-up boots poking out from under their robes, fervently bobbing the smoking censers, and the loveliness of the forest and its light and shadow and the call of the cuckoos parting to the stride of the priest dressed in gold who lifts the shining monstrance with the glowing white circle (the most perfect plane figure of the ancient Greeks) in its glittering center and holds it suspended over the bowed heads in kerchiefs and the gray hair of old farmers so that it seems to float on wisps of smoke from the burning incense, flooded by the glow of sun and forest light like a symbol of that eternal human longing and hope which will be realized here and on this earth, but which is unattainable, unthinkable without this poetic folk faith in the goodness which rules the world in the long run, faith in love, faith in justice; a faith, hope, and love that had never entered the mind of this drunken, vulgar, dense Cultural Guide.

In our room that night the schoolteacher said to me, "Seems to me you're not very good at handling women. That's no way to go after a broad. Religion and dinosaurs? At that rate you'll never get her to bed within the week, you can bet your life on it."

Later, Emöke told me about him. The schoolteacher had got up early and prowled around under her window, baring his yellow teeth at her, yelling his wisecracks up to her whenever she appeared at the window to take down the white socks she washed each evening and hung out below on a taut string to dry. The schoolteacher rutted under the window while she gave him a cool and polite good morning, and he made his proposition, "Don't you want to flush out your lungs, miss, the woods are full of ozone of a morning!" and she shook her head and told him No and he went off by himself and then all day he circled around her, his eyes glowing in his self-indulgent face, his brain chewing the cud of the few ideas at his command, not ideas, conversational stereotypes, and from time to time he would come up to her, pull one out and lay it on her, and having failed go off again, his eyes still glowing, observing her hungrily from a distance, circling around her like a ruffled rooster around an inaccessible hen from another barnyard. She told me her story, her legend. It was like the confidences that prostitutes are said to impart to their clients of girlhoods in aristocratic households, the fall and the poverty and the sorrowful selling of one's body. She told me how they had stayed in Slovakia after the war, about her Hungarian father, a small-time official and a fascist, who had been a supporter of the Nazis and was destroyed after the war, no pension, no livelihood, too old and sick to take a job digging ditches or cutting down trees, and her mother, broken and loathing physical work, and herself, sixteen, in her sixth year at the Hungarian lyceum that the Slovaks closed down, when along came this man, the owner of a farm, and vineyards, he was rich, forty-five, with a hotel in Bratislava, and she had given in to him to save her family from misery or death by starvation or old age in the poorhouse, he was overbearing, mean, dense, he didn't believe in anything, God, democracy, human decency, nothing, just himself, and he wanted a son to inherit his farm and hotel and vineyards, but he wasn't prejudiced, he didn't mind that she was Hungarian. She bore him a daughter and that day he stormed out and drank himself dumb, he didn't speak to her for a week and then he began to beat her when he was drunk; that was when a hearty, hard-drinking bunch began to meet at the farm, cars would drive up from Bratislava, from Košice, from Turčanský Svatý Martin, there were meetings in his study and he became a member of a right-wing party, but she didn't pay any attention and when he came to her at night, his breath stinking like a wine cellar, he would force her to do what for him might still have been pleasure but for her was suffering and shame; as she got to know this man with the bull neck and the heavy breath, she also discovered her Truth: she had met another man, a gardener who had tuberculosis and who later died, and he lent her books about the path to God, the developing of one's spiritual strength, the spiritual universe and life beyond the grave, and she came to believe that everything here is nothing but one immense process of purging oneself of the stain of evil, and evil is matter and man must purge himself of matter, of the body, of desire, his goal must be the spirit, but not even that, for the spirit is just another stage, a higher stage than the physical one, and the ultimate aim is to reach God, to become one with Him, to dissolve one's own self in the infinite horizon of bliss that radiates mystical divine Love and Goodness.

Soon after, her husband was killed. After the Communist coup in February 1948 they nationalized his hotel, then his farm, and then they arrested him; he escaped, but they shot him as he tried to swim the Danube to Austria. She got a job in an office and learned bookkeeping, becoming a good bookkeeper; she went to live in Košice with her little girl (her parents were both dead) and she wanted to raise her little girl in the truth that she herself had discovered.

She lent me some of those books. They were bound collections of various parapsychological and theosophical journals; I found an article on the powers of amulets and the effectiveness of copper circlets which, when worn on the naked skin at the perihelion of Mars, will protect the wearer from rheumatism and bleeding, and I asked her whether it didn't seem strange to her that people who place so much emphasis on the spirit should be so concerned with the body since three quarters of those theosophical formulas concerned protection against disease, and whether she believed it all. She replied that at each stage of one's existence one must obey the laws that come from God, and the laws of physical existence call for attention to one's physical well-being. And as for the formulas, she asked how I could admit I had never tried them yet claim I doubted their effectiveness. So you too, she said, are imperfect and reject the truth, everyone rejects the truth, but in the end everyone will discover it, because God is Mercy. And with those words, a curious look came into her eyes, a flash of anxiety, as if she were afraid I wanted to rob her of something, of the certainty she possessed and without which she couldn't survive, couldn't bear the burden of her widowhood, the burden of death and of a sad, destroyed life; it was the expression of an ensnared little woodland animal, begging you with its eyes not to torture it and let it go, to release it from your power.

The schoolteacher asked me how I was making out. I knew that I had her, like the little animal in the woods, strangely in my power, the way men sometimes capture women without deserving to and without really trying, by the simple inscrutable effect of attraction and submission, but I didn't understand it the way I had at other times, or as I did with the ordinary, erotic, and uncomplicated Margit; this time it was as if the invisible nerves that linked us were nourishing some sort of drama, some possible fulfillment that might wipe out the desperate and vicious illusion which had made of that slender body and that lovely face and those delicate dancer's breasts and that creative force a chimerical existence imprisoned in a vicious circle.

The schoolteacher frowned, growled, and rolled over in bed so hard that the springs creaked.

Two days before our week's vacation was due to end, it rained, and the vacationers played Ping-Pong or cards or sat around in the dining room, chatting about things, trying for a while to find someone to play the piano; the Cultural Guide awoke from the previous day's drunkenness and tried to bring the group together with some game he called French Mail, but the only ones he could interest were an old married couple: he, paunchy, with baggy knee breeches, a former owner of a haberdashery, now manager of a state-owned clothing store in Pardubice, and she, fat, benign, at fifty still emitting the naïve peeps of surprise that she used to emit at eighteen on the merry-go-round: she always revived at lunchtime, not out of gluttony but because food was the only thing she understood, otherwise she moved through life in a mist, guided by the light of secure conventions, maternal admonitions, dancing lessons, nice boys carefully picked by her parents, courtship, marriage, two or three births, and Sunday mass (but if anyone were to ask her about even the most basic theological terms, she wouldn't know what to say, she simply went to mass, sang the hymns in the hymnal, genuflected, beat her breast, made the sign of the cross with the tips of her fingers moistened in holy water, and had requiem masses served in memory of her late mother); her kitchen too was an island of security where she became an artist, a virtuoso with absolute pitch for tastes and odors, like a violinist can tell a quarter tone and even an eighth, not rationally but intuitively, with a sense that others don't have and can't have, something that isn't the result of the five or seven years of apprenticeship in a mother's kitchen but a gift of grace, a piece of immortality given to a person in addition to the simple ordinary skills and the sleepy brain with its few stunted thoughts, and a heart submerged in lard, capable of no dishonesty or evil, capable only of an animal love for its young, its spouse, its family, for people, for life, and of resignation to death—the last of those beacons of security that border the path from the first moment of awakening in the mists of life. Then the Cultural Guide also found an old seamstress for the game, an old maid, a worker laureate of the state enterprise called Gentlemen's Linens, who was spending her first vacation away from her home in Prague's working-class Žižkov district, and who had spent the entire week so far sitting around, standing around, walking around, not knowing what to do, with nothing to talk about because she didn't know anyone there and in all her life hadn't known anything but men's shirts, had never known a man and love, had lived frozen between the prose of shirts and the primitive poetry of the dreams of old maids. He also got hold of a pimply young hotshot who had tried in vain the first three days to gain the affections of a pigtailed Slovak girl, who in turn had given preference to a black-haired technician, a former gunner in the R.A.F., who had a wife and child at home but had learned the art in which the schoolteacher would never be more than a rank amateur and had taken it to the very pinnacle that that limited art could ever reach, and the hotshot had got riled, retreating to the stubborn solitude of the recreation hall along with his striped socks and his black silk shirt, and now, sulky and defiant, he had been half talked into playing the game of French Mail. And finally the Cultural Guide had rooted out an uncertain, silent man who may have been a foreman in a factory or something but who never said a word to anyone, and with these people—people dominated by both the feeling of being obliged to enjoy themselves for a whole week, for the duration of this cheap if not entirely free vacation, and a feeling of helplessness as to how to go about it since they had all fallen victim to the fallacy that on vacation you can enjoy yourself in a manner different from the one to which you are accustomed, people who knew nothing but work, and for whom work was as essential as air and food, and who had been suddenly called upon to live the life of men and women from a bygone era, men and women unfamiliar with work: wives of wealthy businessmen, of officers, physicians, stockbrokers, sons of rich fathers, or tanned daughters of the sweet bourgeoisie for whom free time was all the time and amusement a vocation that they understood—and now, with these people burdened with the onus of vacationing, the Cultural Guide, with his hangover, and a cup of black coffee in his hand, began a collective game in order to maintain the impression of his productivity, the illusion of having honestly earned the twelve hundred crowns of his monthly pay.

The schoolteacher lolled around the Ping-Pong room, glaring across the green table and through the glass wall into the dark, wood-paneled corner where I was sitting on a bench with Emöke; then he and a bespectacled self-taught Ping-Pong player played a game, the schoolteacher executing pseudovirtuoso drives and smashes, most of them ending up in the net, but when once in a while he pulled something off after all, he would stab his hungry gaze in Emöke's direction to see if she was looking, and, taking long shots with the elegance of a lifeguard, low and easy, with an expression of bored pity, he beat the pants off the bespectacled enthusiast who played for fun and not for effect but lacked all talent for the game and kept chasing balls under the pool tables into all corners of the room.

I sat with Emöke in the dim light of the wood-paneled corner, drinking a toddy—although Emöke had Chinese tea because one shouldn't drink alcohol, alcohol debases one to the lowest level of physical being, transforms one back to the animal that one once was—and she talked about medical treatment by Paracelsus's methods, about trees that take upon themselves the diseases of men, just a small cut on a fingertip, a drop of blood pressed into a cut in the bark of a tree, and a bond is formed, a fine thread of delicate and invisible matter by means of which the man remains forever joined to the tree, as he remains forever joined to everything that ever left his body, a fallen hair, a breath, a clipped fingernail, and the illness travels along that thread to the tree and the tree fights the illness and overcomes it or sometimes perishes and dries up, but the man regains his health and his strength and lives on. She told about possession by evil spirits, exorcism by means of holy water and prayers, about black magic and evil powers that serve a person if he has the courage to stand in the center of concentric circles inscribed with the secret names of the Supreme One and intone evil prayers from the Satanic psalter, backward, and she told about werewolves, vampires, haunted houses, and witches' sabbaths and her spirit stumbled in those dangerous worlds that you don't believe in and you laugh at, but once you have heard of them there is always a tiny drop of horror in you, terror and fear. She forgot about me and I was silent, she talked on and in the gray light of the rain her eyes shone with a sort of feverish, unhealthy, unnatural enthusiasm, and I was silent and watched those eyes and she noticed it and the feverish shine faded and I shook off the strange evil enchantment of that magic rainy moment too, made a sarcastic face and said, You don't mean to say you want to devote yourself to black magic? Why, it's the epitome of Evil and you're striving to attain Goodness. And she dropped her gaze and said, Not anymore I don't want to, but once I did. When? I asked. When I couldn't stand it anymore, she replied, when I began to feel God didn't hear me, that He'd turned against me. I wanted to ask the Evil One for help, to—

to help me get rid of him. And did you? Did you make those concentric circles with consecrated chalk? I asked. No, she said, God was protecting me. I understand now that God is constantly testing man, and many people don't pass the test. But why does He test them? I asked. To see if man is worthy of the supreme grace of being delivered from everything physical, to see if he's ready. But man never asked God to create him, I said. By what right does God test him? God has the right to do anything, she said, because God is Love. Is He supremely merciful? I asked. Yes, she said. Then why did He create man? Because He loved him, she said. And why did He create him, then? Why did He send him into this world full of suffering? To test him, to see if he is deserving of His grace, she explained. But isn't He torturing him that way? I asked. Why didn't He just leave him alone from the outset, if He loves him? Or, once He created him, why didn't He go ahead and create him perfect right off? Ready for eternal bliss? Why all the martyrdom of the pilgrimage from Matter to Spirit? Oh, you're still imperfect, she said. You reject the truth. I don't reject it, I said, but I want to have proof. And if not proof, then at least logic. Logic is also the work of God, she said. Then why doesn't God use logic Himself? He doesn't have to, she said. Some day you will understand. Some day everyone will understand and everyone will be saved. But don't talk about it anymore, please, she said, and her eyes again had the look of a little animal in the woods, afraid of losing that one certainty of forest freedom; so I stopped talking about it and went over to the piano; Emöke came and leaned against the top and I began to play "Riverside Blues," which she liked, and then I sang "St. James Infirmary," and the schoolteacher came over from the light and darkness of the Ping-Pong room and stood behind Emöke and I was singing

I went down to Saint James Infirmary
For to see my baby there
Stretched out on a cold white table
So sweet, so cold, so fair.

And the pentatonic melody born of that basic human sorrow that can only end in a convulsive lament—the sorrow of two people who are parting ways forever—slid into Emöke's heart and she said, That's a beautiful song. What is it? It's a Negro blues, I replied, and Emöke said, Yes, I've heard that Negro people are very spiritual people, I heard them sing some religious songs on a record, one of the men at the office has records from America. Ah, I said, blacks are lecherous rascals, but they've got a great sense of music. It just seems they're that way, she retorted. They are spiritual people. And I played and sang some more, and when I had finished, the schoolteacher said, "Come on, beef it up a little and put some life into it, a little jive so we can cut a rug, right, miss? This is Dullsville, not a vacation!" So Emöke laughed and told me to give up my place at the piano, and she sat down and started to play with sure, naturally harmonizing fingers, a slow but rhythmical song that held the distant echo of a czardas, the pulse of Hungarian music as unmistakable as the blue notes in Negro blues, and she sang in an alto that sounded like the level tone of a shepherd's flute, that cannot be modulated, strengthened or weakened, sure and straight and with a primitive beauty; she sang in hard sweet Hungarian a song that was neither sad nor happy but just desperate, her cheeks flushed, and the song wasn't the chanting of a black magician in concentric chalk circles but the call of a shepherd on the steppe, ignorant of black sabbaths and black masses, living a natural life on sheep's milk and cheese, sleeping in a wooden shack, aware of a few superstitions but not associating them with God or the Devil, possessed once in his life by such an insurmountable longing that he goes off and sings this desperate, yearning, level, unmodulated loud song in his unmodulated and sweetly hard language and finds a mate and with her conceives new shepherds and lives on, eating cheese and whey by his evening fire, among the smell of hides and charcoal in his shack. And then I realized that that vulgar exhortation of the adulterous schoolteacher had liberated her as if by magic from the spectral world of things spiritual, and that this song sprang from the immense sensuality in her, but I also knew it was just the schoolteacher's words, not the schoolteacher himself, and suddenly I understood the catharsis toward which her drama was progressing, the fact that the Evil One in her life was that middle-aged owner of the hotel and the farm who had driven her into the realm of dangerous shades, into the unreal but frightening world of specters, so that she was now seeking the Supreme Good, Love, spiritual, nonphysical, divine; but that perhaps it would take very little for all that warped symbolism of obscure parapsychological magazines to be turned upside down by a strange, incomprehensible, and yet entirely comprehensible, flip of the soul, that the Good and the Supreme could perfectly well be me that maybe that's what I already was, even if she wouldn't admit it to herself, even if she didn't realize it yet, that maybe I was there already, in the deep, unknown cellar rooms of her unconscious, or at least getting there and at one stroke I might now be able to change the story, the legend, I might really become the Supreme One, the Creator, and create something human of this beautiful shade retreating slowly and surely into the mists of madness, that this mind was still capable, though not for much longer, of turning from its blind alley of uncertain imagery back onto the firm track of things concrete—but not for much longer, soon it would be lost in the twilight of the fogs that rise from terra firma and, having lost all knowledge of the law of gravity and all corollaries to that law, swoop according to the law of fogs to the abyss of senseless heights, possessing their own truth which is not a lie because it is simply another world and there is no communicating between this world and that one: a girl becomes a woman and a woman a crone, closing herself off in that world, encased in a network of wrinkles, her womb wasted and her soul slowly becoming a mournful litany of cracked old voices in the musty Gothic corridor from this world to the next, of which we know nothing and which perhaps is nothing.

"That was swell, miss!" said the schoolteacher when she stopped singing, and he started to applaud. "Now how about a czardas, what do you say?" She laughed and really began to play a czardas, emphasizing the beat with her entire body, her eyes glowing but not with the shiny feverish glow that they had had earlier in the wood-paneled corner. The schoolteacher stepped away from the piano and, yelping, performed a clumsy mock czardas (missing the beat entirely, and stamping his feet out of rhythm too) and as he wriggled ludicrously in front of the piano, Emöke began to sing again. Her singing attracted the group that had been playing French Mail and the athletic young girls and boys from the Ping-Pong room, and soon people began to enjoy themselves; I had to sit down at the piano again and play popular hits and some of the girls and boys and the schoolteacher and Emöke began to dance. Emöke had changed, like a bright butterfly's wing slipping out of a gray and mysterious cocoon, and this was she, not a legend but the real Emöke, for the primitive and unconscious schoolteacher had primitively and unconsciously found the right way to her buried heart and her path to the future; but I knew that path and future weren't destined to be his, because he wasn't interested in her future, just in the brief present of the week's vacation, in a lecherous thrill and a lewd memory. I was the one who could follow that path, but I'd gone too far along the path of my own life to be able to throw myself into the future without stopping to think it over. The yellow piano keys didn't want to return to their original position and I pounded them to produce song after song, watching her, and all of a sudden, like the schoolteacher, I began to desire that body, that slender, firm body, those breasts that didn't disturb its symmetry. Yet I realized it was all very, very complicated; I knew that there's a prescription for such fevers (and the schoolteacher would certainly prescribe it: sleep with her—it'll solve everything) that is, by and large, an effective prescription, but I also knew that in Emöke's case this particular goal, the physical act, would have to be preceded by something far finer and more complex than the schoolteacher's technique, and that it wasn't really a matter of the act at all but of the commitment that it represents, the act being merely a confirmation, a confirmation of the union that people conclude against life and against death, just the stigma of the act of creation which, if I wanted to, I might perhaps bring off; yet it wasn't that act of confirmation I yearned for (it would mean years and years of my life and one knows that every enchantment finally dissipates over the landscapes of the past and all that remains is the present, everyday reality) but rather the body, the pleasant, unusual vacation adventure, the womanly secret between the girlish thighs; but that way, of course, if I didn't take upon myself her whole life I would destroy her, and so as Emöke danced with the schoolteacher, I began to hate him with all my heart, this specimen who was not a man but a mere sum total of screws, and as for her, I was mad at her, a primitive masculine anger that she was dancing with him and so wasn't what she had appeared to be until a while ago; although I didn't agree with that world of hers created of desperate wishes, I still preferred it to the world of the schoolteacher.

So that when we met on the stairs on the way to dinner, I asked her sarcastically why she showed so much interest in the schoolteacher since he was obviously a basely physical person; and she said innocently, I know, he is a physical man, I felt sorry for him. We must feel compassion for people as unfortunate as he, and I asked her whether she didn't feel any compassion for me, after all I was physical too. Not entirely, she said. You at least have an interest in things spiritual, he doesn't; suddenly she was again entirely different from the way she had been with the schoolteacher, that cloud from another world obscured her face, she sat down at the table with a monastic absence of mind, and the schoolteacher's hungry glances went unnoticed as did the stares of the hotshot, who was beginning to weaken although he still clung to his role of offended lover of solitude.

The Cultural Guide announced that after dinner, at half past eight, there would be movies. Emöke went to her room and I went outside to the garden. It was damp, moldy, neglected. I sat down on a rotting bench wet through by the rain. Across from me stood the painted dwarf, his face rain-smudged, the tip of his nose knocked off, with a pipe between his teeth like the one my grandpa used to smoke; Grandpa used to have a dwarf like that in his garden too, with a pipe like that, and a white castle with lots of carved turrets and towers and real glass in the windows, and every spring he would paint the tin roof of the castle with red paint because at seventy-odd years the old man was still thrilled by the ideas that thrilled me when I was small, and thrilled me again at that moment when I remembered my grandfather's little castle: I believed that the castle was real—small maybe, but real—and that perhaps sometimes the half-inch steps were climbed by a royal procession of people two inches tall, like Lilliputians, that there were chambers behind the real glass windows, and salons and banquet halls just as realistic as the castle itself; and then there was the fairy tale of Tom Thumb: I dreamed of being Tom Thumb, riding around in a car wound up with a key, or sailing the bathtub in a little boat that when you poured some chemical into the stern sailed silently and regularly around the miniature ocean of the enameled bathtub. I stared at the ruddy, lecherous, beat-up face of the clay dwarf and in a way it was me, myself, thirty years old, still single, mixed up in the affair with Margit, a married woman, a guy who didn't believe in anything anymore or take anything very seriously, who knew what the world was all about, life, politics, fame and happiness and everything, who was alone, not from incapacity but of necessity, quite successful, with a good salary and reasonable health, for whom life held no surprises and with nothing left to learn that I didn't already know, at an age when the first minor physical problems begin to herald the passing of time, at an age when people get married at the last moment so as still to be able to have children and watch them grow up only to find out equally fast exactly what life's all about, and she, pretty and still young, with a child, Hungarian and hence a fairly novel being, relatively unfamiliar, but then again old enough at twenty-eight, but with a child which I supposed would mean an entirely different lifestyle, and a foreigner, Hungarian, not too intelligent, slightly warped by that parapsychological madness, out to proselytize, but heaven knows how holy, the ideal object for a vacation adventure, nothing more than that, and yet with that terrible look of a little animal of the woods, with that immense self-destructive defense mechanism against the world, in a fog of mystical superstition. For her it was a matter of life and death, not a matter of a hot evening, a meadow soft enough to lie in comfortably, a few tried-and-tested words, a well-chosen moment when the desire of summer and the mood of the week's vacation blend to form a favorable constellation of discarded inhibitions and the will to risk and to surrender; it was in fact a matter of a lifetime of love and self-sacrifice, or of death in the mist of mysticism, in the lunacy of midnight circles that meet around round tables and summon the spirits of their visions to come to earth, circles of faded middle-aged people, misfits, psychopaths, in this twentieth century still believing in goblins and the power of frog hair over cancer, recopying Satanic psalters and speaking backward the terrible black prayers of men who had sold their souls to the Prince of Darkness—men who didn't die a natural death but were torn asunder by the Devil, their souls ripped out from the shreds of their bodies and the tatters of bone and flesh, broken ribs, gouged eyes, flayed skins, ripped out and carried off to the eternal fire in the rotting guts of hell—or praying piously and not eating meat and treating ailments resulting from the constant immobility of praying by placing copper circlets against their bare skin and kissing pictures of saints, although death should be desirable, since death is presumably the gateway to a more perfect plane of life, closer to the Divine and eternal Bliss; that's what it was a matter of, not a matter of a single night but of all nights over many years, and not a matter of nights at all but of days and mutual care, marital love and good and evil until death do you part. That's what it was a matter of with that girl, that girl, that girl Emöke.

But later, sitting in the darkened auditorium where the Cultural Guide was showing a film (after several vain attempts to make the projector work, and only after the silent fellow, who was perhaps a factory foreman, had taken over, adjusting a screw here and there, and the projector had rattled to a start), a film that was precisely calculated for the maximum possible nonentertainment (and yet the people were entertained, because it was a movie and the projector was rattling away behind their backs and they were here to spend a week enjoying themselves), and as the room vanished in the smoky dusk I took Emöke's hand, warm and soft, and because tomorrow was the last day of our stay at the recreation center and I had to do something—or at any rate I succumbed to instinct or to that social obligation to seduce young women on vacation, single, married, or widowed—I asked her to come outside for a stroll. She acquiesced, I got up, she got up too and in the flickering of the projector I glimpsed the schoolteacher's gaze following her as she left the room by my side and went out into the night light of the August evening outside the building.

We walked through the night, along the white road between the fields, bordered by cherry trees and white milestones, the sweet smell of the blossoms and the countless voices of tiny creatures in the grass and the trees. I took Emöke's hand, she didn't object, I wanted to talk but I couldn't think of anything to talk about. There was nothing I might say, since my conscience kept me from opening the dam that held back my usual August evening rhetoric (irresistible to any lone woman on vacation providing the speaker is sufficiently young and not overly ugly) because I once again realized that it was a matter of life and death and that she was different, deeper, more inaccessible than other girls. I merely stopped and said Emöke, she stopped too, and said Yes? and then I took her in my arms or I moved as if to take her in my arms, but she slipped out of the incomplete embrace. I tried again, I put my arm around her slender, very firm waist and drew her toward me but she disengaged herself, turned and walked quickly away. I hurried after her, took her hand and again she didn't object, and I said Emöke, don't be angry. She shook her head and said, I'm not angry. But really, I insisted. Really, she said. It's just that I'm disappointed. Disappointed? I asked. That's right, replied Emöke. I'd begun to think you were different after all, but you aren't, you're just a prisoner of your body like all men. Don't be angry at me for it, Emöke, I said. I'm not angry, she answered, I know that men are usually like that. It's not your fault. You're still imperfect. I thought you were on the way, but you aren't, not yet. Not quite. And what about you, Emöke, I said, have you entirely given up everything physical already? Yes, replied Emöke. But you're so young, I said. Don't you want to marry again? She shook her head. Men are all the same, she said. I thought that I might find someone, some friend that I could live with, but just as a friend, you know, nothing physical, it disgusts me—no, I don't feel contempt for it, I know that physical people need it, there's nothing essentially bad about it, but it's derived from badness, from imperfection, from the body, from matter, and man progresses only by reaching toward the spirit. But now I've stopped believing that I'll ever be able to find a friend like that, so I'd rather be alone, with my little girl. She spoke, and her face was like milk, lovely in the light of the stars and the moon and the August night. I said, You won't find a friend like that. Not you. Not unless it's someone like that consumptive gardener of yours, the one who used to lend you those books because he wasn't capable of anything else— Don't talk about him like that, she interrupted me, don't be like that, please. But Emöke, really, I said, don't you ever long for someone—I mean the way girls do when they're as young as you and as pretty? Do you honestly think you could find a friend who wouldn't want that of you unless he were a poor wretch, somehow disabled or crippled? Oh, but it's not a matter of longing, Emöke replied. Everyone has temptation, but one must overcome it. But why? I said. What for? Longing needn't be exclusively and solely physical. It can be an expression of love, a yearning for oneness. Longing is at the very source of existence, insofar as people are born of love. You love your little daughter, don't you? And don't you want to have any more children? You could have them, I'm sure of that. Do you want to give all that up, voluntarily? Emöke echoed, Give it up? Everything is the will of God, she said. But is God standing in your way? I asked. He gave you so much, more than other women. You are young, pretty, healthy, all men aren't like that first husband of yours, not all marriages are based on reasons like yours. There are men who love their wives for more than just the physical side of marriage, even though that too is a part of love—But it's not a part of true love, she exclaimed. True love is love of the soul. But how would you have children then? I asked. Or are you against children? Oh, no, she said, children are innocent and need love. But they're burdened with sin, and woman must suffer for that sin when she brings them into the world. That doesn't answer my question, I said, and besides, childbirth can be painless nowadays. But are you in favor of children being born at all? Wouldn't it be better just to give it up and not keep bringing new objects of sin or whatever into the world, new beings burdened by matter and physicality, because that's what most people are. Wouldn't it be better to let people die out? No, she retorted quickly. It's God's will that they live. In His infinite goodness, God wants all people to find salvation. And all of them will, one day. But what do you mean by "all"? I said. And when will they all find salvation? Wouldn't it be better to stop now, so that "all" would be "all those now living in the world"? No, no, no, she said. No, you don't understand. You're the one that doesn't understand, I replied. You don't understand your own self, you're full of inconsistencies. You haven't resolved a single thing for yourself, let alone thought about the logical flaws in your mystical system. Oh, what's logic! she said. Just a subject in school. No, it's everything, I answered. It's your appealing to me terribly, it's . . . my liking you a lot, and it's my . . . Don't say it, she whispered, ridding me of the need to pronounce that fatal set of words which in her case could not be taken back, which would carry its full meaning and not be just a vague promise to be broken or simply forgotten, because it was she, Emöke, that story, that legend, that poem, the past, the future.

We were standing in front of the illuminated entrance to the recreation center. She stared at the dark shadows of the trees against the night, and the expression in her eyes was no longer that of a forest animal but of a woman fighting off the primal damnation that is the root of her feelings of inferiority and the source of her life-giving force, and that can in one red flash blind thought and reason although it may end up in—well, in all that painful business and possibly the shame of being an unwed mother and the worry and the risk of getting fat and losing one's charms and one's life and everything. But that damnation overcomes a woman all the same, and she gives in the way she's always given in and always will give in, and it's of this damnation that a new human being is born. Good night, said Emöke, reaching out to shake my hand. Emöke, I said, think about it. Good night, she said and disappeared inside the hotel. I caught a glimpse of her slender legs on the stairway and then nothing. For a while I stood in front of the hotel and at last I went upstairs to my room.

The schoolteacher was lying in bed, his pants, shirt, shorts, socks, everything neatly hung up to air along the back of the chair and the foot of the bed. He was awake and he measured me with a mean look. "Well?" he said. I didn't answer him, I sat down on my bed and began to undress. The schoolteacher watched me with eyes like two dried-up black figs. "Well, I'll be damned," he said, "don't tell me you're going to sleep with a hard-on!" Aw, nuts, I said, turned off the light and lay down in bed. For a while there was silence. Then the schoolteacher said, "Seems to me that you're a dud. That you don't know how to handle women. Admit it!" Good night, I said. Beyond the window a rooster crowed, aroused from his night's sleep by a bad dream.

At the farewell party, I drank red wine and watched Emöke who was wearing a close-fitting summer dress with a white collar, her arms bare, dressed like any other attractive girl of her age. When the vacationers saw I was just sitting there drinking, they gradually grew bolder and asked her to dance (they hadn't dared before, because according to the rules of vacationers she and I comprised a couple, and such a couple is a holy thing to these one- or two-week collectives), and so Emöke was constantly on the dance floor, one time with the Cultural Guide, who was only half sober, once with the hotshot, who had given up sulking but hadn't quite given up hope of living it up in what was left of his vacation (specifically with one of the four or five available girls in the group), once with the paunchy manager of the clothing store, whose pudgy wife observed her with the loving gaze of matrons who would never think of being jealous but who view young girls full of erotic charm as sort of mystical sisters in the delusive destiny of womankind, once with the leader of the jazz band, who didn't dance or even put down his fiddle at any other time during the evening, and with several others, and I sat over my third glass of red wine, for I was possessed by the strange indecisiveness of a man who feels a sense of responsibility but is still too much a man of his times not to have to fight off indifference, frivolity, irresponsibility. Emöke, the wine rose slowly to my head, Emöke on the dance floor looked altogether different from the five or six other girls on the dance floor; she was the most graceful, youthful yet ripe, without the imperfection of the seventeen-year-old face that hasn't yet made up its mind whether to trade in the loveliness of childhood for the shallow and uninteresting beauty of adulthood or for the charm of youth, the female charm of the age of courtship and the first natural swell of fertility; she laughed like they did, but hers was a deep alto laugh, and she danced with the natural assurance of women who know how to dance the way birds know how to sing or bees to make a honeycomb, the body of a dancer curving under the thin summer fabric of her August dress; I looked at her and a wave of longing and fondness for that desperate soul and, fortified by the wine, a longing for the body and the breasts swelled inside me until finally the wine which man substitutes for woman's damnation (risking fatherhood, matrimony, his career, his whole life for the deception of a brief moment) released me from all bonds of reason and wisdom, and when I saw the schoolteacher, his eyes lit up like those of a witch's tomcat, emerge from somewhere in the dark recesses of the hall and ask Emöke to dance and saw him dance with her, pressing close to her body, half a head shorter than she, a satyr with a satyr's lecherous face but none of the mythic poetry, I rose and broke onto the dance floor with a drunkard's energetic gait and cut in and took Emöke away from the schoolteacher. I hadn't seen her since morning. I had spent the whole day in my room; the schoolteacher had taken off but I had stayed in, dozing and thinking about that girl, about all the possibilities and my own insecurity and indecisiveness, but now I was with her, holding her around the waist as I had last night only she wasn't pulling away from me this time, and I had the wine in my head and her eyes had lost their mystical mildness, the cloistered resignation of anaesthetized passions, and they were the eyes of a Hungarian girl, like stars over the *puszta,* and the inner rhythm that yesterday had made the keys of the old piano tremble now flowed through her slender legs and was transformed at her hips into the circular motion of a prelude to love.

The schoolteacher withdrew to a table with a small glass of white wine and wet his muzzle in that sourish liquid of village dances that infuses the stench of lust pantingly relieved with hot whispers and abandoned cries in fragrant orchards behind taverns or, when there isn't enough tail to go around, that simply goes the way of all liquids, flowing into the stinking tarred troughs of caustic smelling tavern toilets and from there to cesspools and from there into the earth which purifies the liquid and transforms it back into the crystal flow of the spring in the valley. He raised his heavy, mean, bloodshot eyes to the dance floor and followed me with the resentful stare of an outsider as I danced with the Hungarian girl; he knew I was young and single and an intellectual from Prague, one who had mastered that vague miscellany of information that evokes the impression of erudition he too was striving to evoke, and so at night, in private, he would rail contemptuously against yokels who get together at recreation centers, dumb-ass shopgirls, mechanics who barely know how to sign their names, and it never occurred to him that he himself was capable of little more than signing his own name in the heavy-handed calligraphy that was a throwback to the days of the Austrian Empire, that he didn't know much more than the four rudimentary operations of arithmetic, the solution of a quadratic equation and a brief review of Czech history (memorized a long time ago by rote in the so-called heroical-patriotic form of idealistic bourgeois stories about heroes and national spirit, and now confused with a Marxism he had failed to grasp), how to tell the male blossom from the female on a few plants and how to classify the common fauna of this planet into mammals, birds, and invertebrates, but he didn't know a blessed thing about Dollo's Law of Irreversibility or the amazing evolution of turtles' shells, or the semilegendary archaeopteryx; he wouldn't believe you if you told him that the brontosaurus had two nerve centers in its spine and hence two brains, and if he did happen to half believe you he'd transform it into a crude joke. And yet he could stand in front of runny-nosed children at their schooldesks, and with an expression of extreme erudition lecture them how, according to an English scholar named Darwin, man is descended from the monkey, and over the years he had grown used to feeling intellectually superior to the six- to eleven-year-old pupils around him, to the weary farmers who dropped in to the tavern on Saturdays for a drink, and village blacksmiths whose hands, accustomed to the weight of iron sledgehammers, were unable to sign their names in the box marked "parental signature" in their children's weekly reports without smearing the page with axle grease and without the uneven signature creeping beyond the narrow printed rectangle; he never considered that it is just as hard, if not harder, and just as worthy, if not worthier, and probably far more beautiful to be able to control the delicate mechanism of a precision lathe, to turn out silvery shining bolts and nuts, to observe the milky flow of oils and other fluids that flush and lubricate the cutters and drills, than it is to scratch out the natural expressions of childhood with red ink, molding them into uniform monstrosities of correct grammar and acceptable style, and to implant in children's souls such deep-rooted subconscious convictions as "i before e except after c," yet he did know that my erudition (even though it was only a glorified nonerudition, the kind of intellectual fraud committed by ninety-nine percent of all high school graduates with the exception of the one percent that become theoretical physicists, astronomers, paleontologists, paleographers, chemists, and experimental pathologists) was greater, more impressive than his—as was my suit, made by a good Prague tailor, while his pudgy body, half a head shorter than Emöke's, slouched in a Sunday suit of a style beyond style that had never even been in style, aggravated by a necktie in that eternal pattern of indeterminate slots and slashes; and so with his baleful, helpless eyes, eyes of the weak, the outcast, the handicapped, he followed me around the dance floor as I danced with Emöke.

For a long time, we didn't speak. I could feel her body, feverish with the inner warmth of young women, of the music, the stuffy room, the wine, and the dance. We didn't speak to each other, and then the fiddler cut loose with a wailing, rapid Gypsy melody in a spasmodic rhythm, first a long drawn-out note, growing stronger, finally exploding into a brief syncopation, almost a dead end, to continue on another note, and Emöke began to sing in Hungarian, a hard, beautiful, primitive song of her nomadic ancestors, she was transformed once again into what she really was, a young girl concentrating all her energy in the essence of her female life, and we wheeled in some wild Hungarian dance, smudges of faces and figures and silver musical instruments spinning past as when a camera turns too quickly in a movie panorama.

I don't know for how long. For quite a while. Then toward midnight they began to play a tearful and sentimental slow fox-trot, from his alto sax the saxophone player drew the most heartrending sobs that could ever be wrung from that most perfect product of instrumental inbreeding, and Emöke stopped singing and I began to talk, from somewhere out of my subconscious memory of the innumerable blues that have never failed to thrill me came lines of verse, in triads, as they must come to black guitarists high like I was high on wine, and into Emöke's happy, lovely little ear I spoke line upon line of the only blues I ever composed in all my life, colored by that rural sax player who didn't even know the secret of black syncopation and who transformed the saxophone into a wailing instrument of cheap saccharine emotion made beautiful by the primitive and eternal beauty of that convulsive, alcoholic moment, when the alcohol, man's enemy but a greater friend, reveals to him the truth about his own self, the truth about Emöke. First time, first time, baby, last time, only time too. Short time, short time, baby, first and last time too. We wait such a hard long time for this time, what else can we do? and Emöke stopped short, in the smokescreen of nicotine and spotlights above the tables I could see her long charcoal lashes and I said, Like a dying fire we wait to die, die in the flame. In a living death we burn, burn in the cold rain. Fire and ashes everything changes, still is the same. Now is the time, I continued, for us to meet somehow, Just this time, lady, can we meet somehow? Listen, little darlin', to the sweet sound of now, and Emöke's lips, usually wilting, a convent rose of frosty asceticism, had broken into a smile, I said, Let me see you smile, laugh the whole night through. Smile for me now, smile the whole night through. Nobody for years, now he's here to save you, she looked at me, the smile on her lips, her eyes smiling the same smile, the saxophone wailing and moaning. Listen! See that flame glimmer in the night, see in infinite black, love's flickering light, Dark rain's over, love's season is in sight, and then Emöke laughed aloud and said, That's a nice poem! Who wrote it? But I shook my head and continued, This time, baby, this is my this time song. Coming at you from nowhere, it's here and then it's gone. Sing it for my little lady this time, this time song. Emöke threw her head back, the saxophone sobbed and groaned and the words flowed through me, on and on, from a strange inspiration never before and never since encountered, at that moment as beautiful as the Song of Solomon because this girl had never heard the like in her life, no one had ever called her the Rose of Sharon, no one had ever addressed her with that Pythagorean axiom of love, O thou fairest among women, because for all her short life she'd been no more than purchased property, a hot-water bottle of flesh and blood and bones, but now she was hearing it, a poem composed just for her by a man, a poem flowing from a man's heart, borne by the strange magic of this crazy age of telecommunications from the heart and throat of a half-stoned black shouter of the Memphis periphery to the vocal chords of a Prague intellectual in this social hall in a recreation center in the Socialist state of Czechoslovakia, but then she didn't know anything about the picturesque genealogy of the song, she perceived it only in the ideal manner of perceiving poetry, because every poem is created ad hoc, for some woman, and if it isn't, it's not a poem, it's not worth reading or hearing since it doesn't come from that unique, genuine, and true inspiration of all poetry; it seemed that she was happy and she said in a whisper, May I believe you? Do you really mean it? Yes, Emöke, I said, and my soul or my heart or whatever it was, brought forth more and more verses of those alcoholic, triadic blues. I don't know, but at that moment I entered into matrimony with her, at that moment I gained a wisdom long forgotten by this age, an awareness that marriage—the life of a man with a woman—isn't, can't be, must not be that odd jumble of passion and sentimentality, smut, and gastronomic indulgence, complementary souls and common interests, since it isn't a matter of understanding, equality of intellect, dovetailing personalities and support and a balanced diet and the way to a heart through a stomach, and it isn't that ludicrous relationship canonized by Hollywood in the twenties and still adhered to in socialist-realist novels of the fifties—a relationship valid at best for the instinctive eroticism of adolescent infatuations or for the fossils of middle-class Victorianism—and that winds up in loathsome divorce proceedings claiming the no less ludicrous relationship of conjugal incompatibility, but it is the relationship between a male of the species and a female of the species, the primal cave couple of two equal but totally different individuals, one of whom has mastered the club and the other the fire, one of whom brings home the game and the other kneads the bread, together bringing their young into the world according to the primal laws of the species, for the unique beauty of perpetual regeneration, the joy of sunlight on naked skin and of digestive juices and the poetry of the blood and that finer joy of hearts obedient to the law that man must again attain the level of animals, but higher by one twist of the spiral, and rid himself of the psychoneurotic dross of conventional sentimentality that has been sloughed off on the relationship of the human pair by centuries of war and thievery and perverse mysticism and male servitude and male dominance *(Frauendienst ist Gottesdienst).*

But when I returned to the room (I had left for a moment, and in the corridor to the toilet—where I was singing blues without words, the way youth since the beginning of time has given voice to the joy of motion and rhythm by chanting unintelligible nonsense syllables in rapid succession—I got to talking with the leader of the jazz band who was making his way there too, fiddle in hand, and who recognized in me a brother in the international brotherhood of rhythmic, antiracist, antifascist syncopated music) I found Emöke dancing in the arms of the schoolteacher, who was telling her something with great urgency, and when he caught sight of me (I had stopped and was leaning against a column, watching them) the expression on his face changed unwittingly to that of someone caught doing something he shouldn't; when the piece ended he bowed to Emöke and went with untoward willingness over to his table and his white wine, fixing on me the black hate-filled eyes of a man avenging a defeat in the eternal struggle. I went over to Emöke and asked her to dance; she came but she was suddenly different, the membrane of monastic reserve once again obscuring her pupils. What is it, Emöke? What happened to you? I asked. Nothing, she said, but she was dancing lifelessly, passively submitting to my movements like an indifferent dance partner casually asked to dance in some dance hall into which a lonely young man has wandered foolishly seeking diversion, seeking to fill a lonely city afternoon with a casual dance with a partner he doesn't know and who doesn't know him, they dance a set of foxtrots together, in silence or exchanging a few conventional phrases, neither appeals to the other, they nod a bow and he leads her to her table where there is a glass of soda-pop and he says, Thank you, she nods again, they part and forget each other's existence and he just sits there looking at the half-empty dance floor of the half-empty dance hall and he doesn't dance after that and he goes home alone and lonely and goes to sleep, devoured and torn by the indifferent isolation of big cities. What happened to you? I insisted. Something happened. There's something on your mind, Emöke, tell me what it is. Then she turned to me, and in her eyes, around her eyes, in the configuration of the fine lines that comprise immediate expression, there was painful surprise, the sorrowful self-deriding reproof of a woman who suddenly realizes that she has once again done something she swore she would never do again, and she said to me, I'm sorry, but could you show me your identity folder? For a millisecond I was startled, not painfully or offendedly, simply startled by that almost official request, whereupon I felt a surge of fondness for the simplicity, the straightforward, ordinary, honorable way in which she took my offer of marriage so matter-of-factly, the only right way, without the movie mysticism of fragile emotions, and instantly I knew it was the schoolteacher, that in his impotent rage the schoolteacher had convinced her I was a cheat, a married man taking a vacation from his marriage, and his dirty mind had transformed the fictional tale of my forthcoming marriage to a widow and the legend of Emöke into this ugly and yet logically credible tale, and immediately I felt a wave of tenderness toward Emöke, who had encountered that kind of man in her own marriage and was now terrified that I might be the same. I said, Emöke! Who gave you that idea? Of course I can show you my identity folder, and I reached into my inside breast pocket for that document that would confirm the truthfulness of my actions, my countenance, and she said, with an inexpressible sadness in her voice, Why are you lying to me? You don't have to show me anything. I know everything. But what? What? Emöke! There isn't anything to know! I said. Why do you deny it? she replied. I thought you were different, but you aren't. You aren't. You aren't. You're just the same as all the rest, she said. But Emöke! No, don't say anything, I know it all. Why don't you at least consider your fiancée's feelings, if you don't consider mine. Basically, I'm just a stranger, you've only known me a few days. But her feelings . . . Emöke! That's nonsense! I exclaimed. It was that idiot schoolteacher who made you believe that. But he's lying! Can't you tell he's just a dirty old man? Don't call him names, she said. It was honorable of him to call my attention to it. But it's not true! Emöke! Don't lie, please. You showed him her photograph. But . . . (I had shown the schoolteacher a picture of Margit and her two-year-old son, Peter, I don't know why, maybe out of stupid male vanity). Then show me your identity folder if you say it isn't true, said Emöke, and that was when I remembered that the picture was in my identity folder; I had taken it out to show to the schoolteacher, and he had even told her that—Margit with the flirty bangs, the cleavage in the neckline of her summer dress, and with that sweet little blond two-year-old in the grass among the dandelions. I can't, I said weakly. But it isn't true. Don't lie, said Emöke. Please, don't lie at least. I'm not, I insisted, I'm not lying, but I can't show you the identity folder. Why not? I just can't. Because . . . Why? said Emöke with a penetrating look, and once again it was the little animal looking at me, but this time it was as if someone really had taken something away from it, an illusion of forest freedom, as if it were staring into the maw of a wild beast it hadn't known existed in its green and sunny world. Why can't you? she said urgently, in an excited voice that I hadn't heard her use before and the eyes of the little animal grew large as in the final, ultimate flash of comprehension beneath the yellowed fangs of the beast, and then the monastic pallor of her cheeks flushed an unnatural crimson and nervously, painfully, almost weeping, Emöke said quickly, Let me go, I have to leave. I'm taking the train at one o'clock in the morning. Goodbye! and she tore herself away and left the room swiftly, she disappeared while I stood there, she vanished.

I turned and saw the schoolteacher, squatting at the table, his face smoldering with wounded righteousness.

I was waiting for her at half-past midnight in front of the building, but she came out with her roommate, another Hungarian girl, in a group of about five Slovaks who were all taking the night train. It was obvious that she had asked the other girl not to leave her alone with me because she stayed close beside us the whole way. So I couldn't say anything to Emöke, I just asked her if I might write to her. Of course, she said, why not? And will you write to me? Why? she said. I lowered my voice so the other girl wouldn't hear and said, Because I love you, Emöke. Believe me. I don't believe you, she replied. The other girl had stepped aside a bit but she was still within hearing distance so I had to keep my voice down. Believe me, I repeated, I'll come to see you in Košice. May I? Why not? she said. But will you speak to me? May I visit you? Of course, she said. Then will you believe me? She didn't reply. Will you believe me, Emöke? She was silent a while longer. I don't know. Maybe, she said after a pause, and by then we were at the station, a little village station with the train already waiting, and the uniformed stationmaster standing beside it. The vacationers boarded, a Slovak helped Emöke get her suitcase inside and then she appeared like a black silhouette at the carriage window. Emöke, I said, aiming my words upward as if I were casting a spell on her, as if I could draw from her an answer to the eternal and monotonous question of my life, so empty with its eternal variations on the love ritual, so sleazy, so lacking in values, in honesty, in love, and yet so bound up in the self-indulgent habit of illusory freedom that I was unable to make up my mind. Emöke, I said in the darkness, upward toward that silhouette, that legend that was ending, and I heard her Yes softly and from a great distance. Believe me, please, I called weakly. Emöke! Yes, she said. Goodbye, but it was no longer the call of a lonely animal in the forest wilderness but the voice of disappointed and skeptical wisdom, the voice of a woman who is being transformed into the image of time lost, and the engine started to rumble, the train moved, and a slender white arm waved to me out of the window, the arm of that girl, that dream, that madness, that truth, Emöke.

Overnight, the wine and the wisdom, the awareness or the vacation infatuation or whatever it was, evaporated and I awoke to the cold sober reality of Sunday morning, my imminent departure for Prague, my office, my colleagues, my pitiful affair with Margit, and all the rest. The schoolteacher lay snoring on the other bed, his shorts, his shirt, everything carefully hung up to air again. I didn't say a thing. He disgusted me, for all the hygiene of his clean underwear, because the grime of his soul couldn't be aired out of his jockey shorts, his trousers, or his shirt; he wasn't even human, just living breathing filth, an egotist, a lecher, an idiot, an enemy.

I didn't say a thing to him. He might have even denied it. It wouldn't have proved anything, and I wouldn't have achieved anything by an angry confrontation. I was silent. Yet in fact my time was coming, my moment of revenge—the only possible revenge, for it wounded him where he was most vulnerable, a revenge that he dug for himself like a grave, and into which he lowered himself helplessly.

But maybe it was Fate, the miller, the avenger, tyrant, friend, and lord who provided the means on that train rolling through the ripe August landscape, in pursuit of the curving track of the eternal sun, eternal within the bounds of human eternity, its shiny, reddening glory lighting up the faces in the compartment like kerosene lamps, transforming them into golden portraits: a childless couple of about thirty (a technical draftsman and his wife, who was a clerk at the State Statistical Agency), the taciturn factory foreman, the hotshot, the manager of the clothing store, his wife, myself, and the schoolteacher. And the game began. It was the idea of the draftsman and his wife. They often played it; they had no children and they killed time by paying visits to other childless white-collar couples—every Thursday the wife played bridge and he played poker, and since they were members of a Hiking Club they would also go every Sunday in spring to a chalet in Skochovice where they played volleyball with the people from the neighboring chalets, and other games, when it grew dark, such as this familiar parlor game. It has a hundred names and like chess is played by everyone at some time or another; but this parlor game is more human than the empty and perverted feudal logic of chess which sucks so much energy from the human brain for the sake of the silly movement of bizarre figurines: here one person goes out of the room while the others decide on a certain object, person, animal, the Pope, Mars, the fruit preserves in one of the suitcases, or even the player himself (the one who went out of the room) and then they let him back in and he must eliminate everything, progressively and by using indirect questions requiring affirmative or negative replies, until by logic he arrives at the thing or the animal or person. The draftsman went out, and the clothing-store manager—as often happens with people who once in their lives stumble on something unusual, something which brightens their dull world of daily routine and polite clichés with a ray of wit, and which they'll then repeat at every possible opportunity—suggested that we choose him, the draftsman himself, as our subject, but the hotshot, with little consideration for the man's feelings, declared that everybody does that and any fool would guess it right off; his own suggestion was that we take the Pope's left shoe as the subject. But the draftsman's wife decided that too few attributes of the object were known, such as the material, the shape, the color, and so forth. "No," she said. "We have to use something easier, so the ones who've never played the game will see how it's done." The schoolteacher and the wife of the clothing-store manager had declared they didn't know the game. The manager's wife was probably telling the truth, but not so the schoolteacher. I looked at him; he had the expression of a fat man forced to be It in a game of tag, totally at the mercy of slimmer players and destined to plod heavy and wheezing among human bodies tauntingly flitting past until someone takes pity on his helplessness and allows himself to be caught. He was lying. Obviously and visibly. He knew how to play the game. But he probably didn't like to play it. I knew why some people didn't like to play it. Not fat people, people who are slow in other ways. He was nervous. Then he noticed I was looking at him and suggested his suitcase, to keep up appearances.

"No," said the draftsman's wife, "that would be too easy. How about the Ping-Pong table in the recreation center?"

The draftsman was called in and he started with a query as to the concrete or abstract nature of the object.

"It's concrete," said his wife. A second later, the schoolteacher nodded. The wife of the clothing-store manager looked at the draftsman's wife with an uncertain questioning smile. Her eyes showed as much intelligence as those of the schoolteacher, but they lacked the nervousness. She displayed only wondering ignorance.

"Is it in Czechoslovakia?" asked the draftsman.

"It is," replied the schoolteacher, the manager's wife, and the hotshot in unison.

"Is it in Prague?" asked the draftsman.

"No," replied the chorus, this time without the schoolteacher.

"Is it in K.?" asked the draftsman. (K. was the place we had just left, where the recreation center was.)

"No," replied the schoolteacher quickly.

"Oh, but it is!" the wife of the clothing-store manager corrected him with wondering reproof. "We said it's the—"

"Shhh, Mrs. M.!" exclaimed the draftsman's wife. "Yes, it's in K.," she told her husband.

"Then why did you say it wasn't?" the manager's wife asked, in the petulant voice of the naïve. "When it really is?"

"I just wanted to mix him up a bit," said the schoolteacher.

"But that's against the rules," said the draftsman's wife. "It wouldn't work that way."

"That's just what makes it exciting," he replied.

"Oh, no," said the draftsman's wife. "The point of the game is in having to answer truthfully, but in not being able to ask directly. So it's up to the person to show how smart he is at asking indirect questions."

"But if he gets a little mixed up it would be much more fun," said the schoolteacher.

"And then how would you want him to guess what it is, smart aleck?" asked the hotshot. "You just wait till you're the one asking questions."

"All right, let's go on," said the draftsman's wife.

"Is it in the recreation center building?" continued the draftsman, and then with several practiced questions he determined what the object was. To someone new at the game it looked almost like clairvoyance, but it was simply the result of logic and experienced instinct. All the same, some were surprised.

"You really are clever, Mr. N.!" exclaimed the store manager's wife.

"It's not cleverness," the draftsman replied modestly, "you just have to ask the right questions, from the general down to the specific, and in a little while you've got it."

Then it was the hotshot's turn. I suggested as a subject Louis Armstrong's trumpet. Some voices were raised in opposition—the store manager's wife because she didn't know who Armstrong was, and the schoolteacher who didn't know either—but my suggestion was accepted in the end all the same. I had to answer most of the questions myself. The road to success was not an easy one for the hotshot's foggy mind, but once he had determined the approximate size of the object and had ingeniously asked whether you could use it for something, and then thought of asking if it was in Czechoslovakia and then if it was on the earth, and after the third question in this series (Was it in America? since in addition to Czechoslovakia, where he was obliged to live, and the earth, where we are all obliged to live, he knew and loved and was interested in just one other place in the world) he was suddenly inspired or perhaps the focus of his interests suggested the question and he asked if it was used to play on. As soon as he was told that it was, he was home free. By precise reasoning, resulting from his scale of values and his devotion to this love that was, apart from himself, his sole raison d'être, he determined that it was a brass instrument, that this instrument was the property of an outstanding jazz musician, that this musician was black, and then victoriously but also piously he pronounced the name, the whole name, as if he were pronouncing a long and awe-inspiring royal title: Louis Satchmo Dippermouth Armstrong.

I looked at the schoolteacher. He glanced at his watch and was silent. When the hotshot made his guess, the schoolteacher suggested hoarsely that we play something else.

"Oh, no you don't," said the hotshot insolently. "Not until everybody gets a turn!"

"Yes," said the wife of the clothing-store manager.

"And how about your taking a turn now, Mrs. M.?" said the draftsman's wife.

"Who, me?" asked the wife of the store manager.

"Well?"

"But I don't know how!" exclaimed the fat lady.

"But it's easy," said the draftsman's wife. "You'll catch on."

"Oh, golly, I'll never get it!" said the fat lady and raised her hands to her lips. "Oh, gosh, I don't know how!" She shook her head in the panic of simple women, inexorably convinced they are dumb, ignorant of the wisdom of life that is in them. Everyone started to persuade her. The fat lady kept shaking her head, until finally she began to thaw. "But I don't know," she kept saying, "I won't know what to ask."

"Oh, go on, lady," the hotshot urged. "We're each as stupid as the next one here, right?" He turned to me.

I laughed and looked at the schoolteacher. He had not joined in the persuading. "Oh, go ahead, Mrs. M.," I said. "Nothing's going to happen to you."

"Well, if you say so," said the store manager's wife, rising with difficulty, and with difficulty pressed her way between the knees in the compartment and went outside. Through the glass door, you could see her broad, benign, and sweetly simple face puckered in an effort to catch something of the conversation inside.

The group in the compartment decided on a sack of coffee that the lady's husband told us she had in her suitcase. The manager's wife was let in, she giggled, sat down heavily, and opened her mouth.

After much visible effort, she asked, "Wha—what is it?"

"You can't ask like that, Mrs. M. You have to ask questions like my husband did, or Mr. P. here," said the draftsman's wife, nodding toward the hotshot.

"But I don't know how, like that," implored the fat lady.

"Come on. Try it. Slowly," the draftsman's wife soothed her. The fat lady concentrated. Beads of sweat formed on her oily skin and ran down her round cheeks, and after a long moment of intense effort, she blurted out, "Is it here?"

"See how easy it is," said the draftsman's wife. "Yes, it's here in the compartment."

The fat lady looked around. Her little eyes, half lost in the simple face, so simple that the simplicity was almost a decoration, drifted from object to object, from person to person, rested on the hotshot's yellow-and-black leather suitcase, the portable radio of the draftsman's wife, the introverted face of the factory foreman, my nylon socks, and finally on the pale face of the schoolteacher, who glared back venomously.

"Is it—is it something to eat?"

"Yes!" exclaimed the chorus. The manager's wife smiled happily.

"So I guessed it!" she said.

"Yes," said the draftsman's wife, "but you still have to keep on guessing."

"How come?" wondered the fat lady.

"So far, you've only guessed the nature of the thing, but you still don't know what it is."

"What nature?" said the manager's wife, bewildered.

"Like you know it's something to eat, but like you don't know what it is," explained the hotshot.

"Ah," said the lady and looked around again. "But there isn't anything to eat here."

"It doesn't have to be something you can see, does it?" said the draftsman. "It can be put away somewhere."

"But how am I supposed to guess it if it's put away somewhere?" asked the fat lady.

"That's why you've got to ask questions," said the draftsman's wife.

"Questions?"

"That's right. You have to find out exactly where in the compartment it is."

"Exactly?" The wife of the clothing-store manager looked pleadingly at the draftsman's wife.

"Well, you have to find out if it's on the floor or on the seat or in the luggage rack—"

"Is it in a suitcase?" the manager's wife interrupted her.

"It is!" came the chorus.

"So it's doughnuts!" exclaimed the fat lady delightedly. Whereupon she was shattered to discover that she was mistaken. Then she named the edible contents of her suitcase item by item, disregarding protests that you can't ask direct questions, until she guessed it. She glowed with pride. "I guessed it," she said blissfully, and cast her ingenuous smile on the entire company.

"You see!" said the draftsman's wife. The fat lady clasped her husband's arm and said, "Goodness, this game is fun!"

My moment had come. It was as if I could feel Emöke's presence, somewhere in another train compartment and yet almost here, sitting terribly alone, surrounded and harassed again by the spirits of chalk circles, returning to the world of her past, to the fearful solitude of that Hungarian ultima Thule, condemned there forever to the superstitions of the consumptive gardener and to nightmares of the owner of the hotel and farm. I said, "And now the schoolteacher here could take his turn."

The schoolteacher winced. He objected. He said he had never played the game. He even said he wasn't interested but that turned everyone against him. Finally he had to leave, grumbling, and wait behind the glass with his vacant face and his outthrust lower lip, his dull, mean eyes. We agreed on him as the subject. An old trick, easy to guess. This time no one protested. We nodded to him. The schoolteacher came inside.

"Well, what is it?" he said, trying to evoke an impression of jocularity.

"Come on, just ask questions the way you're supposed to," said the store manager's wife.

The schoolteacher sat down. I could sense the gears grinding in his brain accustomed to processing ready-made bits of information and to the endless, fruitless contemplation of ways and means of achieving physical satisfaction. He was incapable of anything. Incapable of the simplest logic. I knew it.

"Is it . . . a house?" he squeezed out of himself. The others, not as well acquainted with him as I, were embarrassed. They didn't know if the schoolteacher was still joking. I knew he was stupid.

"Quit kidding and play it right," the hotshot said after a pause.

The schoolteacher began to sweat. His black pupils mirrored an inner effort that was more than the organism was used to.

"Is it . . ." he said slowly, "or . . . is it a train?"

"Come on, mister," the hotshot was irritated, "what d'you think you're doing? Ask right, will you?"

The schoolteacher flushed with fury.

"What do you think I'm doing?" he said, and his eyes flashed with the yearning to be able to exert his schoolroom authority over this conceited puppy in striped socks who was scarcely older than the particular breed of human beings he was used to having in his absolute power.

"You're not doing what you're supposed to be doing," said the hotshot. "You're asking stupid questions. You can't ask plain out, like is it a dumbbell or is it a crumb-bun. You have to ask is it like this or that, is it here or there, and like that, don't you see?"

"Is it here or there?" the schoolteacher asked quickly.

"For cripes'—" the hotshot began, but the draftsman's wife interrupted him.

"It's like this. You can only ask questions that we can answer 'Yes' or 'No' to, do you understand?"

"Naturally," said the schoolteacher. Everyone fell silent. The silence dragged on. The schoolteacher was floundering in embarrassment.

"Come on!" exclaimed the store manager's wife, anxious to get on with the game in which she had been so successful.

The schoolteacher rolled his eyes. "Is it something to eat?" he said.

Everyone burst out laughing and the schoolteacher flushed again. This time it was apparent that he was offended.

"No!" exclaimed the two women.

"Sure it is," said the hotshot.

"How come?" demanded the fat lady.

"Sure it is. Like there are people in the world as would eat it too."

"Yes, but we can't use that," said the draftsman's wife, "because it isn't customary here."

"So what?" said the hotshot. "So what if we don't eat it here. He asked is it something to eat and I say it is, like if they can eat it in Borneo, it's something to eat, isn't it?"

I observed the schoolteacher. His gaze was flitting from face to face, in complete confusion. His cheeks seemed to have swollen with rage. The dispute between the hotshot and the draftsman's wife continued. The schoolteacher squirmed and said, "I give up, then."

"Oh, but you can't do that!" squealed the fat lady.

"Why not?" said the schoolteacher. "You don't even know if it's something to eat or not."

"That's 'cause we never tasted it, right?" said the hotshot. "Maybe it's tough, or maybe it tastes awful and you might get sick to your stomach." I noticed his voice held something more than its usual singsong intonation; it seemed to contain hatred for the schoolteacher, probably the legacy of years of being derided by some similar member of the teaching profession for his ostentatious adherence to brightly colored clothing, and total self-indulgence as the only possible way of life (whereas his teacher—kindred to this one, paunchy, with soft hands, and a covert lecherousness of mind—would naturally have preached the importance of the work ethic).

"It's like this," the factory foreman interjected (until then he had been silent; in his youth he probably hadn't assimilated much of that negligible store of information that the schoolteacher peddled for a decent month's salary, perhaps he hadn't even finished school and had had to work all his life to make a living, but every day in his few free hours he found time to think, perhaps he read—books of nonfiction, nature, travel; a slow man without too much of a sense of humor but capable of honest logical thought and lacking only in words). "It's like this, sir," he said. "Where we live, it is not eaten, but there are countries of the world where some people might eat it. That's how it is."

The schoolteacher focused his baleful gaze on this new enemy who spoke to him with respect, a respect for the teaching profession and for a teacher's erudition, wisdom, and justice that he had acquired from his elderly parents in his childhood and had passed on to his own children. But the schoolteacher was disdainful.

"I give up," he said again, wearily.

"Don't do that," said the draftsman's wife. "It isn't hard at all."

"No, I give up. It doesn't make sense for me to guess if you think up things that you don't even know if they're something to eat," said the schoolteacher. Once more they tried to persuade him. The fat lady was close to weeping in her impatient pleasure in the game. The schoolteacher, almost black with rage by now, finally gave in and immersed himself again in fruitless thought. It had the external form of something almost Aristotelian, but it was nothing but the gray, impotent pounding of a sledgehammer on an empty anvil.

"Is it . . . a car?" he finally came up with.

The hotshot broke into a rude laugh. "Are you stupid or something?" Everything that he felt for the schoolteacher burst out of him openly and directly, without restraint, with the supreme honesty that is perhaps the sole virtue of young hotshots such as he, apart from a strong fidelity to an ideal. "You ever hear of anybody eating a car, for cripes' sake?"

"Watch your language, you!" the schoolteacher snapped at him.[1]

"C'mon," said the hotshot, "you don't have to be so touchy. I didn't say anything all that bad, did I?"

"I'm not playing," said the schoolteacher, indignantly making it clear that he was offended. "I don't have to let myself be insulted."

1. [The hotshot has used a Czech synonym for "eat" that in polite language refers only to animals.]

Supported by a new wave of protest, I entered the fray. "Look," I said, "it's just a matter of thinking your questions over, logically, understand?"

The schoolteacher stabbed me with his eyes. "I said I'm not playing," he repeated.

"But that would be a shame," squealed the manager's wife. "You wouldn't want a disgrace like that!" She had characterized the situation precisely, she was still a little child who couldn't see the Emperor's new clothes.

"Let our friend here explain it to you," said the draftsman's wife, indicating me. "You don't want to be a spoilsport."

The schoolteacher muttered something under his breath.

"You have to start from general terms," I said, "and get increasingly specific as your questions give you more information, understand?"

The schoolteacher didn't say anything.

"Do you see?" I said sweetly. "Start out with something very general, the best is to localize the subject, and then get more and more specific until you determine, shall I say, the exact coordinates." I glanced at him. He didn't understand at all. "The best of all is to find out at the very outset whether it is abstract or concrete."

The schoolteacher was silent.

"So try it. Pose an initial inquiry," I babbled, "and try to localize the subject."

The schoolteacher moved his lips in hatred. "Is . . . is it black?" he said.

The hotshot guffawed, laughed so hard his spidery legs lifted off the floor and nearly kicked the schoolteacher in the nose.

"That is a very specific premise," I prattled affably, "and it cannot tell you anything about the localization. Localize, localize!" I kept on.

"Is it . . ." said the teacher dully, "is it a train carriage?"

"Ah, no, it's not." I raised my eyebrows. "And that doesn't tell you anything about the localization either."

The hotshot whinnied. "Dammit, so ask where it is already!"

The schoolteacher glared at him. "I asked already."

"Yeah, but how! You can't ask 'Is it here or there?' " he mimicked—very successfully—the inane melody of the schoolteacher's questions. "You have to say 'Is it here?' or 'Is it . . . is it . . .' " he searched his mind quickly for something clever. The only thing that occurred to him was what to his comrades, and many others, is the epitome of all humor. "Is it up your ass, maybe?"

"But Mr. P.!" giggled the wife of the clothing-store manager.

"I'm not playing," said the schoolteacher. "I don't play with people who don't know anything about polite behavior," he declared virtuously.

But he did play. They forced him to, and it lasted all the way to Pardubice, where he and the manager of the clothing store got off. It was the greatest fun that this parlor game had ever given me or the hotshot or the wife of the draftsman, because it wasn't fun, it was the mill of God grinding him between its stone wheels. Slowly, with an immense series of silly questions that finally lost all semblance of system, he got himself into the mental state known in boxing circles as "punch-drunk." With questions like "Does it stink?" he elicited a remarkable and copious flow of sarcasm from the soul of the hotshot, whose brightly colored socks rose more and more frequently like fireworks toward the ceiling. With the question "Is it anything at all?" he gave me food for thought, because I truly didn't know what it was, this schoolteacher, lifelong proclaimer of a morality that was founded on no law whatsoever, not Christ's, not Marx's, and himself living without morality, without even the morality of a human animal which recognizes the ageless law of the herd—don't do things you don't want people to do to you—living a life without meaning or content, a mere system of bowels and reflexes, more pitiful than a silky little hamster caught in a cage, trying in vain with its pink claws to dig its way out through the metal cage floor, to the only thing of value—sweet freedom. This creature here didn't need freedom, which is certainly of supreme value in our life but cannot be achieved except in the wisdom that understands our necessity, even though he often spouted the word "freedom" at Party meetings; he didn't need the freedom that we need to remain sane if we are human beings, because he wasn't human. Naturally there is no such thing as a superman, but it always seemed to me that there is such a thing as a subman. He exists, he is among us for all the days of the world, like Jesus's poor, except that the submen aren't poor. Small or large, fat or skinny mammals unfamiliar with love, fidelity, honesty, altruism—all those virtues and attributes that make up a human being and justify the survival of the species of animals and men (conscious in humans, unconscious in animals, in armadillos, or white mice that in their natural state would never in all their short lives think of killing each other)—who with no qualms assert the absolute priority of their bellies, their imagined (but to them indisputable) rights, and broadcast their own inanity in speeches about their infallibility, always ready to judge others, to condemn others, not for an instant doubting their own perfection, not for a moment contemplating the meaning of their own existence, deriding Christianity and morality as outdated but in the depths of their souls hating Communism, which robs them of the freedom to be parasites, although some occasionally even win out over that because they find they can sponge off it equally well, and they never realize that they are simply a terrible emptiness bounded by skin and bone, leaving in their wake traces of lesser or greater pain, ruined lives, wrecked existences, jobs spoiled, tasks undone, wretched divorces, crimes, and dull and sordid cynicism. They are the ones for whom hell and eternal punishment must exist, at least the punishment of human memory, if everything in the world is not to become one immense injustice, because perhaps not even the entire future of Communism-come-to-pass can make up for the oceans of suffering they have precipitated upon the world in the eight or nine thousand years of their existence, for the subhumans have always succeeded in accommodating themselves while others suffered, have always been quick to advocate Truths, for they are indifferent to truth, insidiously forging pain in the hearts of betrayed friends, mauled wives, deserted mistresses, battered children, destroyed competitors who stood in their way, victims of their mean hatred which needs no motive, only blood, only revenge cruel and direct or dressed in the juridical verdict of a juridical society. Yes, they are among us still, more so than Jesus's poor, like an evil reproach and a derision of our pretty words, like a memento of our conceit, a warning to the peace of our self-satisfaction.

Finally the factory foreman took pity on the schoolteacher, and using his ordinary common sense and patient simplicity led him to the humiliating mark: to the recognition that the object of his quest was himself, that it was his own person that was the inane answer to the collection of idiotic questions he had posed and that cost him the greatest humiliation of his life, or whatever it was he lived. He got off at Pardubice, and didn't even say goodbye to me.

That was my revenge. But then, when I arrived in Prague and strode with the crowd down the underground corridor of the railway station toward the exit where clusters of girls' faces awaited me, powdered and delicate, beautiful Prague faces, and when the motley, somber streets took me into their noisy gullets, brightened by the colorful bells of full-skirted summer dresses and hemmed in by the racket of everyday disagreements, when I met again, furtively, with Margit in her blue-and-white striped dress at a discreet booth-table at Myšák's Café, Margit, who lived on crème caramel and turned to me with tender amorous eyes, when I began again to take part in that great game of petty cruelties, artifices, pretenses, and lies born of a longing for a paradise lost, for a different, more perfect Man who might once have been and may once again be but is perhaps only just being born by the great and difficult Caesarean section of socialism (or maybe he is toddling around in diapers already in the wake of the factory foreman, but I don't know, I can't tell, I couldn't say), then Emöke was only a dream again, only a legend that perhaps never was, a distant echo of an alien destiny, and soon I had almost ceased to believe in her existence. I didn't write to her, I didn't send her the books I had planned to—philosophy, a short private course in the history of thought from Socrates to Engels—I never went to Košice.

And in time, very quickly, I was permeated with an indifference toward the legend, the indifference that allows us to live in a world where creatures of our own blood are dying every day of tuberculosis and cancer, in prisons and concentration camps, in distant tropics and on the cruel and insane battlefields of an Old World drunk on blood, in the lunacy of disappointed love, under the burden of ludicrously negligible worries, that indifference that is our mother, our salvation, our ruin.

And that is how a story, a legend, comes to pass and no one tells it. And yet, somewhere, someone lives on, afternoons are hot and idle, and the person grows older, is deserted, dies. All that is left is a slab, a name. Maybe not even a slab, not even a name. The story is borne for a few more years by another, and then that person dies too. And other people know nothing, as they never, never, never knew anything. The name is lost. As is the story, the legend. Neither a name nor a memory nor even an empty space is left. Nothing.

But perhaps somewhere at least an impression is left, at least a trace of the tear, the beauty, the loveliness of the person, the legend, Emöke.

I wonder, I wonder, I wonder. ~

Interpretive Questions for Discussion

Why does the narrator find satisfaction and revenge in the schoolteacher's humiliating failure at the guessing game?

1. Why does the schoolteacher's depiction of his relations with women evoke in the narrator a profound depression, "as if the hand of Death were reaching out" to him? (81–82)

2. Why does the narrator have more contempt for the schoolteacher than he has for simple and uneducated people, or even for those who are deluded, like Emöke, by parapsychology and theosophy?

3. Why does the schoolteacher want to destroy the relationship between Emöke and the narrator? (112–113)

4. Why can't the schoolteacher understand that players of the guessing game must answer truthfully, but cannot ask direct questions? (119)

5. Why is the story told so that both the simple wife of the clothing-store manager and the schoolteacher have trouble understanding and playing the game, but the manager's wife is able to guess accurately and enjoy the experience? (121–123)

6. Why does the narrator feel the presence of Emöke, haunted by her past, as he calls for the schoolteacher to take his turn at the game? (123)

7. Why does the group turn against the schoolteacher when he says he isn't interested in playing the game? Why do they make him the object he must guess? (123)

8. Why do the hotshot and the draftsman's wife take such great pleasure in the schoolteacher's disgrace? (128)

9. Why does the group force the schoolteacher to play the game against his will and let his torture go on throughout the train trip? Why does the narrator see the schoolteacher's humiliation as "the mill of God grinding him between its stone wheels"? (128)

10. Why is the patient and simple factory foreman the only one to take pity on the schoolteacher? (130)

Suggested textual analyses

Pages 123–126: beginning, "My moment had come," and ending, "the gray, impotent pounding of a sledgehammer on an empty anvil."

Pages 128–130: beginning, "But he did play," and ending, "a warning to the peace of our self-satisfaction."

Why does the narrator lose his love for Emöke after he returns to Prague?

1. Why does the narrator feel timid around Emöke and find that with her most conversation topics are trivial and irrelevant? (83)

2. Why does the narrator think that he captured Emöke by the "simple inscrutable effect of attraction and submission"? (91)

3. Why does sorrowful, "desperate" music break down the barrier between Emöke and the narrator? (95–96, 110–111)

4. Why does music bring out the "real Emöke" as called forth by the "primitive and unconscious" schoolteacher? (98) Why does Emöke's own Hungarian music awaken her "immense sensuality"? (96–97, 107, 109)

5. Why does the narrator come to think that "the Good and the Supreme" that Emöke is searching for could be himself? Why does he imagine himself as "the Creator" who could "create something human" out of Emöke? (97)
6. Why does the narrator think that "the primitive and eternal beauty" of his drunken dance with Emöke revealed to him "the truth about his own self," and "the truth about Emöke"? (110)
7. Why does the narrator think that he entered into matrimony with Emöke and gained a higher awareness of what marriage is all about when he sang the song he composed just for her? (111–112)
8. Why does the narrator, a Prague intellectual, come to see marriage as a relationship of "the primal cave couple of two equal but totally different individuals, one of whom has mastered the club and the other the fire"? (111–112)
9. Why "can't" the narrator show Emöke his identity card and explain away the picture of Margit and her son? (114)
10. Why does the narrator look to Emöke to answer "the eternal and monotonous question" of his empty life? (116)
11. Why does the narrator's infatuation with Emöke evaporate in the "cold sober reality of Sunday morning"? (116)
12. Why does the narrator end up thinking of Emöke as "that dream, that madness, that truth," "a legend that perhaps never was, a distant echo of an alien destiny"? (116, 131) Why does he grow indifferent, not only to Emöke herself, but to her "legend" as well? (131; cf. 104)

Suggested textual analyses

Pages 96–99: beginning, "And the pentatonic melody," and ending, "I still preferred it to the world of the schoolteacher."

Pages 109–112: beginning, "For a long time, we didn't speak," and ending, "male servitude and male dominance. . . ."

Are we meant to equate Emöke's personal religious "truth" with the narrator's dedication to socialism?

1. Why does Emöke seek refuge from her painful past in religion and parapsychology?

2. Why does Emöke resist the narrator's logical analysis of Darwinian nature by saying he is merely an imperfect, physical person? Why does the narrator feel a "desperate fury" when he is unable to convince her that she is deluded? (85)

3. Why does the atheist narrator have more sympathy for the ritualistic beliefs of the Mariatal Catholics than he has for the "pseudoscience" of the socialist Cultural Guide? (87–88)

4. Why does Emöke strike the narrator as "an ensnared little woodland animal" when he points out a contradiction in her beliefs—that her emphasis on the physical self is not in keeping with spiritual goals? (90–91)

5. Why does the narrator see all people—both those he loves and those he despises—as animals acting out of instinct?

6. Why are we told that Emöke's horror of her husband almost led her to practice black magic and devil worship? (94–95)

7. After imagining he could be like God to Emöke, why does the narrator begin to think he is instead like the dwarf in the garden, with a "ruddy, lecherous, beat-up face . . . a guy who didn't believe in anything anymore or take anything very seriously"? (97, 100)

8. Why does the narrator return to his life in Prague if he sees it as "that great game of petty cruelties, artifices, pretenses, and lies born of a longing for a paradise lost"? (130)

9. Why does the narrator see the establishment of socialism as the birth of a "more perfect Man"? Why does he think of the factory foreman, "a slow man without too much of a sense of humor but capable of honest logical thought," as the precursor of a more perfect Man? (130; cf. 125)

10. Does the narrator think that love between man and woman is impossible in our violent and disease-ridden world? Why does he call indifference "our mother, our salvation, our ruin"? (131)

Suggested textual analyses

Pages 82–88: beginning, "The girl," and ending, "you can bet your life on it."

Pages 130–131: from "That was my revenge," to the end of the epilogue.

For Further Reflection

1. Is the narrator simply a more intelligent, better-educated schoolteacher? Is there much difference between his "love" for Emöke and the schoolteacher's lust for her?

2. Was the narrator wise or foolish to think over the decision to marry Emöke? Were their paths too different, or should he have committed to a future with her?

3. Is there any such thing as "truth" when one probes the nature of love?

4. Is love basically physical attraction, a relationship of "the primal cave couple . . . one of whom has mastered the club and the other the fire," or is true love "of the soul"?

5. Is ardent religious faith or dogged adherence to a political system no different from infatuation or love?

6. Is spirituality antithetical to sensuality? Can one be a spiritual being and still be concerned with the body and "things physical"?

7. Is Emöke right that "men are all the same"—that all are prisoners of their bodies?

Tom-Tit-Tot

~

Caporushes

Two English folktales as told by

Flora Annie Steel

FLORA ANNIE STEEL (1847–1929) was born in England and as the wife of an Indian civil servant spent many years in India, where she was an advocate of education for Indian women. Steel wrote several novels and was a noted reteller of English and Indian folktales. Her collections of folktales include *English Fairy Tales* and *Tales of the Punjab*.

Tom-Tit-Tot

ONCE UPON A TIME there was a woman and she baked five pies. But when they came out of the oven they were overbaked, and the crust was far too hard to eat. So she said to her daughter:

"Daughter," says she, "put them pies onto the shelf and leave 'em there awhile. Surely they'll come again in time."

By that, you know, she meant that they would become softer. But her daughter said to herself, "If Mother says the pies will come again, why shouldn't I eat these now?" So, having good young teeth, she set to work and ate the lot, first and last.

Now when supper time came the woman said to her daughter, "Go you and get one of the pies. They are sure to have come again by now."

Then the girl went and looked, but of course there was nothing but the empty dishes.

So back she came and said, "No, Mother, they ain't come again."

"Not one o' them?" asked the mother, taken aback like.

"Not one o' them," says the daughter, quite confident.

"Well," says the mother, "come again, or not come again, I will have one of them pies for my supper."

"But you can't," says the daughter. "How can you if they ain't come? And they ain't, as sure's sure."

"But I can," says the mother, getting angry. "Go you at once, child, and bring me the best of them. My teeth must just tackle it."

"Best or worst is all one," answered the daughter, quite sulky, "for I've ate the lot, so you can't have one till it comes again—so there!"

Well, the mother she bounced up to see, but half an eye told her there was nothing save the empty dishes, so she was dished up herself and done for.

So, having no supper, she sat her down on the doorstep and, bringing out her distaff, began to spin. And as she spun she sang:

My daughter ha' ate five pies today,
My daughter ha' ate five pies today,
My daughter ha' ate five pies today,

for you see, she was quite flabbergasted and fair astonished.

Now the King of that country happened to be coming down the street, and he heard the song going on and on, but could not quite make out the words. So he stopped his horse and asked:

"What is that you are singing, my good woman?"

Now the mother, though horrified at her daughter's appetite, did not want other folk, leastwise the King, to know about it, so she sang instead:

My daughter ha' spun five skeins today,
My daughter ha' spun five skeins today,
My daughter ha' spun five skeins today.

"Five skeins!" cried the King. "By my garter and my crown, I never heard tell of anyone who could do that! Look you here, I have been searching for a wife, and your daughter who can spin five skeins a day is the very one for me. Only mind you, though for eleven months of the year she shall be Queen indeed, and have all she likes to eat, all the gowns she likes to get, all the company she likes to keep, and everything her heart desires, in the twelfth month she must set to work and spin five skeins a day, and if she does not she must die. Come! is it a bargain?"

So the mother agreed. She thought what a grand marriage it was for her daughter. And as for the five skeins? Time enough to bother about them when the year came round. There was many a slip between cup and lip, and likely as not, the King would have forgotten all about it by then.

Anyhow, her daughter would be Queen for eleven months. So they were married, and for eleven months the bride was happy as happy could be. She had everything she liked to eat, and all the gowns she liked to get, all the company she cared to keep, and everything her heart desired. And her husband the King was kind as kind could be. But in the tenth month she began to think of those five skeins and wonder if the King remembered. And in the eleventh month she began to dream about them as well. But never a word did the King, her husband, say about them, so she hoped he had forgotten.

But on the very last day of the eleventh month, the King, her husband, led her into a room she had never set eyes on before. It had one window, and there was nothing in it but a stool and a spinning wheel.

"Now, my dear," he said quite kind-like, "you will be shut in here tomorrow morning with some food and some flax, and if by evening you have not spun five skeins, your head will come off."

Well, she was fair frightened, for she had always been such a senseless, thoughtless girl that she had never learned to spin at all. So what she was to do on the morrow she could not tell. For you see she had no one to help her, for of course now that she was Queen her mother didn't live nigh her. So she just locked the door of her room, sat down on a stool, and cried and cried and cried until her pretty eyes were all red.

Now as she sat sobbing and crying she heard a queer little noise at the bottom of the door. At first she thought it was a mouse. Then she thought it must be something knocking.

So she upped and opened the door and what did she see? Why! a small, little, black Thing with a long tail that whisked round and round ever so fast.

"What are you crying for?" said that Thing, making a bow and twirling its tail so fast that she could scarcely see it.

"What's that to you?" said she, shrinking a bit, for that Thing was very queer-like.

"Don't look at my tail if you're frightened," says That, smirking. "Look at my toes. Ain't they beautiful?"

And sure enough, That had on buckled shoes with high heels and big bows, ever so smart.

So she kind of forgot about the tail, and wasn't so frightened, and when That asked her again why she was crying, she upped and said, "It won't do no good if I do."

"You don't know that," says That, twirling its tail faster and faster, and sticking out its toes. "Come, tell me, there's a good girl."

"Well," says she, "it can't do any harm if it doesn't do good." So she dried her pretty eyes and told That all about the pies, and the skeins, and everything from first to last.

And then that little, black Thing nearly burst with laughing. "If that is all, it's easy mended!" it says. "I'll come to your window every morning, take the flax, and bring it back spun into five skeins at night. Come! shall it be a bargain?"

Now she, for all she was so senseless and thoughtless, said, cautious-like:

"But what is your pay?"

Then That twirled its tail so fast you couldn't see it, and stuck out its beautiful toes, and smirked and looked out of the corners of its eyes. "I will give you three guesses every night to guess my name, and if you haven't guessed it before the month is up, why"—and That twirled its tail faster and stuck out its toes further, and smirked and sniggered more than ever—"you shall be mine, my beauty."

Three guesses every night for a whole month! She felt sure she would be able for so much. And there was no other way out of the business, so she just said, "Yes! I agree!"

And oh! how That twirled its tail, and bowed, and smirked, and stuck out its beautiful toes.

Well, the very next day her husband led her to the strange room again, and there was the day's food, and a spinning wheel, and a great bundle of flax.

"There you are, my dear," says he as polite as polite. "And remember! if there are not five whole skeins tonight, I fear your head will come off!"

At that she began to tremble, and after he had gone away and locked the door, she was just thinking of a good cry when she heard a queer knocking at the window. She upped at once and opened it, and sure enough there was the small, little, black Thing sitting on the window ledge, dangling its beautiful toes and twirling its tail so that you could scarcely see it.

"Good morning, my beauty," says That. "Come! hand over the flax, sharp, there's a good girl."

So she gave That the flax and shut the window and, you may be sure, ate her food, for as you know she had a good appetite and the King, her husband, had promised to give her everything she liked to eat. So she ate to her heart's content, and when evening came and she heard that queer knocking at the window again, she upped and opened it, and there was the small, little, black Thing with five spun skeins on his arm!

And it twirled its tail faster than ever, and stuck out its beautiful toes, and bowed and smirked and gave her the five skeins.

Then That said, "And now, my beauty, what is That's name?"

And she answered quite easy-like:

"That is Bill."

"No, it ain't," says That, and twirled its tail.

"Then That is Ned," says she.

"No, it ain't," says That, and twirled its tail faster.

"Well," says she a bit more thoughtful, "That is Mark."

"No, it ain't," says That, and laughs and laughs and laughs, and twirls its tail so as you couldn't see it, as away it flew.

Well, when the King, her husband, came in, he was fine and pleased to see the five skeins all ready for him, for he was fond of his pretty wife.

"I shall not have to order your head off, my dear," says he. "And I hope all the other days will pass as happily." Then he said good night and locked the door and left her.

But next morning they brought her fresh flax and even more delicious foods. And the small, little, black Thing came knocking at the window, and stuck out its beautiful toes and twirled its tail faster and faster, and took away the bundle of flax and brought it back all spun into five skeins by evening. Then That made her guess three times what That's name was, but she could not guess right, and That laughed and laughed and laughed as it flew away.

Now every morning and evening the same thing happened, and every evening she had her three guesses, but she never guessed right. And every day the small, little, black Thing laughed louder and louder and smirked more and more, and looked at her quite maliceful out of the corners of its eyes until she began to get frightened, and instead of eating all the fine foods left for her, spent the day in trying to think of names to say. But she never hit upon the right one.

So it came to the last day of the month but one, and when the small, little, black Thing arrived in the evening with the five skeins of flax all ready spun, it could hardly say for smirking:

"Ain't you got That's name yet?"

So says she—for she had been reading her Bible:

"Is That Nicodemus?"

"No, it ain't," says That, and twirled its tail faster than you could see.

"Is That Samuel?" says she, all of a flutter.

"No, it ain't, my beauty," chuckles That, looking maliceful.

"Well—is That Methuselah?" says she, inclined to cry.

Then That just fixes her with eyes like a coal afire and says, "No, it ain't that neither, so there is only tomorrow night and then you'll be mine, my beauty."

And away the small, little, black Thing flew, its tail twirling and whisking so fast that you couldn't see it.

Well she felt so bad she couldn't even cry, but she heard the King, her husband, coming to the door, so she made bold to be cheerful and tried to smile when he said, "Well done, wife! Five skeins again! I shall not have to order your head off after all, my dear, of that I'm quite sure, so let us enjoy ourselves." Then he bade the servants bring supper, and a stool for him to sit beside his Queen, and down they sat, lover-like, side by side.

But the poor Queen could eat nothing. She could not forget the small, little, black Thing. And the King hadn't eaten but a mouthful or two when he began to laugh, and he laughed so long and so loud that at last the poor Queen, all lackadaisical as she was, said:

"Why do you laugh so?"

"At something I saw today, my love," says the King. "I was out a-hunting, and by chance I came to a place I'd never been in before. It was in a wood, and there was an old chalk pit there, and out of the chalk pit there came a queer kind of a sort of a humming, bumming noise. So I got off my horse to see what made it, and went quite quiet to the edge of the pit and looked down. And what do you think I saw? The funniest, queerest, smallest, little black Thing you ever set eyes upon. And it had a little spinning wheel and it was spinning away for dear life, but the wheel didn't go so fast as its tail, and that spun round and round—ho-ho-ha-ha!—you never saw the like. And its little feet had buckled shoes and bows on them, and they went up and down in a desperate hurry. And all the time that small, little, black Thing kept humming and booming away at these words:

Name me, name me not,
Who'll guess it's Tom-Tit-Tot.

Well, when she heard these words the Queen nearly jumped out of her skin for joy. She managed to say nothing, but ate her supper quite comfortably.

And she said no word when next morning the small, little, black Thing came for the flax, though it looked so gleeful and maliceful that she could hardly help laughing, knowing she had got the better of it. And when night came and she heard That knocking against the windowpanes, she put on a wry face and opened the window slowly as if she was afraid. But that Thing was as bold as brass and came right inside, grinning from ear to ear. And oh, my goodness! how That's tail was twirling and whisking!

"Well, my beauty," says That, giving her the five skeins all ready spun, "what's my name?"

Then she put down her lip and says, tearful-like, "Is—is—That—Solomon?"

"No, it ain't," laughs That, smirking out of the corner of That's eye. And the small, little, black Thing came further into the room.

So she tried again—and this time she seemed hardly able to speak for fright.

"Well—is That—Zebedee?" she says.

"No, it ain't," cried the imp, full of glee. And it came quite close and stretched out its little black hands to her, and Oh-Oh-ITS TAIL . . . ! ! !

"Take time, my beauty," says That, sort of jeering-like, and its small, little, black eyes seemed to eat her up. "Take time! Remember! next guess and you're mine!"

Well, she backed just a wee bit from it, for it was just horrible to look at. But then she laughed out and pointed her finger at it and said, says she:

Name me, name me not,
Your name is
TOM
TIT
TOT.

And you never heard such a shriek as that small, little, black Thing gave out. Its tail dropped down straight, its feet all crumpled up, and away That flew into the dark, and she never saw it no more.

And she lived happy ever after with her husband, the King. ~

Caporushes

ONCE UPON A TIME, a long, long while ago, when all the world was young and all sorts of strange things happened, there lived a very rich gentleman whose wife had died, leaving him three lovely daughters. They were as the apple of his eye, and he loved them exceedingly.

Now one day he wanted to find out if they loved him in return, so he said to the eldest, "How much do you love me, my dear?"

And she answered as pat as may be, "As I love my life."

"Very good, my dear," said he, and gave her a kiss. Then he said to the second girl, "How much do you love me, my dear?"

And she answered as swift as thought, "Better than all the world beside."

"Good!" he replied, and patted her on the cheek. Then he turned to the youngest, who was also the prettiest.

"And how much do *you* love me, my dearest?"

Now the youngest daughter was not only pretty, she was clever. So she thought a moment, then she said slowly: "I love you as fresh meat loves salt!"

Now when her father heard this he was very angry, because he really loved her more than the others.

"What!" he said. "If that is all you give me in return for all I've given you, out of my house you go." So there and then he turned her out of the home where she had been born and bred, and shut the door in her face.

Not knowing where to go, she wandered on, and she wandered on, till she came to a big fen where the reeds grew ever so tall and the rushes swayed in the wind like a field of corn. There she sat down and plaited herself an overall of rushes and a cap to match, so as to hide her fine clothes and her beautiful golden hair that was all set with milk-white pearls. For she was a wise girl and thought that in such lonely country, mayhap, some robber might fall in with her and kill her to get her fine clothes and jewels.

It took a long time to plait the dress and cap, and while she plaited she sang a little song:

Hide my hair, O cap o' rushes,
Hide my heart, O robe o' rushes.
Sure! my answer had no fault,
I love him more than he loves salt.

And the fen birds sat and listened and sang back to her:

Cap o' rushes, shed no tear,
Robe o' rushes, have no fear.
With these words if fault he'd find,
Sure your father must be blind.

When her task was finished she put on her robe of rushes, and it hid all her fine clothes. And she put on the cap, and it hid all her beautiful hair, so that she looked quite a common country girl. But the fen birds flew away, singing as they flew:

Cap o' rushes! we can see,
Robe o' rushes! what you be,
Fair and clean, and fine and tidy,
So you'll be whate'er betide ye.

By this time she was very, very hungry, so she wandered on, and she wandered on. But ne'er a cottage or a hamlet did she see, till just at sunsetting she came on a great house on the edge of the fen. It had a fine front door to it, but mindful of her dress of rushes she went round to the back. And there she saw a strapping fat scullion washing pots and pans with a very sulky face. So, being a clever girl, she guessed what the maid was wanting and said: "If I may have a night's lodging, I will scrub the pots and pans for you."

"Why! Here's luck," replied the scullery maid, ever so pleased. "I was just wanting badly to go walking with my sweetheart. So if you will do my work you shall share my bed and have a bite of my supper. Only mind you scrub the pots clean, or Cook will be at me."

Now next morning the pots were scraped so clean that they looked like new, and the saucepans were polished like silver, and the cook said to the scullion, "Who cleaned these pots? Not you, I'll swear." So the maid had to up and out with the truth. Then the cook would have turned away the old maid and put on the new, but the latter would not hear of it.

"The maid was kind to me and gave me a night's lodging," she said. "So now I will stay without wages and do the dirty work for her."

So Caporushes—for so they called her since she would give no other name—stayed on and cleaned the pots and scraped the saucepans.

Now it so happened that her master's son came of age, and to celebrate the occasion a ball was given to the neighbourhood, for the young man was a grand dancer and loved nothing so well as a country measure. It was a very fine party, and after supper was served, the servants were allowed to go and watch the quality from the gallery of the ballroom.

But Caporushes refused to go, for she also was a grand dancer, and she was afraid that when she heard the fiddles starting a merry jig, she might start dancing. So she excused herself by saying she was too tired with scraping pots and washing saucepans, and when the others went off she crept up to her bed.

But alas! and alack-a-day! The door had been left open, and as she lay in her bed she could hear the fiddlers fiddling away and the tramp of dancing feet.

Then she upped and off with her cap and robe of rushes, and there she was, ever so fine and tidy. She was in the ballroom in a trice, joining in the jig, and none was more beautiful or better dressed than she. While as for her dancing . . . !

Her master's son singled her out at once and with the finest of bows engaged her as his partner for the rest of the night. So she danced away to her heart's content, while the whole room was agog, trying to find out who the beautiful young stranger could be. But she kept her own counsel and, making some excuse, slipped away before the ball finished. So when her fellow servants came to bed, there she was in hers, in her cap and robe of rushes, pretending to be fast asleep.

Next morning, however, the maids could talk of nothing but the beautiful stranger.

"You should have seen her," they said. "She was the loveliest young lady as ever you see, not a bit like the likes o' we. Her golden hair was all silvered with pearls, and her dress—law! You wouldn't believe how she was dressed. Young master never took his eyes off her."

And Caporushes only smiled and said, with a twinkle in her eye, "I should like to see her, but I don't think I ever shall."

"Oh, yes, you will," they replied, "for young master has ordered another ball tonight in hopes she will come to dance again."

But that evening Caporushes refused once more to go to the gallery, saying she was too tired with cleaning pots and scraping saucepans. And once more when she heard the fiddlers fiddling she said to herself, "I must have one dance—just one with the young master: he dances so beautifully." For she felt certain he would dance with her.

And sure enough, when she had upped and offed with her cap and robe of rushes, there he was at the door waiting for her to come. For he had determined to dance with no one else.

So he took her by the hand, and they danced down the ballroom. It was a sight of all sights! Never were such dancers! So young, so handsome, so fine, so gay!

But once again Caporushes kept her own counsel and just slipped away on some excuse in time, so that when her fellow servants came to their beds they found her in hers, pretending to be fast asleep; but her cheeks were all flushed and her breath came fast. So they said, "She is dreaming. We hope her dreams are happy."

But next morning they were full of what she had missed. Never was such a beautiful young gentleman as young master! Never was such a beautiful young lady! Never was such beautiful dancing! Everyone else had stopped theirs to look on.

And Caporushes, with a twinkle in her eyes, said, "I should like to see her, but I'm *sure* I never shall!"

"Oh yes!" they replied. "If you come tonight you're sure to see her, for young master has ordered another ball in hopes the beautiful stranger will come again. For it's easy to see he is madly in love with her."

Then Caporushes told herself she would not dance again, since it was not fit for a gay young master to be in love with his scullery maid. But, alas! the moment she heard the fiddlers fiddling, she just upped and offed with her rushes, and there she was, fine and tidy as ever! She didn't even have to brush her beautiful golden hair!

And once again she was in the ballroom in a trice, dancing away with young master, who never took his eyes off her and implored her to tell him who she was. But she kept her own counsel and only told him that she never, never, never would come to dance anymore, and that he must say goodbye. And he held her hand so fast that she had a job to get away, and lo and behold! his ring came off his finger, and as she ran up to her bed there it was in her hand! She had just time to put on her cap and robe of rushes, when her fellow servants came trooping in and found her awake.

"It was the noise you made coming upstairs," she made excuse. But they said, "Not we! It is the whole place that is in an uproar searching for the beautiful stranger. Young master he tried to detain her, but she slipped from him like an eel. But he declares he will find her, for if he doesn't he will die of love for her."

Then Caporushes laughed. "Young men don't die of love," said she. "He will find someone else."

But he didn't. He spent his whole time looking for his beautiful dancer, but go where he might, and ask whom he would, he never heard anything about her. And day by day he grew thinner and thinner, and paler and paler, until at last he took to his bed.

And the housekeeper came to the cook and said, "Cook the nicest dinner you can cook, for young master eats nothing."

Then the cook prepared soups and jellies and creams and roast chicken and bread sauce, but the young man would none of them.

And Caporushes cleaned the pots and scraped the saucepans and said nothing.

Then the housekeeper came crying and said to the cook, "Prepare some gruel for young master. Mayhap he'd take that. If not he will die for love of the beautiful dancer. If she could see him now, she would have pity on him."

So the cook began to make the gruel, and Caporushes left scraping saucepans and watched her.

"Let me stir it," she said, "while you fetch a cup from the pantry room."

So Caporushes stirred the gruel, and what did she do but slip young master's ring into it before the cook came back!

Then the butler took the cup upstairs on a silver salver. But when the young master saw it he waved it away, till the butler, with tears, begged him just to taste it.

So the young master took a silver spoon and stirred the gruel, and he felt something hard at the bottom of the cup. And when he fished it up, lo! it was his own ring! Then he sat up in bed and said quite loud, "Send for the cook!"

And when she came he asked her who made the gruel.

"I did," she said, for she was half-pleased and half-frightened.

Then he looked at her all over and said, "No, you didn't! You're too stout! Tell me who made it and you shan't be harmed!"

Then the cook began to cry. "If you please, sir, I *did* make it. But Caporushes stirred it."

"And who is Caporushes?" asked the young man.

"If you please, sir, Caporushes is the scullion," whimpered the cook.

Then the young man sighed and fell back on his pillow. "Send Caporushes here," he said in a faint voice, for he really was very near dying.

And when Caporushes came he just looked at her cap and her robe of rushes and turned his face to the wall. But he asked her in a weak little voice, "From whom did you get that ring?"

Now when Caporushes saw the poor young man so weak and worn with love for her, her heart melted, and she replied softly: "From him that gave it me," and offed with her cap and robe of rushes. And there she was as fine and tidy as ever, with her beautiful golden hair all silvered over with pearls.

And the young man caught sight of her with the tail of his eye, and sat up in bed as strong as may be, and drew her to him and gave her a great big kiss. So, of course, they were to be married in spite of her being only a scullery maid, for she told no one who she was.

Now everyone far and near was asked to the wedding. Among the invited guests was Caporushes' father, who from grief at losing his favourite daughter had lost his sight and was very dull and miserable. However, as a friend of the family, he had to come to the young master's wedding.

Now the marriage feast was to be the finest ever seen. But Caporushes went to her friend the cook and said: "Dress every dish without one mite of salt."

"That'll be rare and nasty," replied the cook. But because she prided herself on having let Caporushes stir the gruel and so saved the young master's life, she did as she was asked and dressed every dish for the wedding breakfast without one mite of salt.

Now when the company sat down to table their faces were full of smiles and content, for all the dishes looked so nice and tasty. But no sooner had the guests begun to eat than their faces fell, for nothing can be tasty without salt.

Then Caporushes' blind father, whom his daughter had seated next to her, burst out crying.

"What is the matter?" she asked.

Then the old man sobbed, "I had a daughter whom I loved dearly, dearly. And I asked her how much she loved me, and she replied, 'As fresh meat loves salt.' And I was angry with her and turned her out of house and home, for I thought she didn't love me at all. But now I see she loved me best of all."

And as he said the words his eyes were opened, and there beside him was his daughter, lovelier than ever.

And she gave him one hand, and her husband the young master the other, and laughed, saying, "I love you both as fresh meat loves salt." And after that they were all happy for evermore.

Interpretive Questions for Discussion

If the King in "Tom-Tit-Tot" is fond of his wife, why does he insist that she spin five skeins a day or lose her life?

1. Why does the King want to marry a girl who spins five skeins a day?
2. Why does the King give the girl everything her heart desires for eleven months before she has to spin the skeins? Why does the King let eleven months pass before he says anything about the bargain?
3. Why does the King speak so kindly and politely when he tells the girl that she must spin the five skeins a day or die? Why does he suggest that he has no choice but to order the girl's head off if she fails to spin the skeins?
4. Why does the King give the girl everything she likes to eat during her month of spinning?
5. Why does the King dine with his wife on the evening before the last day of spinning and tell her about seeing Tom-Tit-Tot? Why is the story told so that she is saved through this lucky accident?

Suggested textual analysis
Pages 145–146: beginning, "Well, the very next day her husband led her to the strange room again," and ending, "Then he said good night and locked the door and left her."

Why does Tom-Tit-Tot frighten the girl but make the King laugh?

1. Why does Tom-Tit-Tot's spinning tail frighten the girl? Why is she less afraid when she looks at Tom-Tit-Tot's shoes?
2. Why does Tom-Tit-Tot wear beautiful shoes with fancy bows? Why does he tend to bow and smirk and stick out his beautiful toes?
3. Why does Tom-Tit-Tot laugh when the girl can't guess his name? Why does he laugh more and more, and grow more "maliceful" as the month goes on?
4. Why is the girl able to laugh at the horrible Tom-Tit-Tot when she says his name?
5. Why does Tom-Tit-Tot's tail drop down straight and his feet crumple up when the girl says his name aloud?
6. Why does Tom-Tit-Tot end up defeating himself?

Suggested textual analysis
Pages 148–149: beginning, "And she said no word," and ending, "and she never saw it no more."

Why does Caporushes' answer make her father so angry that he banishes her from the house?

1. Why does Caporushes' father want his daughters to tell him how much they love him?
2. Why does Caporushes answer her father by saying that she loves him "as fresh meat loves salt"?
3. Why does the father get so angry at Caporushes when he loves her more than the other daughters?

4. Why does Caporushes' father complain that her answer is all he gets in return for all he's given her?
5. Why does Caporushes' father go blind as a result of losing her?
6. Why does eating food without salt help Caporushes' father see that she loved him "best of all"?
7. Why does the father regain his sight when he admits that Caporushes loved him?
8. Why doesn't Caporushes' father know what "I love you as fresh meat loves salt" means until the end of the story?

Suggested textual analysis
Pages 151–152: beginning, "Now one day he wanted to find out if they loved him in return," and ending, "and shut the door in her face."

After she is banished, why does Caporushes decide to hide her heart as well as her identity, wealth, and beauty?

1. Why do the birds sing that Caporushes' father must be blind not to understand what she said to him?
2. On the third night of dancing, why does Caporushes tell the young master that she will never dance with him again?
3. Why does Caporushes laugh when she is told that the young master will die of love for the girl he danced with?
4. Why does Caporushes take pity on the young master only when she sees how weak he is?
5. Why does Caporushes want the reunion with her father to take place in front of all the wedding guests?

6. Why does Caporushes wait until her father admits he misunderstood her before she reveals who she is?

7. Why does the story end with Caporushes saying to her father and her husband, "I love you both as fresh meat loves salt"?

Suggested textual analysis
Pages 157–158: from "Now everyone far and near was asked to the wedding," to the end of the story.

Why must both girls trick the men in their lives in order to achieve happiness?

1. Why do both girls have foolish parents who put their daughters in danger? Why do both stories begin with a misunderstanding between parent and child?

2. Why doesn't Caporushes say that it was she who danced with the young master, even when he is dying of hunger?

3. Why does Caporushes hide the young master's ring in the gruel, instead of presenting it to him?

4. Why does Caporushes keep saying that she is a scullery maid, even when she is to be married?

5. Why does the King in "Tom-Tit-Tot" get the girl both into and out of her dilemma?

6. Why does the Queen act cheerful in front of her husband when he comes to see her on the evening before the last day of spinning?

7. Why is the "senseless, thoughtless" girl able to outsmart both the King and Tom-Tit-Tot?

8. Why does one marriage begin with the shedding of a deception while the other is preserved by the maintaining of a deception?

Suggested textual analyses
Pages 147–148: beginning, "Well she felt so bad she couldn't even cry," and ending, "but ate her supper quite comfortably."

Pages 155–156: beginning, "Then Caporushes told herself she would not dance again," and ending, "until at last he took to his bed"; and page 157: beginning, "Then the young man sighed," and ending, "for she told no one who she was."

For Further Reflection

1. Does Caporushes treat the young master fairly? Does the Queen treat the King fairly?
2. Do all happy marriages have an element of deception?
3. Does a girl's relationship with her father dictate the kind of relationship she will have with her husband?
4. Does the mother in "Tom-Tit-Tot" have the right attitude toward the marriage of her daughter—that it will all work out somehow?

PATRIOTISM

Yukio Mishima

YUKIO MISHIMA (1925–1970) was noted in his native Japan as a brilliant literary figure and conservative political activist, producing more than twenty novels, dozens of plays, and hundreds of essays. He was also a master of the short story. Mishima's political position and personal ethics led him to publicly commit *seppuku,* or ritual suicide, in a manner prefigured in this story.

1

ON THE TWENTY-EIGHTH of February, 1936 (on the third day, that is, of the February 26 Incident[1]), Lieutenant Shinji Takeyama of the Konoe Transport Battalion—profoundly disturbed by the knowledge that his closest colleagues had been with the mutineers from the beginning, and indignant at the imminent prospect of Imperial troops attacking Imperial troops—took his officer's sword and ceremonially disemboweled himself in the eight-mat room of his private residence in the sixth block of Aoba-chō, in Yotsuya Ward. His wife, Reiko, followed him, stabbing herself to death. The lieutenant's farewell note consisted of one sentence: "Long live the Imperial Forces." His wife's, after apologies for her unfilial conduct in thus preceding her parents to the grave, concluded: "The day which, for a soldier's wife, had to come, has come. . . ." The last moments of this heroic and dedicated couple were such as to make the

1. [The February 26 Incident was a revolt of military extremists in Japan that was suppressed by the conservative military faction.]

gods themselves weep. The lieutenant's age, it should be noted, was thirty-one, his wife's twenty-three; and it was not half a year since the celebration of their marriage.

2

Those who saw the bride and bridegroom in the commemorative photograph—perhaps no less than those actually present at the lieutenant's wedding—had exclaimed in wonder at the bearing of this handsome couple. The lieutenant, majestic in military uniform, stood protectively beside his bride, his right hand resting upon his sword, his officer's cap held at his left side. His expression was severe, and his dark brows and wide-gazing eyes well conveyed the clear integrity of youth. For the beauty of the bride in her white over-robe no comparisons were adequate. In the eyes, round beneath soft brows, in the slender, finely shaped nose, and in the full lips, there was both sensuousness and refinement. One hand, emerging shyly from a sleeve of the over-robe, held a fan, and the tips of the fingers, clustering delicately, were like the bud of a moonflower.

After the suicide, people would take out this photograph and examine it, and sadly reflect that too often there was a curse on these seemingly flawless unions. Perhaps it was no more than imagination, but looking at the picture after the tragedy it almost seemed as if the two young people before the gold-lacquered screen were gazing, each with equal clarity, at the deaths which lay before them.

Thanks to the good offices of their go-between, Lieutenant General Ozeki, they had been able to set themselves up in a new home at Aoba-chō in Yotsuya. "New home" is perhaps misleading. It was an old three-room rented house backing onto a small garden. As neither the six- nor the four-and-a-half-mat room downstairs was favored by the sun, they used the upstairs eight-mat room as both bedroom and guest room. There was no maid, so Reiko was left alone to guard the house in her husband's absence.

The honeymoon trip was dispensed with on the grounds that these were times of national emergency. The two of them had spent the first night of their marriage at this house. Before going to bed, Shinji, sitting erect on the floor with his sword laid before him, had bestowed upon his wife a soldierly lecture. A woman who had become the wife of a soldier should know and resolutely accept that her husband's death might come at any moment. It could be tomorrow. It could be the day after. But, no matter when it came—he asked—was she steadfast in her resolve to accept it? Reiko rose to her feet, pulled open a drawer of the cabinet, and took out what was the most prized of her new possessions, the dagger her mother had given her. Returning to her place, she laid the dagger without a word on the mat before her, just as her husband had laid his sword. A silent understanding was achieved at once, and the lieutenant never again sought to test his wife's resolve.

In the first few months of her marriage Reiko's beauty grew daily more radiant, shining serene like the moon after rain.

As both were possessed of young, vigorous bodies, their relationship was passionate. Nor was this merely a matter of the night. On more than one occasion, returning home straight from maneuvers, and begrudging even the time it took to remove his mud-splashed uniform, the lieutenant had pushed his wife to the floor almost as soon as he had entered the house. Reiko was equally ardent in her response. For a little more or a little less than a month, from the first night of their marriage Reiko knew happiness, and the lieutenant, seeing this, was happy too.

Reiko's body was white and pure, and her swelling breasts conveyed a firm and chaste refusal; but, upon consent, those breasts were lavish with their intimate, welcoming warmth. Even in bed these two were frighteningly and awesomely serious. In the very midst of wild, intoxicating passions, their hearts were sober and serious.

By day the lieutenant would think of his wife in the brief rest periods between training; and all day long, at home, Reiko would recall the image of her husband. Even when apart, however, they had only to look at the wedding photograph for their happiness to be once more confirmed. Reiko felt not the slightest surprise that a man who had been a complete stranger until a few months ago should now have become the sun about which her whole world revolved.

All these things had a moral basis, and were in accordance with the Education Rescript's injunction that "husband and wife should be harmonious." Not once did Reiko contradict her husband, nor did the lieutenant ever find reason to scold his wife. On the god shelf below the stairway, alongside the tablet from the Great Ise Shrine, were set photographs of their Imperial Majesties, and regularly every morning, before leaving for duty, the lieutenant would stand with his wife at this hallowed place and together they would bow their heads low. The offering water was renewed each morning, and the sacred sprig of *sasaki* was always green and fresh. Their lives were lived beneath the solemn protection of the gods and were filled with an intense happiness which set every fiber in their bodies trembling.

3

Although Lord Privy Seal Saitō's house was in their neighborhood, neither of them heard any noise of gunfire on the morning of February 26. It was a bugle, sounding muster in the dim, snowy dawn, when the ten-minute tragedy had already ended, which first disrupted the lieutenant's slumbers. Leaping at once from his bed, and without speaking a word, the lieutenant donned his uniform, buckled on the sword held ready for him by his wife, and hurried swiftly out into the snow-covered streets of the still darkened morning. He did not return until the evening of the twenty-eighth.

Later, from the radio news, Reiko learned the full extent of this sudden eruption of violence. Her life throughout the subsequent two days was lived alone, in complete tranquillity, and behind locked doors.

In the lieutenant's face, as he hurried silently out into the snowy morning, Reiko had read the determination to die. If her husband did not return, her own decision was made: she too would die. Quietly she attended to the disposition of her personal possessions. She chose her sets of visiting kimonos as keepsakes for friends of her schooldays, and she wrote a name and address on the stiff paper wrapping in which each was folded. Constantly admonished by her husband never to think of the morrow, Reiko had not even kept a diary and was now denied the pleasure of assiduously rereading her record of the happiness of the past few months and consigning each page to the fire as she did so. Ranged across the top of the radio were a small china dog, a rabbit, a squirrel, a bear, and a fox. There were also a small vase and a water pitcher. These comprised Reiko's one and only collection. But it would hardly do, she imagined, to give such things as keepsakes. Nor again would it be quite proper to ask specifically for them to be included in the coffin. It seemed to Reiko, as these thoughts passed through her mind, that the expressions on the small animals' faces grew even more lost and forlorn.

Reiko took the squirrel in her hand and looked at it. And then, her thoughts turning to a realm far beyond these childlike affections, she gazed up into the distance at the great sunlike principle which her husband embodied. She was ready, and happy, to be hurtled along to her destruction in that gleaming sun chariot—but now, for these few moments of solitude, she allowed herself to luxuriate in this innocent attachment to trifles. The time when she had genuinely loved these things, however, was long past. Now she merely loved the memory of having once loved them, and their place in her heart had been filled by more intense passions, by a more frenzied happiness. . . . For Reiko had never, even to herself, thought of those soaring joys of the flesh as a mere pleasure. The February cold, and the icy touch of the china squirrel, had numbed Reiko's slender fingers; yet, even so, in her lower limbs, beneath the ordered repetition of the pattern which crossed the skirt of her trim *meisen* kimono, she could feel now, as she thought of the lieutenant's powerful arms reaching out toward her, a hot moistness of the flesh which defied the snows.

She was not in the least afraid of the death hovering in her mind. Waiting alone at home, Reiko firmly believed that everything her husband was feeling or thinking now, his anguish and distress, was leading her—just as surely as the power in his flesh—to a welcome death. She felt as if her body could melt away with ease and be transformed to the merest fraction of her husband's thought.

Listening to the frequent announcements on the radio, she heard the names of several of her husband's colleagues mentioned among those of the insurgents. This was news of death. She followed the developments closely, wondering anxiously, as the situation became daily more irrevocable, why no Imperial ordinance was sent down, and watching what had at first been taken as a movement to restore the nation's honor come gradually to be branded with the infamous name of mutiny. There was no communication from the regiment. At any moment, it seemed, fighting might commence in the city streets, where the remains of the snow still lay.

Toward sundown on the twenty-eighth Reiko was startled by a furious pounding on the front door. She hurried downstairs. As she pulled with fumbling fingers at the bolt, the shape dimly outlined beyond the frosted-glass panel made no sound, but she knew it was her husband. Reiko had never known the bolt on the sliding door to be so stiff. Still it resisted. The door just would not open.

In a moment, almost before she knew she had succeeded, the lieutenant was standing before her on the cement floor inside the porch, muffled in a khaki greatcoat, his top boots heavy with slush from the street. Closing the door behind him, he returned the bolt once more to its socket. With what significance, Reiko did not understand.

"Welcome home."

Reiko bowed deeply, but her husband made no response. As he had already unfastened his sword and was about to remove his greatcoat, Reiko moved around behind to assist. The coat, which was cold and damp and had lost the odor of horse dung it normally exuded when exposed to the sun, weighed heavily upon her arm. Draping it across a hanger, and cradling the sword and leather belt in her sleeves, she waited while her husband removed his top boots and then followed behind him into the "living room." This was the six-mat room downstairs.

Seen in the clear light from the lamp, her husband's face, covered with a heavy growth of bristle, was almost unrecognizably wasted and thin. The cheeks were hollow, their luster and resilience gone. In his normal good spirits he would have changed into old clothes as soon as he was home and have pressed her to get supper at once, but now he sat before the table still in his uniform, his head drooping dejectedly. Reiko refrained from asking whether she should prepare the supper.

After an interval the lieutenant spoke.

"I knew nothing. They hadn't asked me to join. Perhaps out of consideration, because I was newly married. Kanō, and Homma too, and Yamaguchi."

Reiko recalled momentarily the faces of high-spirited young officers, friends of her husband, who had come to the house occasionally as guests.

"There may be an Imperial ordinance sent down tomorrow. They'll be posted as rebels, I imagine. I shall be in command of a unit with orders to attack them. . . . I can't do it. It's impossible to do a thing like that."

He spoke again.

"They've taken me off guard duty, and I have permission to return home for one night. Tomorrow morning, without question, I must leave to join the attack. I can't do it, Reiko."

Reiko sat erect with lowered eyes. She understood clearly that her husband had spoken of his death. The lieutenant was resolved. Each word, being rooted in death, emerged sharply and with powerful significance against this dark, unmovable background. Although the lieutenant was speaking of his dilemma, already there was no room in his mind for vacillation.

However, there was a clarity, like the clarity of a stream fed from melting snows, in the silence which rested between them. Sitting in his own home after the long two-day ordeal, and looking across at the face of his beautiful wife, the lieutenant was for the first time experiencing true peace of mind. For he had at once known, though she said nothing, that his wife divined the resolve which lay beneath his words.

"Well, then . . ." The lieutenant's eyes opened wide. Despite his exhaustion they were strong and clear, and now for the first time they looked straight into the eyes of his wife. "Tonight I shall cut my stomach."

Reiko did not flinch.

Her round eyes showed tension, as taut as the clang of a bell.

"I am ready," she said. "I ask permission to accompany you."

The lieutenant felt almost mesmerized by the strength in those eyes. His words flowed swiftly and easily, like the utterances of a man in delirium, and it was beyond his understanding how permission in a matter of such weight could be expressed so casually.

"Good. We'll go together. But I want you as a witness, first, for my own suicide. Agreed?"

When this was said a sudden release of abundant happiness welled up in both their hearts. Reiko was deeply affected by the greatness of her husband's trust in her. It was vital for the lieutenant, whatever else might happen, that there should be no irregularity in his death. For that reason there had to be a witness. The fact that he had chosen his wife for this was the first mark of his trust. The second, and even greater mark, was that though he had pledged that they should die together he did not intend to kill his wife first—he had deferred her death to a time when he would no longer be there to verify it. If the lieutenant had been a suspicious husband, he would doubtless, as in the usual suicide pact, have chosen to kill his wife first.

When Reiko said, "I ask permission to accompany you," the lieutenant felt these words to be the final fruit of the education which he had himself given his wife, starting on the first night of their marriage, and which had schooled her, when the moment came, to say what had to be said without a shadow of hesitation. This flattered the lieutenant's opinion of himself as a self-reliant man. He was not so romantic or conceited as to imagine that the words were spoken spontaneously, out of love for her husband.

With happiness welling almost too abundantly in their hearts, they could not help smiling at each other. Reiko felt as if she had returned to her wedding night.

Before her eyes was neither pain nor death. She seemed to see only a free and limitless expanse opening out into vast distances.

"The water is hot. Will you take your bath now?"

"Ah yes, of course."

"And supper . . . ?"

The words were delivered in such level, domestic tones that the lieutenant came near to thinking, for the fraction of a second, that everything had been a hallucination.

"I don't think we'll need supper. But perhaps you could warm some sake?"

"As you wish."

As Reiko rose and took a *tanzen* gown from the cabinet for after the bath, she purposely directed her husband's attention to the opened drawer. The lieutenant rose, crossed to the cabinet, and looked inside. From the ordered array of paper wrappings he read, one by one, the addresses of the keepsakes. There was no grief in the lieutenant's response to this demonstration of heroic resolve. His heart was filled with tenderness. Like a husband who is proudly shown the childish purchases of a young wife, the lieutenant, overwhelmed by affection, lovingly embraced his wife from behind and implanted a kiss upon her neck.

Reiko felt the roughness of the lieutenant's unshaven skin against her neck. This sensation, more than being just a thing of this world, was for Reiko almost the world itself, but now—

with the feeling that it was soon to be lost forever—it had freshness beyond all her experience. Each moment had its own vital strength, and the senses in every corner of her body were reawakened. Accepting her husband's caresses from behind, Reiko raised herself on the tips of her toes, letting the vitality seep through her entire body.

"First the bath, and then, after some sake . . . lay out the bedding upstairs, will you?"

The lieutenant whispered the words into his wife's ear. Reiko silently nodded.

Flinging off his uniform, the lieutenant went to the bath. To faint background noises of slopping water Reiko tended the charcoal brazier in the living room and began the preparations for warming the sake.

Taking the *tanzen,* a sash, and some underclothes, she went to the bathroom to ask how the water was. In the midst of a coiling cloud of steam the lieutenant was sitting cross-legged on the floor, shaving, and she could dimly discern the rippling movements of the muscles on his damp, powerful back as they responded to the movement of his arms.

There was nothing to suggest a time of any special significance. Reiko, going busily about her tasks, was preparing side dishes from odds and ends in stock. Her hands did not tremble. If anything, she managed even more efficiently and smoothly than usual. From time to time, it is true, there was a strange throbbing deep within her breast. Like distant lightning, it had a moment of sharp intensity and then vanished without trace. Apart from that, nothing was in any way out of the ordinary.

The lieutenant, shaving in the bathroom, felt his warmed body miraculously healed at last of the desperate tiredness of the days of indecision and filled—in spite of the death which lay ahead—with pleasurable anticipation. The sound of his wife going about her work came to him faintly. A healthy physical craving, submerged for two days, reasserted itself.

The lieutenant was confident there had been no impurity in that joy they had experienced when resolving upon death. They had both sensed at that moment—though not, of course in any clear and conscious way—that those permissible pleasures which they shared in private were once more beneath the protection of Righteousness and Divine Power, and of a complete and unassailable morality. On looking into each other's eyes and discovering there an honorable death, they had felt themselves safe once more behind steel walls which none could destroy, encased in an impenetrable armor of Beauty and Truth. Thus, so far from seeing any inconsistency or conflict between the urges of his flesh and the sincerity of his patriotism, the lieutenant was even able to regard the two as parts of the same thing.

Thrusting his face close to the dark, cracked, misted wall mirror, the lieutenant shaved himself with great care. This would be his death face. There must be no unsightly blemishes. The clean-shaven face gleamed once more with a youthful luster, seeming to brighten the darkness of the mirror. There was a certain elegance, he even felt, in the association of death with this radiantly healthy face.

Just as it looked now, this would become his death face! Already, in fact, it had half departed from the lieutenant's personal possession and had become the bust above a dead soldier's memorial. As an experiment he closed his eyes tight. Everything was wrapped in blackness, and he was no longer a living, seeing creature.

Returning from the bath, the traces of the shave glowing faintly blue beneath his smooth cheeks, he seated himself beside the now well-kindled charcoal brazier. Busy though Reiko was, he noticed, she had found time lightly to touch up her face. Her checks were gay and her lips moist. There was no shadow of sadness to be seen. Truly, the lieutenant felt, as he saw this mark of his young wife's passionate nature, he had chosen the wife he ought to have chosen.

As soon as the lieutenant had drained his sake cup he offered it to Reiko. Reiko had never before tasted sake, but she accepted without hesitation and sipped timidly.

"Come here," the lieutenant said.

Reiko moved to her husband's side and was embraced as she leaned backward across his lap. Her breast was in violent commotion, as if sadness, joy, and the potent sake were mingling and reacting within her. The lieutenant looked down into his wife's face. It was the last face he would see in this world, the last face he would see of his wife. The lieutenant scrutinized the face minutely, with the eyes of a traveler bidding farewell to splendid vistas which he will never revisit. It was a face he could not tire of looking at—the features regular yet not cold, the lips lightly closed with a soft strength. The lieutenant kissed those lips, unthinkingly. And suddenly, though there was not the slightest distortion of the face into the unsightliness of sobbing, he noticed that tears were welling slowly from beneath the long lashes of the closed eyes and brimming over into a glistening stream.

When, a little later, the lieutenant urged that they should move to the upstairs bedroom, his wife replied that she would follow after taking a bath. Climbing the stairs alone to the bedroom, where the air was already warmed by the gas heater, the lieutenant lay down on the bedding with arms outstretched and legs apart. Even the time at which he lay waiting for his wife to join him was no later and no earlier than usual.

He folded his hands beneath his head and gazed at the dark boards of the ceiling in the dimness beyond the range of the standard lamp. Was it death he was now waiting for? Or a wild ecstasy of the senses? The two seemed to overlap, almost as if the object of this bodily desire was death itself. But, however that might be, it was certain that never before had the lieutenant tasted such total freedom.

There was the sound of a car outside the window. He could hear the screech of its tires skidding in the snow piled at the side of the street. The sound of its horn re-echoed from nearby walls. . . . Listening to these noises he had the feeling that this house rose like a solitary island in the ocean of a society going as restlessly about its business as ever. All around, vastly and untidily, stretched the country for which he grieved. He was to give his life for it. But would that great country, with which he was prepared to remonstrate to the extent of destroying himself, take the slightest heed of his death? He did not know; and it did not matter. His was a battlefield without glory, a battlefield where none could display deeds of valor: it was the front line of the spirit.

Reiko's footsteps sounded on the stairway. The steep stairs in this old house creaked badly. There were fond memories in that creaking, and many a time, while waiting in bed, the lieutenant had listened to its welcome sound. At the thought that he would hear it no more he listened with intense concentration, striving for every corner of every moment of this precious time to be filled with the sound of those soft footfalls on the creaking stairway. The moments seemed transformed to jewels, sparkling with inner light.

Reiko wore a Nagoya sash about the waist of her *yukata,* but as the lieutenant reached toward it, its redness sobered by the dimness of the light, Reiko's hand moved to his assistance and the sash fell away, slithering swiftly to the floor. As she stood before him, still in her *yukata,* the lieutenant inserted his hands through the side slits beneath each sleeve, intending to embrace her as she was; but at the touch of his fingertips upon the warm naked flesh, and as the armpits closed gently about his hands, his whole body was suddenly aflame.

In a few moments the two lay naked before the glowing gas heater.

Neither spoke the thought, but their hearts, their bodies, and their pounding breasts blazed with the knowledge that this was the very last time. It was as if the words "The Last Time" were spelled out, in invisible brushstrokes, across every inch of their bodies.

The lieutenant drew his wife close and kissed her vehemently. As their tongues explored each other's mouths, reaching out into the smooth, moist interior, they felt as if the still-unknown agonies of death had tempered their senses to the keenness of red-hot steel. The agonies they could not yet feel, the distant pains of death, had refined their awareness of pleasure.

"This is the last time I shall see your body," said the lieutenant. "Let me look at it closely." And, tilting the shade on the lampstand to one side, he directed the rays along the full length of Reiko's outstretched form.

Reiko lay still with her eyes closed. The light from the low lamp clearly revealed the majestic sweep of her white flesh. The lieutenant, not without a touch of egocentricity, rejoiced that he would never see this beauty crumble in death.

At his leisure, the lieutenant allowed the unforgettable spectacle to engrave itself upon his mind. With one hand he fondled the hair, with the other he softly stroked the magnificent face, implanting kisses here and there where his eyes lingered. The quiet coldness of the high, tapering forehead, the closed eyes with their long lashes beneath faintly etched brows, the set of the finely shaped nose, the gleam of teeth glimpsed between full, regular lips, the soft cheeks and the small, wise chin . . . these things conjured up in the lieutenant's mind the vision of a truly radiant death face, and again and again he pressed his lips tight against the white throat—where Reiko's own hand was soon to strike—and the throat reddened faintly beneath his kisses. Returning to the mouth he laid his lips against it with the gentlest of pressures, and moved them rhythmically over Reiko's with the light rolling motion of a small boat. If he closed his eyes, the world became a rocking cradle.

Wherever the lieutenant's eyes moved his lips faithfully followed. The high, swelling breasts, surmounted by nipples like the buds of a wild cherry, hardened as the lieutenant's lips closed about them. The arms flowed smoothly downward from each side of the breast, tapering toward the wrists, yet losing nothing of their roundness or symmetry, and at their tips were those delicate fingers which had held the fan at the wedding ceremony. One by one, as the lieutenant kissed them, the fingers withdrew behind their neighbor as if in shame. . . . The natural hollow curving between the bosom and the stomach carried in its lines a suggestion not only of softness but of resilient strength, and while it gave forewarning of the rich curves spreading outward from here to the hips it had, in itself, an appearance only of restraint and proper discipline. The whiteness and richness of the stomach and hips was like milk brimming in a great bowl, and the sharply shadowed dip of the navel could have been the fresh impress of a raindrop, fallen there that very moment. Where the shadows gathered more thickly, hair clustered, gentle and sensitive, and as the agitation mounted in the now no longer passive body there hung over this region a scent like the smoldering of fragrant blossoms, growing steadily more pervasive.

At length, in a tremulous voice, Reiko spoke.

"Show me. . . . Let me look too, for the last time."

Never before had he heard from his wife's lips so strong and unequivocal a request. It was as if something which her modesty had wished to keep hidden to the end had suddenly burst its bonds of constraint. The lieutenant obediently lay back and surrendered himself to his wife. Lithely she raised her white, trembling body, and—burning with an innocent desire to return to her husband what he had done for her—placed two white fingers on the lieutenant's eyes, which gazed fixedly up at her, and gently stroked them shut.

Suddenly overwhelmed by tenderness, her cheeks flushed by a dizzying uprush of emotion, Reiko threw her arms about the lieutenant's close-cropped head. The bristly hairs rubbed painfully against her breast, the prominent nose was cold as it dug into her flesh, and his breath was hot. Relaxing her embrace, she gazed down at her husband's masculine face. The severe brows, the closed eyes, the splendid bridge of the nose, the shapely lips drawn firmly together . . . the blue, clean-shaven cheeks reflecting the light and gleaming smoothly. Reiko kissed each of these. She kissed the broad nape of the neck, the strong, erect shoulders, the powerful chest with its twin circles like shields and its russet nipples. In the armpits, deeply shadowed by the ample flesh of the shoulders and chest, a sweet and melancholy odor emanated from the growth of hair, and in the sweetness of this odor was contained, somehow, the essence of young death. The lieutenant's naked skin glowed like a field of barley, and everywhere the muscles showed in sharp relief, converging on the lower abdomen about the small, unassuming navel. Gazing at the youthful, firm stomach, modestly covered by a vigorous growth of hair, Reiko thought of it as it was soon to be, cruelly cut by the sword, and she laid her head upon it, sobbing in pity, and bathed it with kisses.

At the touch of his wife's tears upon his stomach the lieutenant felt ready to endure with courage the cruelest agonies of his suicide.

What ecstasies they experienced after these tender exchanges may well be imagined. The lieutenant raised himself and enfolded his wife in a powerful embrace, her body now limp with exhaustion after her grief and tears. Passionately they held their faces close, rubbing cheek against cheek. Reiko's body was trembling. Their breasts, moist with sweat, were tightly joined, and every inch of the young and beautiful bodies had become so much one with the other that it seemed impossible there should ever again be a separation. Reiko cried out. From the heights they plunged into the abyss, and from the abyss they took wing and soared once more to dizzying heights. The lieutenant panted like the regimental standard-bearer on a route march. . . . As one cycle ended, almost immediately a new wave of passion would be generated, and together—with no trace of fatigue—they would climb again in a single breathless movement to the very summit.

4

When the lieutenant at last turned away, it was not from weariness. For one thing, he was anxious not to undermine the considerable strength he would need in carrying out his suicide. For another, he would have been sorry to mar the sweetness of these last memories by overindulgence.

Since the lieutenant had clearly desisted, Reiko too, with her usual compliance, followed his example. The two lay naked on their backs, with fingers interlaced, staring fixedly at the dark ceiling. The room was warm from the heater, and even when the sweat had ceased to pour from their bodies they felt no cold. Outside, in the hushed night, the sounds of passing traffic had ceased. Even the noises of the trains and streetcars around Yotsuya station did not penetrate this far. After echoing through the region bounded by the moat, they were lost in the heavily wooded park fronting the broad driveway before Akasaka Palace. It was hard to believe in the tension gripping this whole quarter, where the two factions of the bitterly divided Imperial Army now confronted each other, poised for battle.

Savoring the warmth glowing within themselves, they lay still and recalled the ecstasies they had just known. Each moment of the experience was relived. They remembered the taste of kisses which had never wearied, the touch of naked flesh, episode after episode of dizzying bliss. But already, from the dark boards of the ceiling, the face of death was peering down. These joys had been final, and their bodies would never know them again. Not that joy of this intensity—and the same thought had occurred to them both—was ever likely to be reexperienced, even if they should live on to old age.

The feel of their fingers intertwined—this too would soon be lost. Even the wood-grain patterns they now gazed at on the dark ceiling boards would be taken from them. They could feel death edging in, nearer and nearer. There could be no hesitation now. They must have the courage to reach out to death themselves, and to seize it.

"Well, let's make our preparations," said the lieutenant. The note of determination in the words was unmistakable, but at the same time Reiko had never heard her husband's voice so warm and tender.

After they had risen, a variety of tasks awaited them.

The lieutenant, who had never once before helped with the bedding, now cheerfully slid back the door of the closet, lifted the mattress across the room by himself, and stowed it away inside.

Reiko turned off the gas heater and put away the lamp standard. During the lieutenant's absence she had arranged this room carefully, sweeping and dusting it to a fresh cleanness, and now—if one overlooked the rosewood table drawn into one corner—the eight-mat room gave all the appearance of a reception room ready to welcome an important guest.

"We've seen some drinking here, haven't we? With Kanō and Homma and Noguchi . . ."

"Yes, they were great drinkers, all of them."

"We'll be meeting them before long, in the other world. They'll tease us, I imagine, when they find I've brought you with me."

Descending the stairs, the lieutenant turned to look back into this calm, clean room, now brightly illuminated by the ceiling lamp. There floated across his mind the faces of the young officers who had drunk there, and laughed, and innocently bragged. He had never dreamed then that he would one day cut open his stomach in this room.

In the two rooms downstairs husband and wife busied themselves smoothly and serenely with their respective preparations. The lieutenant went to the toilet, and then to the bathroom to wash. Meanwhile Reiko folded away her husband's padded robe, placed his uniform tunic, his trousers, and a newly cut bleached loincloth in the bathroom, and set out sheets of paper on the living-room table for the farewell notes. Then she removed the lid from the writing box and began rubbing ink from the ink tablet. She had already decided upon the wording of her own note.

Reiko's fingers pressed hard upon the cold gilt letters of the ink tablet, and the water in the shallow well at once darkened, as if a black cloud had spread across it. She stopped thinking that this repeated action, this pressure from her fingers, this rise and fall of faint sound, was all and solely for death. It was a routine domestic task, a simple paring away of time until death should finally stand before her. But somehow, in the increasingly smooth motion of the tablet rubbing on the stone, and in the scent from the thickening ink, there was unspeakable darkness.

Neat in his uniform, which he now wore next to his skin, the lieutenant emerged from the bathroom. Without a word he seated himself at the table, bolt upright, took a brush in his hand, and stared undecidedly at the paper before him.

Reiko took a white silk kimono with her and entered the bathroom. When she reappeared in the living room, clad in the white kimono and with her face lightly made up, the farewell note lay completed on the table beneath the lamp. The thick black brushstrokes said simply:

"Long live the Imperial Forces—Army Lieutenant Takeyama Shinji."

While Reiko sat opposite him writing her own note, the lieutenant gazed in silence, intensely serious, at the controlled movement of his wife's pale fingers as they manipulated the brush.

With their respective notes in their hands—the lieutenant's sword strapped to his side, Reiko's small dagger thrust into the sash of her white kimono—the two of them stood before the god shelf and silently prayed. Then they put out all the downstairs lights. As he mounted the stairs the lieutenant turned his head and gazed back at the striking, white-clad figure of his wife, climbing behind him, with lowered eyes, from the darkness beneath.

The farewell notes were laid side by side in the alcove of the upstairs room. They wondered whether they ought not to remove the hanging scroll, but since it had been written by their go-between, Lieutenant General Ozeki, and consisted, moreover, of two Chinese characters signifying "Sincerity," they left it where it was. Even if it were to become stained with splashes of blood, they felt that the lieutenant general would understand.

The lieutenant, sitting erect with his back to the alcove, laid his sword on the floor before him.

Reiko sat facing him, a mat's width away. With the rest of her so severely white the touch of rouge on her lips seemed remarkably seductive.

Across the dividing mat they gazed intently into each other's eyes. The lieutenant's sword lay before his knees. Seeing it,

Reiko recalled their first night and was overwhelmed with sadness. The lieutenant spoke, in a hoarse voice:

"As I have no second to help me I shall cut deep. It may look unpleasant, but please do not panic. Death of any sort is a fearful thing to watch. You must not be discouraged by what you see. Is that all right?"

"Yes."

Reiko nodded deeply.

Looking at the slender white figure of his wife the lieutenant experienced a bizarre excitement. What he was about to perform was an act in his public capacity as a soldier, something he had never previously shown his wife. It called for a resolution equal to the courage to enter battle; it was a death of no less degree and quality than death in the front line. It was his conduct on the battlefield that he was now to display.

Momentarily the thought led the lieutenant to a strange fantasy. A lonely death on the battlefield, a death beneath the eyes of his beautiful wife . . . in the sensation that he was now to die in these two dimensions, realizing an impossible union of them both, there was sweetness beyond words. This must be the very pinnacle of good fortune, he thought. To have every moment of his death observed by those beautiful eyes—it was like being borne to death on a gentle, fragrant breeze. There was some special favor here. He did not understand precisely what it was, but it was a domain unknown to others: a dispensation granted to no one else had been permitted to himself. In the radiant, bride-like figure of his white-robed wife the lieutenant seemed to see a vision of all those things he had loved and for which he was to lay down his life—the Imperial Household, the Nation, the Army Flag. All these, no less than the wife who sat before him, were presences observing him closely with clear and never-faltering eyes.

Reiko too was gazing intently at her husband, so soon to die, and she thought that never in this world had she seen anything so beautiful. The lieutenant always looked well in uniform, but now, as he contemplated death with severe brows and firmly closed lips, he revealed what was perhaps masculine beauty at its most superb.

"It's time to go," the lieutenant said at last.

Reiko bent her body low to the mat in a deep bow. She could not raise her face. She did not wish to spoil her make-up with tears, but the tears could not be held back.

When at length she looked up she saw hazily through the tears that her husband had wound a white bandage around the blade of his now unsheathed sword, leaving five or six inches of naked steel showing at the point.

Resting the sword in its cloth wrapping on the mat before him, the lieutenant rose from his knees, resettled himself cross-legged, and unfastened the hooks of his uniform collar. His eyes no longer saw his wife. Slowly, one by one, he undid the flat brass buttons. The dusky brown chest was revealed, and then the stomach. He unclasped his belt and undid the buttons of his trousers. The pure whiteness of the thickly coiled loincloth showed itself. The lieutenant pushed the cloth down with both hands, further to ease his stomach, and then reached for the white-bandaged blade of his sword. With his left hand he massaged his abdomen, glancing downward as he did so.

To reassure himself on the sharpness of his sword's cutting edge the lieutenant folded back the left trouser flap, exposing a little of his thigh, and lightly drew the blade across the skin. Blood welled up in the wound at once, and several streaks of red trickled downward, glistening in the strong light.

It was the first time Reiko had ever seen her husband's blood, and she felt a violent throbbing in her chest. She looked at her husband's face. The lieutenant was looking at the blood with calm appraisal. For a moment—though thinking at the same time that it was hollow comfort—Reiko experienced a sense of relief.

The lieutenant's eyes fixed his wife with an intense, hawklike stare. Moving the sword around to his front, he raised himself slightly on his hips and let the upper half of his body lean over the sword point. That he was mustering his whole strength was apparent from the angry tension of the uniform at his shoulders. The lieutenant aimed to strike deep into the left of his stomach. His sharp cry pierced the silence of the room.

Despite the effort he had himself put into the blow, the lieutenant had the impression that someone else had struck the side of his stomach agonizingly with a thick rod of iron. For a second or so his head reeled and he had no idea what had happened. The five or six inches of naked point had vanished completely into his flesh, and the white bandage, gripped in his clenched fist, pressed directly against his stomach.

He returned to consciousness. The blade had certainly pierced the wall of the stomach, he thought. His breathing was difficult, his chest thumped violently, and in some far deep region, which he could hardly believe was a part of himself, a fearful and excruciating pain came welling up as if the ground had split open to disgorge a boiling stream of molten rock. The pain came suddenly nearer, with terrifying speed. The lieutenant bit his lower lip and stifled an instinctive moan.

Was this *seppuku?*—he was thinking. It was a sensation of utter chaos, as if the sky had fallen on his head and the world was reeling drunkenly. His will power and courage, which had seemed so robust before he made the incision, had now dwindled to something like a single hairlike thread of steel, and he was assailed by the uneasy feeling that he must advance along this thread, clinging to it with desperation. His clenched fist had grown moist. Looking down, he saw that both his hand and the cloth about the blade were drenched in blood. His loincloth too was dyed a deep red. It struck him as incredible that, amidst this terrible agony, things which could be seen could still be seen, and existing things existed still.

The moment the lieutenant thrust the sword into his left side and she saw the deathly pallor fall across his face, like an abruptly lowered curtain, Reiko had to struggle to prevent herself from rushing to his side. Whatever happened, she must watch. She must be a witness. That was the duty her husband had laid upon her. Opposite her, a mat's space away, she could clearly see her husband biting his lip to stifle the pain. The pain was there, with absolute certainty, before her eyes. And Reiko had no means of rescuing him from it.

The sweat glistened on her husband's forehead. The lieutenant closed his eyes, and then opened them again, as if experimenting. The eyes had lost their luster, and seemed innocent and empty like the eyes of a small animal.

The agony before Reiko's eyes burned as strong as the summer sun, utterly remote from the grief which seemed to be tearing herself apart within. The pain grew steadily in stature, stretching upward. Reiko felt that her husband had already become a man in a separate world, a man whose whole being had been resolved into pain, a prisoner in a cage of pain where no hand could reach out to him. But Reiko felt no pain at all. Her grief was not pain. As she thought about this, Reiko began to feel as if someone had raised a cruel wall of glass high between herself and her husband.

Ever since her marriage her husband's existence had been her own existence, and every breath of his had been a breath drawn by herself. But now, while her husband's existence in pain was a vivid reality, Reiko could find in this grief of hers no certain proof at all of her own existence.

With only his right hand on the sword the lieutenant began to cut sideways across his stomach. But as the blade became entangled with the entrails it was pushed constantly outward by their soft resilience; and the lieutenant realized that it would be necessary, as he cut, to use both hands to keep the point pressed deep into his stomach. He pulled the blade across. It did not cut as easily as he had expected. He directed the strength of his whole body into his right hand and pulled again. There was a cut of three or four inches.

The pain spread slowly outward from the inner depths until the whole stomach reverberated. It was like the wild clanging of a bell. Or like a thousand bells which jangled simultaneously at every breath he breathed and every throb of his pulse, rocking his whole being. The lieutenant could no longer stop himself from moaning. But by now the blade had cut its way through to below the navel, and when he noticed this he felt a sense of satisfaction, and a renewal of courage.

The volume of blood had steadily increased, and now it spurted from the wound as if propelled by the beat of the pulse. The mat before the lieutenant was drenched red with splattered blood, and more blood overflowed onto it from pools which gathered in the folds of the lieutenant's khaki trousers. A spot, like a bird, came flying across to Reiko and settled on the lap of her white silk kimono.

By the time the lieutenant had at last drawn the sword across to the right side of his stomach, the blade was already cutting shallow and had revealed its naked tip, slippery with blood and grease. But, suddenly stricken by a fit of vomiting, the lieutenant cried out hoarsely. The vomiting made the fierce pain fiercer still, and the stomach, which had thus far remained firm and compact, now abruptly heaved, opening wide its wound, and the entrails burst through, as if the wound too were vomiting. Seemingly ignorant of their master's suffering, the entrails gave an impression of robust health and almost disagreeable vitality as they slipped smoothly out and spilled over into the crotch. The lieutenant's head drooped, his shoulders heaved, his eyes opened to narrow slits, and a thin trickle of saliva dribbled from his mouth. The gold markings on his epaulettes caught the light and glinted.

Blood was scattered everywhere. The lieutenant was soaked in it to his knees, and he sat now in a crumpled and listless posture, one hand on the floor. A raw smell filled the room. The lieutenant, his head drooping, retched repeatedly, and the movement showed vividly in his shoulders. The blade of the sword, now pushed back by the entrails and exposed to its tip, was still in the lieutenant's right hand.

It would be difficult to imagine a more heroic sight than that of the lieutenant at this moment, as he mustered his strength and flung back his head. The movement was performed with sudden violence, and the back of his head struck with a sharp crack against the alcove pillar. Reiko had been sitting until now with her face lowered, gazing in fascination at the tide of blood advancing toward her knees, but the sound took her by surprise and she looked up.

The lieutenant's face was not the face of a living man. The eyes were hollow, the skin parched, the once so lustrous cheeks and lips the color of dried mud. The right hand alone was moving. Laboriously gripping the sword, it hovered shakily in the air like the hand of a marionette and strove to direct the point at the base of the lieutenant's throat. Reiko watched her husband make this last, most heart-rending, futile exertion. Glistening with blood and grease, the point was thrust at the throat again and again. And each time it missed its aim. The strength to guide it was no longer there. The straying point struck the collar and the collar badges. Although its hooks had been unfastened, the stiff military collar had closed together again and was protecting the throat.

Reiko could bear the sight no longer. She tried to go to her husband's help, but she could not stand. She moved through the blood on her knees, and her white skirts grew deep red. Moving to the rear of her husband, she helped no more than by loosening the collar. The quivering blade at last contacted the naked flesh of the throat. At that moment Reiko's impression was that she herself had propelled her husband forward; but that was not the case. It was a movement planned by the lieutenant himself, his last exertion of strength. Abruptly he threw his body at the blade, and the blade pierced his neck, emerging at the nape. There was a tremendous spurt of blood and the lieutenant lay still, cold blue-tinged steel protruding from his neck at the back.

5

Slowly, her socks slippery with blood, Reiko descended the stairway. The upstairs room was now completely still.

Switching on the ground-floor lights, she checked the gas jet and the main gas plug and poured water over the smoldering, half-buried charcoal in the brazier. She stood before the upright mirror in the four-and-a-half-mat room and held up her skirts. The bloodstains made it seem as if a bold, vivid pattern was printed across the lower half of her white kimono. When she sat down before the mirror, she was conscious of the dampness and coldness of her husband's blood in the region of her thighs, and she shivered. Then, for a long while, she lingered over her toilet preparations. She applied the rouge generously to her cheeks, and her lips too she painted heavily. This was no longer make-up to please her husband. It was make-up for the world which she would leave behind, and there was a touch of the magnificent and the spectacular in her brushwork. When she rose, the mat before the mirror was wet with blood. Reiko was not concerned about this.

Returning from the toilet, Reiko stood finally on the cement floor of the porchway. When her husband had bolted the door here last night it had been in preparation for death. For a while she stood immersed in the consideration of a simple problem. Should she now leave the bolt drawn? If she were to lock the door, it could be that the neighbors might not notice their suicide for several days. Reiko did not relish the thought of their two corpses putrifying before discovery. After all, it seemed, it would be best to leave it open. . . . She released the bolt, and also drew open the frosted-glass door a fraction. . . . At once a chill wind blew in. There was no sign of anyone in the midnight streets, and stars glittered ice-cold through the trees in the large house opposite.

Leaving the door as it was, Reiko mounted the stairs. She had walked here and there for some time and her socks were no longer slippery. About halfway up, her nostrils were already assailed by a peculiar smell.

The lieutenant was lying on his face in a sea of blood. The point protruding from his neck seemed to have grown even more prominent than before. Reiko walked heedlessly across the blood. Sitting beside the lieutenant's corpse, she stared intently at the face, which lay on one cheek on the mat. The eyes were opened wide, as if the lieutenant's attention had been attracted by something. She raised the head, folding it in her sleeve, wiped the blood from the lips, and bestowed a last kiss.

Then she rose and took from the closet a new white blanket and a waist cord. To prevent any derangement of her skirts, she wrapped the blanket about her waist and bound it there firmly with the cord.

Reiko sat herself on a spot about one foot distant from the lieutenant's body. Drawing the dagger from her sash, she examined its dully gleaming blade intently, and held it to her tongue. The taste of the polished steel was slightly sweet.

Reiko did not linger. When she thought how the pain which had previously opened such a gulf between herself and her dying husband was now to become a part of her own experience, she saw before her only the joy of herself entering a realm her husband had already made his own. In her husband's agonized face there had been something inexplicable which she was seeing for the first time. Now she would solve that riddle. Reiko sensed that at last she too would be able to taste the true bitterness and sweetness of that great moral principle in which her husband believed. What had until now been tasted only faintly through her husband's example she was about to savor directly with her own tongue.

Reiko rested the point of the blade against the base of her throat. She thrust hard. The wound was only shallow. Her head blazed, and her hands shook uncontrollably. She gave the blade a strong pull sideways. A warm substance flooded into her mouth, and everything before her eyes reddened, in a vision of spouting blood. She gathered her strength and plunged the point of the blade deep into her throat. ~

Interpretive Questions for Discussion

Why does being close to death refine the couple's awareness of pleasure?

1. Why does "a sudden release of abundant happiness" well up in both their hearts when the lieutenant and Reiko agree to their suicide pact? (176)

2. Why do the lieutenant and Reiko make passionate love before killing themselves?

3. Why are we told that even "in the very midst of wild, intoxicating passions," the couple's hearts were "sober and serious"? (171)

4. Why does the lieutenant feel "a certain elegance" in the association of death with his healthy face? (179) Why are both he and Reiko concerned about the beauty of their death faces?

5. Why does Reiko's thought of losing the sensation of her husband's unshaven skin give it "freshness beyond all her experience"? (177–178)

6. When waiting for Reiko to join him in bed, why doesn't the lieutenant know whether he is waiting for death or for "a wild ecstasy of the senses"? Why does it seem to him "almost as if the object of this bodily desire was death itself"? (180)

7. Why does Reiko overcome her modesty and ask to look at her husband's body just as he has looked at hers? (183)

8. Why do both the lieutenant and Reiko think that the intensity of their final lovemaking is not likely to be reexperienced, "even if

they should live on to old age"? (185) Are we meant to think that they prefer dying to growing old?

Suggested textual analysis

Pages 181–184: beginning, "In a few moments the two lay naked," and ending, "the cruelest agonies of his suicide."

Why is Reiko determined to follow her husband in death?

1. Does Reiko's desire to die with her husband spring more from her sense of duty or from her feelings of love?

2. Why is the dagger Reiko received from her mother "the most prized of her new possessions"? Why does she communicate her resolve to die with her husband by silently laying the dagger beside his sword? (171)

3. Why does Reiko live in "complete tranquillity" after she learns the true nature of the crisis that has called her husband away? (172) Why is she "not in the least afraid of the death hovering in her mind"? (174)

4. Why does Reiko think of death as "welcome" if she is so happy in her marriage? (174)

5. Why does Reiko think tenderly about her collection of china animals and allow herself to "luxuriate" in her innocent attachment to them as she prepares to die? (173)

6. Why, in Reiko's mind, does her husband embody a "great sunlike principle"? Why is she not only ready but *happy* "to be hurtled along to her destruction in that gleaming sun chariot"? (173)

7. Why does the suicide pact make Reiko feel "as if she had returned to her wedding night"? Why does she see before her eyes "neither pain nor death" but "only a free and limitless expanse opening out into vast distances"? (177)

8. Why does her husband's pain make Reiko feel as if "a cruel wall of glass" had been raised between them? (191) Why does Reiko feel joy at the thought that she will join her husband in the experience of agonizing death pain? (195)

Suggested textual analyses
Pages 172–174: beginning, "Later, from the radio news," and ending, "to the merest fraction of her husband's thought."

Pages 193–195: from "Slowly, her socks slippery with blood," to the end of the story.

Why is the double suicide of the "heroic and dedicated" couple considered an act of patriotism?

1. Why does the lieutenant feel a "bizarre excitement" and a "sweetness beyond words" at knowing he will die in "two dimensions"—in his public capacity as a soldier and before the eyes of his beautiful wife? (188)
2. Why is the lieutenant able to regard "the urges of his flesh" and "the sincerity of his patriotism" as "parts of the same thing"? (179)
3. Why does the lieutenant believe he will be giving his life for his country when he commits suicide? Why doesn't it matter to him whether that country will "take the slightest heed of his death"? (180–181)
4. Why are we told that the lieutenant feels "indignant" at the idea of Imperial troops attacking Imperial troops? (169) Why does he choose to commit suicide rather than obey orders? (175–176)
5. Why is the lieutenant confident that there had been "no impurity" in the joy he and his wife had experienced when they resolved upon death? (178–179)

6. Why does Reiko see her suicide as the only means to "taste the true bitterness and sweetness of that great moral principle in which her husband believed"? (195)

7. Why, at the touch of his wife's tears of pity upon his stomach, does the lieutenant feel "ready to endure with courage the cruelest agonies of his suicide"? (184)

8. Why does the lieutenant choose as his farewell message, "Long live the Imperial Forces"? (187)

9. Why does the author not spare us the ugly, gruesome details of *seppuku,* if his intention is to glorify it?

Suggested textual analyses

Pages 169–171: from the beginning of the story to "and the lieutenant never again sought to test his wife's resolve."

Pages 188–189: beginning, "Looking at the slender white figure of his wife," and ending, "masculine beauty at its most superb."

For Further Reflection

1. Are the deaths of the lieutenant and Reiko meaningless and unnecessary, or noble and inspiring?

2. Do the lieutenant's and Reiko's intense dedication to each other present a model for a good marriage?

3. Does a strong marriage help overcome the fear and confusion human beings feel about death?

4. Why does suicide sometimes have a romantic attraction for young people?

5. Is a sense of duty as important as love in a successful marriage?

6. Is it impossible for westerners to comprehend why the lieutenant and his wife felt it was their duty to commit suicide?

Symposium

Plato

PLATO (427?–347? B.C.) was born in Athens, Greece, of a family prominent in Athenian affairs. His association with the followers of Socrates led Plato to found the Academy, a school dedicated to philosophical and scientific research in Athens that survived for more than 900 years. He taught and officiated there—while also writing his thirty-five dialogues—until his death. In his dialogues, Plato portrayed his master, Socrates, in a leading role. Socrates himself did not leave any writings.

Characters of the Dialogue

Apollodorus, who narrates the story as it was told to him by Aristodemus

Agathon, the host

Socrates

Eryximachus

Aristophanes

Phaedrus

Alcibiades

Pausanias

A troop of revelers

Apollodorus: Oh, if that's what you want to know, it isn't long since I had occasion to refresh my memory. Only the day before yesterday, as I was coming up to the city from my place at Phalerum, a friend of mine caught sight of me from behind, and while I was still a long way ahead he shouted after me, Here, I say, Apollodorus! Can't you wait for me?

So I stopped and waited for him.

Apollodorus, he said as he came up, you're the very man I'm looking for. I want to ask you about this party at Agathon's, when Socrates and Alcibiades and the rest of them were at dinner there. What were all these speeches they were making about Love? I've heard something about them from a man who'd been talking to Phoenix, but his information was rather sketchy and he said I'd better come to you. So you'll have to tell me the whole story, for you know we always count on you, Apollodorus, to report your beloved Socrates. But before you begin, tell me, were you there yourself?

Well, said I, whoever was your informant I can well believe he wasn't very clear about it if you gathered it was such a recent party that I could have been there!

That was my impression, said he.

My dear Glaucon, I protested, how could it have been? Have you forgotten how long Agathon's been away from Athens? And don't you know it's only two or three years since I started spending so much of my time with Socrates, and making it my business to follow everything he says and does from day to day? Because, you know, before that I used to go dashing about all over the place, firmly convinced that I was leading a full and interesting life, when I was really as wretched as could be—much the same as you, for instance, for I know philosophy's the last thing *you'd* spend your time on.

Now don't start girding at me, said Glaucon, but tell me, when was this party, then?

It was given, I told him, when you and I were in the nursery, the day after Agathon's celebrations with the players when he'd won the prize with his first tragedy.

Yes, he admitted, that must have been a good many years ago. But who told you about it—Socrates himself?

No, no, I said. I had it from the same source as Phoenix—Aristodemus of Cydathenaeum, a little fellow who used to go about barefoot. He was there himself; indeed I fancy he was one of Socrates' most impassioned admirers at the time. As a matter of fact I did ask Socrates about one or two points later on, and he confirmed what Aristodemus had told me.

Very well, said Glaucon, then you must tell me all about it before we reach the city. I'm sure it'll pass the time most agreeably.

Well, I told him all about it as we went along, and so, as I was saying, I've got the story pretty pat, and if you want to hear it too I suppose I may as well begin. For that matter I don't know anything that gives me greater pleasure, or profit either, than talking or listening to philosophy. But when it comes to ordinary conversation, such as the stuff you talk about financiers and the money market, well, I find it pretty tiresome personally, and I feel sorry that my friends should think they're being very busy when they're really doing absolutely nothing. Of course, I know your idea of me; you think I'm just a poor unfortunate, and I shouldn't wonder if you're right. But then, I don't *think* that *you're* unfortunate—I know you are.

FRIEND: There you go again, Apollodorus! Always running down yourself and everybody else! You seem to have some extravagant idea that the whole world, with the sole exception of Socrates, is in a state of utter misery—beginning with yourself. You're always the same—perhaps that's why people think you're mad—always girding at yourself and all the rest of us, except Socrates, of course.

APOLLODORUS: My dear man, of course I am! And of course I shouldn't *dream* of thinking such things about myself or about my friends if I weren't completely crazy.

FRIEND: Oh, come now, Apollodorus! We needn't go into that. For heaven's sake, man, don't fly off at a tangent, but simply answer our question. What were these speeches about Love?

APOLLODORUS: Well then, they were something like this—but perhaps I'd better begin at the beginning and tell you in Aristodemus' own words.

I met Socrates, he told me, looking very spruce after his bath, with a nice pair of shoes on although, as you know, he generally goes about barefoot. So I asked him where he was going, cutting such a dash.

I'm going to dinner with Agathon, he said. I kept away from the public celebrations yesterday because I was afraid there'd be a crush, but I promised I'd go along this evening. And I've got myself up like this because I don't want to disgrace such a distinguished host. But what about you? he went on. How would you like to join the party uninvited?

Just as you think, I replied.

Then come along with me, he said, and we'll adapt the proverb, "Unbidden do the good frequent the tables of the good." Though, if it comes to that, Homer himself has not so much adapted that very proverb as exploded it, for after making Agamemnon extremely stout and warlike, and Menelaus a most indifferent spearman, he shows Agamemnon making merry after the sacrifice and Menelaus coming to his table uninvited—that is, the lesser man coming to supper with the greater.

I'm afraid, said I, that Homer's version is the apter so far as I'm concerned—an uninvited ignoramus going to dinner with a man of letters. So you'd better be preparing your excuses on the way, for you needn't think I'll apologize for coming without an invitation—I shall plead that you invited me.

Two heads are better than one, he said, when it comes to excuses. Well, anyway, let's be off.

Having settled this point, continued Aristodemus, we started out, and as we went along Socrates fell into a fit of abstraction and began to lag behind, but when I was going to wait for him he told me to go on ahead. So when I arrived at Agathon's, where the door was standing wide open, I found myself in rather a curious position, for a servant immediately showed me in and announced me to the assembled company, who were already at table and just about to begin.

However, the moment Agathon saw me he cried, Ah! Here's Aristodemus—just in time for dinner, and if you've come on business it'll have to wait, that's flat. I was going to invite you yesterday, only I couldn't get hold of you. But I say, where's Socrates? Haven't you brought him with you?

I looked round, supposing that Socrates was bringing up the rear, but he was nowhere to be seen; so I explained that we'd been coming along together, and that I'd come at his invitation.

Very nice of you, said Agathon, but what on earth can have happened to the man?

He was just coming in behind me; I can't think where he can be.

Here, said Agathon to one of the servants, run along and see if you can find Socrates, and show him in. And now, my dear Aristodemus, may I put you next to Eryximachus?

And so, Aristodemus went on, I made my toilet and sat down, the servant meanwhile returning with the news that our friend Socrates had retreated into the next-door neighbor's porch.

And there he stood, said the man. And when I asked him in he wouldn't come.

This is very odd, said Agathon. You must speak to him again, and insist.

But here I broke in. I shouldn't do that, I said. You'd much better leave him to himself. It's quite a habit of his, you know; off he goes and there he stands, no matter where it is. I've no doubt he'll be with us before long, so I really don't think you'd better worry him.

Oh, very well, said Agathon. I expect you know best. We won't wait then, he said, turning to the servants. Now you understand, you fellows are to serve whatever kind of dinner you think fit; I'm leaving it entirely to you. I know it's a new idea, but you'll simply have to imagine that we've all come here as your guests. Now go ahead and show us what you can do.

Well, we started dinner, and still there was no sign of Socrates; Agathon still wanted to send for him, but I wouldn't let him. And when at last he did turn up, we weren't more than halfway through dinner, which was pretty good for him.

As he came in, Agathon, who was sitting by himself at the far end of the table, called out, Here you are, Socrates. Come and sit next to me; I want to share this great thought that's just struck you in the porch next door. I'm sure you must have mastered it, or you'd still be standing there.

My dear Agathon, Socrates replied as he took his seat beside him, I only wish that wisdom *were* the kind of thing one could share by sitting next to someone—if it flowed, for instance, from the one that was full to the one that was empty, like the water in two cups finding its level through a piece of worsted. If that were how it worked, I'm sure I'd congratulate myself on sitting next to you, for you'd soon have me brimming over with the most exquisite kind of wisdom. My own understanding is a shadowy thing at best, as equivocal as a dream, but yours, Agathon, glitters and dilates—as which of us can forget that saw you the other day, resplendent in your youth, visibly kindled before the eyes of more than thirty thousand of your fellow Greeks.

Now, Socrates, said Agathon, I know you're making fun of me; however, I shall take up this question of wisdom with you later on, and let Bacchus judge between us. In the meantime you must really show a little interest in your food.

So Socrates drew up and had his dinner with the rest of them, and then, after the libation and the usual hymn and so forth, they began to turn their attention to the wine. It was Pausanias, so far as Aristodemus could remember, who opened the conversation.

Well, gentlemen, he began, what do you say? What sort of a night shall we make of it? Speaking for myself, I'm not quite up to form. I'm still a bit the worse for what I had last night, and I don't suppose you're most of you much better—we were all in the same boat. Anyhow, what do you say? How does everybody feel about the drink?

That's a most sensible question of yours, Pausanias, said Aristophanes. We don't want to make a burden of it—I speak as one who was pretty well soaked last night.

I quite agree, observed Eryximachus, and there is just one question I should like to add. What about Agathon? Has he sufficiently recovered to feel like drinking?

Not I, said Agathon. You can count me out.

So much the better for me, then, said Eryximachus, and so much the better for Aristodemus and Phaedrus and one or two more I could mention. We never could keep up with heavy drinkers like the rest of you. I say nothing of Socrates, for we know he's equal to any occasion, drunk or sober. And now, gentlemen, since nobody seems very anxious to get drunk tonight, I may perhaps be pardoned if I take this opportunity of saying a few words on the true nature of inebriation. My own experience in medicine has entirely satisfied me that vinous excess is detrimental to the human frame. And therefore I can never be a willing party to heavy drinking, as regards either myself or my friends—especially when one is only partially recovered from the excesses of the previous night.

But here Phaedrus broke in. My dear Eryximachus, he said, I always do what you tell me to, especially when it really is a case of "doctor's orders," and I think the others would be well advised to do the same.

Whereupon it was unanimously agreed that this was not to be a drunken party, and that the wine was to be served merely by way of refreshment.

Very well, then, said Eryximachus, since it is agreed that we need none of us drink more than we think is good for us, I also propose that we dispense with the services of the flute girl who has just come in, and let her go and play to herself or to the women inside there, whichever she prefers, while we spend our evening in discussion of a subject which, if you think fit, I am prepared to name.

It was generally agreed that he should go on with his proposal. So he continued, If I may preface my remarks by a tag from Euripides, "The tale is not my own," as Melanippe says, that I am going to tell, but properly belongs to my friend Phaedrus here, who is continually coming to me with the following complaint. Is it not, he asks me, an extraordinary thing that, for all the hymns and anthems that have been addressed to the other deities, not one single poet has ever sung a song in praise of so ancient and so powerful a god as Love?

Take such distinguished men of letters as Prodicus, for instance, with their eulogies in prose of Heracles and all the rest of them—not that *they're* so much out of the way either, but do you know, I once came across a book which enumerated the uses of common salt and sang its praises in the most extravagant terms, and not only salt but all kinds of everyday commodities. Now isn't it, as I say, an extraordinary thing, Eryximachus, that while all these screeds have been written on such trivial subjects, the god of love has found no man bold enough to sing his praises as they should be sung—is it not, in short, amazing that there should be so little reverence shown to such a god!

This, gentlemen, is Phaedrus' complaint, and I must say I think it is justified. And, moreover, not only am I willing to oblige him with a contribution on my own account, but also I suggest that this is a most suitable occasion for each one of us to pay homage to the god. If therefore, gentlemen, this meets with your approval, I venture to think we may spend a very pleasant evening in discussion. I suppose the best way would be for each in turn from left to right to address the company and speak to the best of his ability in praise of Love. Phaedrus, I think, should open the debate, for besides being head of the table he is the real author of our discussion.

The motion is carried, Eryximachus, said Socrates, unanimously, I should think. Speaking for myself, I couldn't very well dissent when I claim that love is the one thing in the world I understand—nor could Agathon and Pausanias; neither could Aristophanes, whose whole life is devoted to Dionysus and Aphrodite; no more could any of our friends who are here with us tonight. Of course, your procedure will come very hard on us who are sitting at the bottom of the table, but if the earlier speeches are fine enough, I promise you we shan't complain. So let Phaedrus go ahead with his eulogy of Love—and good luck to him.

Then all the rest of them agreed, and told Phaedrus to begin—but before I go on I must make it quite clear that

Aristodemus did not pretend to reproduce the various speeches verbatim, any more than I could repeat them word for word as I had them from him. I shall simply recount such passages as the speaker or the thought itself made, so far as I could judge, especially memorable.

As I was saying, then, Phaedrus opened with some such arguments as these—that Love was a great god, wonderful alike to the gods and to mankind, and that of all the proofs of this the greatest was his birth.

The worship of this god, he said, is of the oldest, for Love is unbegotten, nor is there mention of his parentage to be found anywhere in either prose or verse, while Hesiod tells us expressly that Chaos first appeared, and then

From Chaos rose broad-bosomed Earth, the sure
And everlasting seat of all that is,
And after, Love. . .

Acusilaus agrees with Hesiod, for he holds that after Chaos were brought forth these twain, Earth and Love, and Parmenides writes of the creative principle,

And Love she framed the first of all the gods.

Thus we find that the antiquity of Love is universally admitted, and in very truth he is the ancient source of all our highest good. For I, at any rate, could hardly name a greater blessing to the man that is to be than a generous lover, or, to the lover, than the beloved youth. For neither family, nor privilege, nor wealth, nor anything but Love can light that beacon which a man must steer by when he sets out to live the better life. How shall I describe it—as that contempt for the vile, and emulation of the good, without which neither cities nor citizens are capable of any great or noble work. And I will say this of the lover, that, should he be discovered in some inglorious act, or in abject submission to ill-usage, he could better bear that anyone—father, friends, or who you will—should witness it than his beloved.

And the same holds good of the beloved—that his confusion would be more than ever painful if he were seen by his lovers in an unworthy light.

If only, then, a city or an army could be composed of none but lover and beloved, how could they deserve better of their country than by shunning all that is base, in mutual emulation? And men like these fighting shoulder to shoulder, few as they were might conquer—I had almost said—the whole world in arms. For the lover would rather anyone than his beloved should see him leave the ranks or throw away his arms in flight—nay, he would sooner die a thousand deaths. Nor is there any lover so faint of heart that he could desert his beloved or fail to help him in the hour of peril, for the very presence of Love kindles the same flame of valor in the faintest heart that burns in those whose courage is innate. And so, when Homer writes that some god "breathed might" into one of the heroes, we may take it that this is what the power of Love effects in the heart of the lover.

And again, nothing but Love will make a man offer his life for another's—and not only man but woman, of which last we Greeks can ask no better witness than Alcestis, for she alone was ready to lay down her life for her husband—for all he had a father and a mother, whose love fell so far short of hers in charity that they seemed to be alien to their own son, and bound to him by nothing but a name. But hers was accounted so great a sacrifice, not only by mankind but by the gods, that in recognition of her magnanimity it was granted—and among the many doers of many noble deeds there is only the merest handful to whom such grace has been given—that her soul should rise again from the Stygian depths.

Thus heaven itself has a peculiar regard for ardor and resolution in the cause of Love. And yet the gods sent Orpheus away from Hades empty-handed, and showed him the mere shadow of the woman he had come to seek. Eurydice herself they would not let him take, because he seemed, like the mere minstrel that he was, to be a lukewarm lover, lacking the courage to die as

Alcestis died for love, and choosing rather to scheme his way, living, into Hades. And it was for this that the gods doomed him, and doomed him justly, to meet his death at the hands of women.

How different was the fate of Achilles, Thetis' son, whom they sent with honors to the Islands of the Blessed, because, after learning from his mother that if he slew Hector he should die, while if he spared him he should end his days at home in the fullness of his years, he made the braver choice and went to rescue his lover Patroclus, avenged his death, and so died, not only *for* his friend, but to be with his friend in death. And it was because his lover had been so precious to him that he was honored so signally by the gods.

I may say that Aeschylus has reversed the relation between them by referring to Patroclus as Achilles' darling, whereas Achilles, we know, was much handsomer than Patroclus or any of the heroes, and was besides still beardless and, as Homer says, by far the younger of the two. I make a point of this because, while in any case the gods display special admiration for the valor that springs from Love, they are even more amazed, delighted, and beneficent when the beloved shows such devotion to his lover, than when the lover does the same for his beloved. For the lover, by virtue of Love's inspiration, is always nearer than his beloved to the gods. And this, I say, is why they paid more honor to Achilles than to Alcestis, and sent him to the Islands of the Blessed.

In short, this, gentlemen, is my theme, that Love is the oldest and most glorious of the gods, the great giver of all goodness and happiness to men, alike to the living and to the dead.

This, to the best of Aristodemus' recollection, was Phaedrus' speech. It was followed by several more which had almost, if not quite, escaped him; so he went straight on to Pausanias, who spoke as follows.

I am afraid, my dear Phaedrus, that our arrangement won't work very well if it means that we are simply to pronounce a eulogy of Love. It would be all very well if there were only one kind of Love, but unfortunately this is not the case, and we should therefore have begun by stipulating which kind in particular was to receive our homage. In the circumstances I will try to set the matter right by first defining the Love whom we are to honor, and then singing his praises in terms not unworthy, I hope, of his divinity.

Now you will all agree, gentlemen, that without Love there could be no such goddess as Aphrodite. If, then, there were only one goddess of that name, we might suppose that there was only one kind of Love, but since in fact there are two such goddesses there must also be two kinds of Love. No one, I think, will deny that there are two goddesses of that name—one, the elder, sprung from no mother's womb but from the heavens themselves, we call the Uranian, the heavenly Aphrodite, while the younger, daughter of Zeus and Dione, we call Pandemus, the earthly Aphrodite. It follows, then, that Love should be known as earthly or as heavenly according to the goddess in whose company his work is done. And our business, gentlemen—I need hardly say that every god must command our homage—our business at the moment is to define the attributes peculiar to each of these two.

Now it may be said of any kind of action that the action itself, as such, is neither good nor bad. Take, for example, what we are doing now. Neither drinking nor singing nor talking has any virtue in itself, for the outcome of each action depends upon how it is performed. If it is done rightly and finely, the action will be good; if it is done basely, bad. And this holds good of loving, for Love is not of himself either admirable or noble, but only when he moves us to love nobly.

Well then, gentlemen, the earthly Aphrodite's Love is a very earthly Love indeed, and does his work entirely at random. It is he that governs the passions of the vulgar. For, first, they are as much attracted by women as by boys; next, whoever they may love, their desires are of the body rather than of the soul; and, finally, they make a point of courting the shallowest people they can find, looking forward to the mere act of fruition and careless whether it be a worthy or unworthy consummation. And hence they take their pleasures where they find them, good and bad alike. For this is the Love of the younger Aphrodite, whose nature partakes of both male and female.

But the heavenly Love springs from a goddess whose attributes have nothing of the female, but are altogether male, and who is also the elder of the two, and innocent of any hint of lewdness. And so those who are inspired by this other Love turn rather to the male, preferring the more vigorous and intellectual bent. One can always tell—even among the lovers of boys—the man who is wholly governed by this elder Love, for no boy can please him until he has shown the first signs of dawning intelligence, signs which generally appear with the first growth of beard. And it seems to me that the man who falls in love with a youth of such an age will be prepared to spend all his time with him, to share his whole life with him, in fact; nor will he be likely to take advantage of the lad's youth and credulity by seducing him and then turning with a laugh to some newer love.

But I cannot help thinking, gentlemen, that there should be a law to forbid the loving of mere boys, a law to prevent so much time and trouble being wasted upon an unknown quantity—for what else, after all, is the future of any boy, and who knows whether he will follow the paths of virtue or of vice, in body and in soul? Of course, your man of principle is a law unto himself, but these followers of the earthly Love should be legally compelled to observe a similar restraint—just as we prevent them, as far as possible, from making love to our own wives and daughters—for it is their behavior that has brought the name of Love into such disrepute that one has even heard it held to be degrading to yield to a lover's solicitation. Anyone who can hold such a view must surely have in mind these earthly lovers, with their offensive importunities, for there can be nothing derogatory in any conduct which is sanctioned both by decency and custom.

Then again, gentlemen, may I point out that, while in all the other states of Hellas the laws that deal with Love are so simple and well defined that they are easy enough to master, our own code is most involved. In Elis and Boeotia, for instance, and wherever else the people are naturally inarticulate, it has been definitely ruled that it is right for the lover to have his way. Nor does anyone, old or young, presume to say that it is wrong—the idea being, I suppose, to save themselves from having to plead with the young men for their favors, which is rather difficult for lovers who are practically dumb.

On the other hand, in Ionia and many other countries under Oriental rule, the very same thing is held to be disgraceful. Indeed, the Oriental thinks ill not only of Love but also of both philosophy and sport, on account of the despotism under which he lives. For I suppose it does not suit the rulers for their subjects to indulge in high thinking, or in staunch friendship and fellowship, which Love more than anything is likely to beget. And those who seized the power here in Athens learned the same lesson from bitter experience, for it was the might of Aristogiton's love and Harmodius' friendship that brought their reign to an end. Thus, wherever the law enacts that it is wrong to yield to the lover, you may be sure that the fault lies with the legislators—that is to say, it is due to the oppression of the rulers and the servility of their subjects. On the other hand, wherever you find the same thing expressly sanctioned, you may blame the legislators' mental inertia.

But in Athens, gentlemen, we have a far more admirable code—a code which, as I was saying, is not nearly so easy to understand. Take for instance our maxim that it is better to love openly than in secret, especially when the object of one's passion is eminent in nobility and virtue, and even if his personal appearance should lack the same distinction. And think how we all love to cheer the lover on, without the least idea that he is doing anything unworthy, and how we see honor in his success and shame in his defeat. And remember, gentlemen, what latitude the law offers to the lover in the prosecution of his suit, and how he may be actually applauded for conduct which, in any other circumstances or in any other cause, would call down upon him the severest censure.

Imagine what would happen to a man who wanted to get money out of someone, or a post, or powers of some kind, and who therefore thought fit to behave as the lover behaves to his beloved—urging his need with prayers and entreaties, and vowing vows, and sleeping upon doorsteps, subjecting himself, in short, to a slavery which no slave would ever endure—why, gentlemen, not only his friends, but his very enemies, would do their best to stop him, for his enemies would accuse him of the most abject servility, while his friends would take him to task because they felt ashamed of him.

But when it is a lover who does this kind of thing people only think the more of him, and the law expressly sanctions his conduct as the means to an honorable end. And, what is the most extraordinary thing of all, it is popularly supposed that the lover is the one man whom the gods will pardon for breaking his vows, for lovers' promises, they say, are made to be forsworn. And so, gentlemen, we see what complete indulgence, not only human but divine, is accorded to the lover by our Athenian code.

In view of this, one would have thought that, here if anywhere, loving and being kind to one's lover would have been positively applauded. Yet we find in practice that if a father discovers that someone has fallen in love with his son, he puts the boy in charge of an attendant, with strict injunctions not to let him have anything to do with his lover. And if the boy's little friends and playmates see anything of that kind going on, you may be sure they'll call him names, while their elders will neither stop their being rude nor tell them they are talking nonsense. So if there were no more to it than that, anyone would think that we Athenians were really shocked at the idea of yielding to a lover.

But I fancy we can account for the apparent contradiction if we remember that the moral value of the act is not what one might call a constant. We agreed that love itself, as such, was neither good nor bad, but only insofar as it led to good or bad behavior. It is base to indulge a vicious lover viciously, but noble to gratify a virtuous lover virtuously. Now the vicious lover is the follower of the earthly Love who desires the body rather than the soul; his heart is set on what is mutable and must therefore be inconstant. And as soon as the body he loves begins to pass the first flower of its beauty, he "spreads his wings and flies away," giving the lie to all his pretty speeches and dishonoring his vows, whereas the lover whose heart is touched by moral beauties is constant all his life, for he has become one with what will never fade.

Now it is the object of the Athenian law to make a firm distinction between the lover who should be encouraged and the lover who should be shunned. And so it enjoins pursuit in certain cases, and flight in others, and applies various touchstones and criteria to discriminate between the two classes of lover and beloved. And this is why it is immoral, according to our code, to yield too promptly to solicitation; there should first be a certain lapse of time, which is generally considered to be the most effective test. Secondly, it is immoral when the surrender is due to financial or political considerations, or to unmanly fear of ill-treatment; it is immoral, in short, if the youth fails to show the contempt he should for any advantage he may gain in pocket or position. For in motives such as these we can find nothing fixed or permanent, except, perhaps, the certainty that they have never been the cause of any noble friendship.

There remains, therefore, only one course open to the beloved if he is to yield to his lover without offending our ideas of decency. It is held that, just as the lover's willing and complete subjection to his beloved is neither abject nor culpable, so there is one other form of voluntary submission that shall be blameless—a submission which is made for the sake of virtue. And so, gentlemen, if anyone is prepared to devote himself to the service of another in the belief that through him he will find increase of wisdom or of any other virtue, we hold that such willing servitude is neither base nor abject.

We must therefore combine these two laws—the one that deals with the love of boys and the one that deals with the pursuit of wisdom and the other virtues—before we can agree that the youth is justified in yielding to his lover. For it is only when lover and beloved come together, each governed by his own special law—the former lawfully enslaving himself to the youth he loves, in return for his compliance, the latter lawfully devoting his services to the friend who is helping him to become wise and good—the one sharing his wealth of wisdom and virtue, and the other drawing, in his poverty, upon his friend for a liberal education—it is then, I say, and only then, when the observance of the two laws coincides, that it is right for the lover to have his way.

There is no shame in being disappointed of such hopes as these, but any other kind of hope, whether it comes true or not, is shameful in itself. Take the case of a youth who gratifies his lover in the belief that he is wealthy and in the hope of making money. Such hopes will be nonetheless discreditable if he finds in the event that he has been the prey of a penniless seducer, for he will have shown himself for what he is, the kind of person, namely, who will do anything for money—which is nothing to be proud of. But suppose that he had yielded because he believed in his lover's virtue, and hoped to be improved by such an association; then, even if he discovered in the end that he had been duped by an unholy blackguard, there would still have been something noble in his mistake, for he, too, would have shown himself for what he was—the kind of person who will do anything for anybody for the sake of progress in the ways of virtue. And what, gentlemen, could be more admirable than that? I conclude, therefore, that it is right to let the lover have his way in the interests of virtue.

Such, then, is the Love of the heavenly Aphrodite, heavenly in himself and precious alike to cities and to men, for he constrains both lover and beloved to pay the most earnest heed to their moral welfare, but all the rest are followers of the other, the earthly Aphrodite. And this, Phaedrus, is all I have to say, extempore, on the subject of Love.

When Pausanias had paused—you see the kind of tricks we catch from our philologists, with their punning derivations—the next speaker, so Aristodemus went on to tell me, should have been Aristophanes; only as it happened, whether he'd been overeating I don't know, but he had got the hiccups so badly that he really wasn't fit to make a speech. So he said to the doctor, Eryximachus, who was sitting next below him, Eryximachus, you'll either have to cure my hiccups or take my turn and go on speaking till they've stopped.

I'm prepared to do both, said Eryximachus. I'll take your turn to speak, and then when you've recovered you can take mine. Meanwhile, you'd better try holding your breath, or if that won't stop your hiccups try gargling with a little water, or if it's particularly stubborn you'll have to get something that you can tickle your nostrils with, and sneeze, and by the time you've done that two or three times you'll find that it will stop, however bad it is.

Go ahead, then, said Aristophanes. You make your speech, and I'll be doing as you say.

Whereupon Eryximachus spoke as follows.

Well, gentlemen, since Pausanias broke off, after an excellent beginning, without having really finished, I must try to wind up his argument myself. I admit that in defining the two kinds of Love he has drawn a very useful distinction, but the science of medicine seems to me to prove that, besides attracting the souls of men to human beauty, Love has many other objects and many other subjects, and that his influence may be traced both in the brute and the vegetable creations, and I think I may say in every form of existence—so great, so wonderful, and so all-embracing is the power of Love in every activity, whether sacred or profane.

I propose, in deference to my own profession, to begin with the medical aspect. I would have you know that the body comprehends in its very nature the dichotomy of Love, for, as we all agree, bodily health and sickness are both distinct and dissimilar, and unlike clings to unlike. And so the desires of health are one thing, while the desires of sickness are quite another. I confirm to what Pausanius has observed, that it is right to yield to the virtuous and wrong to yield to the vicious lover, and similarly, in the case of the body, it is both right and necessary to gratify such desires as are sound and healthy in each particular case, and this is what we call the art of medicine. But it is utterly wrong to indulge such desires as are bad and morbid, nor must anyone who hopes to become expert in this profession lend his countenance to such indulgence. For medicine may be described as the science of what the body loves, or desires, as regards repletion and evacuation, and the man who can distinguish between what is harmful and what is beneficial in these desires may claim to be a physician in the fullest sense of the word. And if he can replace one desire with another, and produce the requisite desire when it is absent, or, if necessary, remove it when it is present, then we shall regard him as an expert practitioner.

Yes, gentlemen, he must be able to reconcile the jarring elements of the body, and force them, as it were, to fall in love with one another. Now, we know that the most hostile elements are the opposites—hot and cold, sweet and sour, wet and dry, and so on—and if, as I do myself, we are to believe these poets of ours, it was his skill in imposing love and concord upon these opposites that enabled our illustrious progenitor Asclepius to found the science of medicine.

And so, gentlemen, I maintain that medicine is under the sole direction of the god of love, as are also the gymnastic and the agronomic arts. And it must be obvious to the most casual observer that the same holds good of music—which is, perhaps, what Heraclitus meant us to understand by that rather cryptic pronouncement, "The one in conflict with itself is held together, like the harmony of the bow and of the lyre." Of course it is absurd to speak of harmony as being in conflict, or as arising out of elements which are still conflicting, but perhaps he meant that the art of music was to create harmony by resolving the discord between the treble and the bass. There can certainly be no harmony of treble and bass while they are still in conflict, for harmony is concord, and concord is a kind of sympathy, and sympathy between things which are in conflict is impossible so long as that conflict lasts. There is, on the other hand, a kind of discord which it is not impossible to resolve, and here we may effect a harmony—as, for instance, we produce rhythm by resolving the difference between fast and slow. And just as we saw that the concord of the body was brought about by the art of medicine, so this other harmony is due to the art of music, as the creator of mutual love and sympathy. And so we may describe music, too, as a science of love, or of desire—in this case in relation to harmony and rhythm.

It is easy enough to distinguish the principle of Love in this rhythmic and harmonic union, nor is there so far any question of Love's dichotomy. But when we come to the application of rhythm and harmony to human activities—as for instance the composition of a song, or the instruction of others in the correct performance of airs and measures which have already been composed—then, gentlemen, we meet with difficulties which call for expert handling. And this brings us back to our previous conclusion, that we are justified in yielding to the desires of the temperate—and of the intemperate insofar as such compliance will tend to sober them, and to this Love, gentlemen, we must hold fast, for he is the fair and heavenly one, born of Urania, the Muse of heaven. But as for that other, the earthly Love, he is sprung from Polyhymnia, the Muse of many songs, and whatever we have to do with him we must be very careful not to add the evils of excess to the enjoyment of the pleasures he affords—just as, in my own profession, it is an important part of our duties to regulate the pleasures of the table so that we may enjoy our meals without being the worse for them. And so in music, in medicine, and in every activity, whether sacred or profane, we must do our utmost to distinguish the two kinds of Love, for you may be sure that they will both be there.

And again, we find these two elements in the seasons of the year, for when the regulating principle of Love brings together those opposites of which I spoke—hot and cold, wet and dry—and compounds them in an ordered harmony, the result is health and plenty for mankind and for the animal and vegetable kingdoms, and all goes as it should. But when the seasons are under the influence of that other Love, all is mischief and destruction, for now plague and disease of every kind attack both herds and crops, and not only these, but frost and hail and blight—and all of them are due to the uncontrolled and the acquisitive in that great system of Love which the astronomer observes when he investigates the movements of the stars and the seasons of the year.

And further, the sole concern of every rite of sacrifice and divination—that is to say, the means of communion between god and man—is either the preservation or the repair of Love. For most of our impiety springs from our refusal to gratify the more temperate Love, and to respect and defer to him in everything we do, and from our following that other Love in our attitude toward our parents, whether alive or dead, and toward the gods. It is the diviner's office to be the guide and healer of these Loves, and his art of divination, with its power to distinguish those principles of human love that tend to decency and reverence, is, in fact, the source of concord between god and man.

And so, gentlemen, the power of Love in its entirety is various and mighty, nay, all-embracing, but the mightiest power of all is wielded by that Love whose just and temperate consummation, whether in heaven or on earth, tends toward the good. It is he that bestows our every joy upon us, and it is through him that we are capable of the pleasures of society, aye, and friendship even, with the gods our masters.

And now, gentlemen, if, as is not unlikely, there are many points I have omitted in my praise of Love, let me assure you that such omissions have been unintentional. It is for you, Aristophanes, to make good my deficiencies, that is unless you're thinking of some other kind of eulogy. But in any case, let us hear what you have to say—now you've recovered from your hiccups.

To which, Aristodemus went on to tell me, Aristophanes replied, Yes, I'm better now, thank you, but not before I'd had recourse to sneezing—which made me wonder, Eryximachus, how your orderly principle of the body could possibly have called for such an appalling union of noise and irritation; yet there's no denying that the hiccups stopped immediately I sneezed.

Now, Aristophanes, take care, retorted Eryximachus, and don't try to raise a laugh before you've even started. You'll only have yourself to thank if I'm waiting to pounce on your silly jokes, instead of giving your speech a proper hearing.

Aristophanes laughed. You're quite right, Eryximachus, he said. I take it all back. But don't be too hard on me. Not that I mind if what I'm going to say is funny—all the better if it is; besides, a comic poet is supposed to be amusing. I'm only afraid of being utterly absurd.

Now, Aristophanes, said Eryximachus, I know the way you loose your shafts of ridicule and run away. But don't forget that anything you say may be used against you—and yet, who knows? Perhaps I shall decide to let you go with a caution.

Well then, Eryximachus, Aristophanes began, I propose, as you suggested, to take quite a different line from you and Pausanias. I am convinced that mankind has never had any conception of the power of Love, for if we had known him as he really is, surely we should have raised the mightiest temples and altars, and offered the most splendid sacrifices, in his honor, and not—as in fact we do—have utterly neglected him. Yet he of all the gods has the best title to our service, for he, more than all the rest, is the friend of man; he is our great ally, and it is he that cures us of those ills whose relief opens the way to man's highest happiness. And so, gentlemen, I will do my best to acquaint you with the power of Love, and you in your turn shall pass the lesson on.

First of all I must explain the real nature of man, and the change which it has undergone—for in the beginning we were nothing like we are now. For one thing, the race was divided into three; that is to say, besides the two sexes, male and female, which we have at present, there was a third which partook of the nature of both, and for which we still have a name, though the creature itself is forgotten. For though "hermaphrodite" is only used nowadays as a term of contempt, there really was a man-woman in those days, a being which was half male and half female.

And secondly, gentlemen, each of these beings was globular in shape, with rounded back and sides, four arms and four legs, and two faces, both the same, on a cylindrical neck, and one head, with one face one side and one the other, and four ears, and two lots of privates, and all the other parts to match. They walked erect, as we do ourselves, backward or forward, whichever they pleased, but when they broke into a run they simply stuck their legs straight out and went whirling round and round like a clown turning cartwheels. And since they had eight legs, if you count their arms as well, you can imagine that they went bowling along at a pretty good speed.

The three sexes, I may say, arose as follows. The males were descended from the Sun, the females from the Earth, and the hermaphrodites from the Moon, which partakes of either sex, and they were round and they *went* round, because they took after their parents. And such, gentlemen, were their strength and energy, and such their arrogance, that they actually tried—like Ephialtes and Otus in Homer—to scale the heights of heaven and set upon the gods.

At this Zeus took counsel with the other gods as to what was to be done. They found themselves in rather an awkward position; they didn't want to blast them out of existence with thunderbolts as they did the giants, because that would be saying goodbye to all their offerings and devotions, but at the same time they couldn't let them get altogether out of hand. At last, however, after racking his brains, Zeus offered a solution.

I think I can see my way, he said, to put an end to this disturbance by weakening these people without destroying them. What I propose to do is to cut them all in half, thus killing two birds with one stone, for each one will be only half as strong, and there'll be twice as many of them, which will suit us very nicely. They can walk about, upright, on their two legs, and if, said Zeus, I have any more trouble with them, I shall split them up again, and they'll have to hop about on one.

So saying, he cut them all in half just as you or I might chop up sorb apples for pickling, or slice an egg with a hair. And as each half was ready he told Apollo to turn its face, with the half-neck that was left, toward the side that was cut away—thinking that the sight of such a gash might frighten it into keeping quiet—and then to heal the whole thing up. So Apollo turned their faces back to front, and, pulling in the skin all the way round, he stretched it over what we now call the belly—like those bags you pull together with a string—and tied up the one remaining opening so as to form what we call the navel. As for the creases that were left, he smoothed most of them away, finishing off the chest with the sort of tool a cobbler uses to smooth down the leather on the last, but he left a few puckers round about the belly and the navel, to remind us of what we suffered long ago.

Now, when the work of bisection was complete it left each half with a desperate yearning for the other, and they ran together and flung their arms around each other's necks, and asked for nothing better than to be rolled into one. So much so, that they began to die of hunger and general inertia, for neither would do anything without the other. And whenever one half was left alone by the death of its mate, it wandered about questing and clasping in the hope of finding a spare half-woman—or a whole woman, as we should call her nowadays—or half a man. And so the race was dying out.

Fortunately, however, Zeus felt so sorry for them that he devised another scheme. He moved their privates round to the front, for of course they had originally been on the outside—which was now the back—and they had begotten and conceived not upon each other, but, like the grasshoppers, upon the earth. So now, as I say, he moved their members round to the front and made them propagate among themselves, the male begetting upon the female—the idea being that if, in all these clippings and claspings, a man should chance upon a woman, conception would take place and the race would be continued, while if man should conjugate with man, he might at least obtain such satisfaction as would allow him to turn his attention and his energies to the everyday affairs of life. So you see, gentlemen, how far back we can trace our innate love for one another, and how this love is always trying to redintegrate our former nature, to make two into one, and to bridge the gulf between one human being and another.

And so, gentlemen, we are all like pieces of the coins that children break in half for keepsakes—making two out of one, like the flatfish—and each of us is forever seeking the half that will tally with himself. The man who is a slice of the hermaphrodite sex, as it was called, will naturally be attracted by women—the adulterer, for instance—and women who run after men are of similar descent—as, for instance, the unfaithful wife. But the woman who is a slice of the original female is attracted by women rather than by men—in fact she is a Lesbian—while men who are slices of the male are followers of the male, and show their masculinity throughout their boyhood by the way they make friends with men, and the delight they take in lying beside them and being taken in their arms. And these are the most hopeful of the nation's youth, for theirs is the most virile constitution.

I know there are some people who call them shameless, but they are wrong. It is not immodesty that leads them to such pleasures, but daring, fortitude, and masculinity—the very virtues that they recognize and welcome in their lovers—which is proved by the fact that in after years they are the only men who show any real manliness in public life. And so, when they themselves have come to manhood, their love in turn is lavished upon boys. They have no natural inclination to marry and beget children. Indeed, they only do so in deference to the usage of society, for they would just as soon renounce marriage altogether and spend their lives with one another.

Such a man, then, gentlemen, is of an amorous disposition,

and gives his love to boys, always clinging to his like. And so, when this boy lover—or any lover, for that matter—is fortunate enough to meet his other half, they are both so intoxicated with affection, with friendship, and with love, that they cannot bear to let each other out of sight for a single instant. It is such reunions as these that impel men to spend their lives together, although they may be hard put to it to say what they really want with one another, and indeed, the purely sexual pleasures of their friendship could hardly account for the huge delight they take in one another's company. The fact is that both their souls are longing for a something else—a something to which they can neither of them put a name, and which they can only give an inkling of in cryptic sayings and prophetic riddles.

Now, supposing Hephaestus were to come and stand over them with his tool bag as they lay there side by side, and suppose he were to ask, Tell me, my dear creatures, what do you really want with one another?

And suppose they didn't know what to say, and he went on, How would you like to be rolled into one, so that you could always be together, day and night, and never be parted again? Because if that's what you want, I can easily weld you together, and then you can live your two lives in one, and, when the time comes, you can die a common death and still be two-in-one in the lower world. Now, what do you say? Is that what you'd like me to do? And would you be happy if I did?

We may be sure, gentlemen, that no lover on earth would dream of refusing such an offer, for not one of them could imagine a happier fate. Indeed, they would be convinced that this was just what they'd been waiting for—to be merged, that is, into an utter oneness with the beloved.

And so all this to-do is a relic of that original state of ours, when we were whole, and now, when we are longing for and following after that primeval wholeness, we say we are in love. For there was a time, I repeat, when we were one, but now, for our sins, God has scattered us abroad, as the Spartans scattered the Arcadians. Moreover, gentlemen, there is every reason to fear that, if we neglect the worship of the gods, they will split us up again, and then we shall have to go about with our noses sawed asunder, part and counterpart, like the basso-relievos on the tombstones. And therefore it is our duty one and all to inspire our friends with reverence and piety, for so we may ensure our safety and attain that blessed union by enlisting in the army of Love and marching beneath his banners.

For Love must never be withstood—as we do, if we incur the displeasure of the gods. But if we cling to him in friendship and reconciliation, we shall be among the happy few to whom it is given in these latter days to meet their other halves. Now, I don't want any coarse remarks from Eryximachus. I don't mean Pausanias and Agathon, though for all I know they may be among the lucky ones, and both be sections of the male. But what I am trying to say is this—that the happiness of the whole human race, women no less than men, is to be found in the consummation of our love, and in the healing of our dissevered nature by finding each his proper mate. And if this be a counsel of perfection, then we must do what, in our present circumstances, is next best, and bestow our love upon the natures most congenial to our own.

And so I say that Love, the god who brings all this to pass, is worthy of our hymns, for his is the inestimable and present service of conducting us to our true affinities, and it is he that offers this great hope for the future—that, if we do not fail in reverence to the gods, he will one day heal us and restore us to our old estate, and establish us in joy and blessedness.

Such, Eryximachus, is my discourse on Love—as different as could be from yours. And now I must ask you again. Will you please refrain from making fun of it, and let us hear what all the others have to say—or rather, the other two, for I see there's no one left but Agathon and Socrates.

Well, you shall have your way, said Eryximachus, and, joking apart, I enjoyed your speech immensely. Indeed, if I were not aware that Socrates and Agathon were both authorities on Love, I should be wondering what they could find to say after being treated to such a wealth and variety of eloquence. But, knowing what they are, I've no doubt we'll find them equal to the occasion.

To which Socrates retorted, It's all very well for you to talk, Eryximachus, after your own magnificent display, but if you were in my shoes now—or rather when Agathon has finished speaking—you'd be just as nervous as I am.

Now, Socrates, said Agathon, I suppose you're trying to upset me by insisting on the great things my public is expecting of me.

My dear Agathon, said Socrates, do you think I don't remember your ease and dignity as you took the stage with the actors the other day, and how you looked that vast audience in the face, as cool as you please, and obviously prepared to show them what you were made of? And am I to suppose that the sight of two or three friends will put you out of countenance?

Ah, but, Socrates, protested Agathon, you mustn't think I'm so infatuated with the theater as to forget that a man of any judgment cares more for a handful of brains than an army of blockheads.

Oh, I should never make such a mistake, Socrates assured him, as to credit *you,* my dear Agathon, with ideas that smacked of the illiterate. I've no doubt that if you found yourself in what you really considered intellectual company, you'd be more impressed by their opinion than by the mob's. But we, alas, can't claim to be your intelligent minority, for we were there too, you know, helping to swell that very crowd. But tell me, if you were with some other set of people whose judgment you respected, I suppose you'd feel uncomfortable if they saw you doing anything you thought beneath you. Am I right?

Perfectly, said Agathon.

And yet, Socrates went on, you wouldn't feel uncomfortable if the *mob* saw you doing something equally unworthy?

But here Phaedrus stepped in. My dear Agathon, he said, if you go on answering his questions he won't care twopence what becomes of our debate, so long as there's someone he can argue with—especially if it's somebody good-looking. Now, much as I enjoy listening to Socrates' arguments, it's my duty as chairman to insist that each man makes his speech. So I must ask you both to pay your tribute to the god, and then you can argue as much as you please.

Phaedrus is right, said Agathon. I'm quite prepared to speak. After all, I can argue with Socrates any day.

Now, before I begin my speech I want to explain what sort of a speech I think it ought to be. For to my way of thinking the speakers we have heard so far have been at such pains to congratulate mankind upon the blessings of Love that they have quite forgotten to extol the god himself, and have thrown no light at all upon the nature of our divine benefactor. Yet surely, if we are to praise anyone, no matter whom, no matter how, there is only one way to go about it, and that is to indicate the nature of him whose praises we are to sing, and of the blessings he is the author of. And so, gentlemen, with Love. Our duty is first to praise him for what he is, and secondly, for what he gives.

And so I shall begin by maintaining that, while all the gods are blessed, Love—be it said in all reverence—is the blessedest of all, for he is the loveliest and the best. The loveliest, I say, because first of all, Phaedrus, he is the youngest of the gods, which is proved by his flight, aye, and his escape, from the ravages of time, who travels fast enough—too fast, at any rate, for us poor mortals. But Love was born to be the enemy of age, and shuns the very sight of senility, clinging always to his like in the company of youth, because he is young himself.

I agreed with most of Phaedrus' speech, but not with his suggestion that Love was older than even Cronus or Iapetus. No, gentlemen, Love, in his imperishable youth, is, I repeat, the youngest of them all. And as for those old stories of the gods we have read in Hesiod and Parmenides, we may be sure that any such proceedings were the work not of Love but of Necessity—if, indeed, such tales are credible at all. For if Love had been among them then, they would neither have fettered nor gelded one another; they would have used no violence at all, but lived together in peace and concord as they do today, and as they have done since Love became their heavenly overlord.

It is clear, then, that he is young, and not only young but dainty, with a daintiness that only a Homer could describe. For it is Homer, is it not, who writes of Ate as being both divine and dainty—dainty of foot, that is. "How delicate," he says—

How delicate her feet who shuns the ground,
Stepping a-tiptoe on the heads of men.

Now, you will agree that to prefer what is soft to what is hard is proof enough of being dainty, and the same argument will demonstrate the daintiness of Love, for he never treads upon the ground, nor even on our heads—which, after all, are not so very soft—but lives and moves in the softest thing in the whole of nature. He makes the dispositions and the hearts of gods and men his dwelling place—not, however, without discrimination, for if the heart he lights upon be hard he flies away to settle in a softer. And so, not only treading on but altogether clinging to the softest of the soft, he must indeed be exquisitely dainty.

We see, then, that Love is for one thing the youngest, and for another the most delicate, thing in the world, and thirdly, gentlemen, we find that he is tender and supple. For if he were hampered by the least inflexibility, how could he wind us in such endless convolutions, and steal into all our hearts so secretly—aye, and leave them, too, when he pleases? And that elegance of his, which all the world confesses, bears witness to his suppleness and symmetry, for Love and unsightliness will never be at peace. Moreover, his life among the flowers argues in himself a loveliness of hue, for Love will never settle upon bodies, or souls, or anything at all where there is no bud to blossom, or where the bloom is faded. But where the ground is thick with flowers and the air with scent, there he will settle, gentlemen, and there he loves to linger.

I shall say no more about Love's loveliness—though much remains to say—because we must now consider his moral excellence, and in particular the fact that he is never injured by, nor ever injures, either god or man. For, whatever Love may suffer, it cannot be by violence—which, indeed, cannot so much as touch him—nor does he need to go to work by force, for the world asks no compulsion, but is glad to serve him, and, as we know, a compact made in mutual good will is held to be just and binding by the sovereign power of the law.

Added to his righteousness is his entire temperance. I may take it, I suppose, for granted that temperance is defined as the power to control our pleasures and our lusts, and that none of these is more powerful than Love. If, therefore, they are weaker, they will be overcome by Love, and he will be their master, so that Love, controlling, as I said, our lusts and pleasures, may be regarded as temperance itself.

Then, as to valor, as the poet sings, "But him not even Ares can withstand." For, as the story goes, it was not Ares that captured Love, but Love that captured Ares—love, that is, of Aphrodite. Now, the captor is stronger than the captive, and therefore Love, by overcoming one who is mightier than all the rest, has shown himself the mightiest of all.

So much, gentlemen, for the righteousness of Love, his temperance, and his valor; there remains his genius, to which I must do such scanty justice as I can. First of all, then—if, like Eryximachus, I may give pride of place to my own vocation—Love is himself so divine a poet that he can kindle in the souls of others the poetic fire, for no matter what dull clay we seemed to be before, we are every one of us a poet when we are in love. We need ask no further proof than this that Love is a poet deeply versed in every branch of what I may define succinctly as creative art, for, just as no one can give away what he has not got, so no one can teach what he does not know.

And who will deny that the creative power by which all living things are begotten and brought forth is the very genius of Love? Do we not, moreover, recognize that in every art and craft the artist and the craftsman who work under the direction of this same god achieve the brightest fame, while those that lack his influence grow old in the shadow of oblivion? It was longing and desire that led Apollo to found the arts of archery, healing, and divination—so he, too, was a scholar in the school of Love. It was thus that the fine arts were founded by the Muses, the smithy by Hephaestus, and the loom by Pallas, and thus it was that Zeus himself attained the "governance of gods and men." And hence the actions of the gods were governed by the birth of Love—love, that is, of beauty, for, as we know, he will have none of ugliness. We are told, as I have already said, that in the beginning there were many strange and terrible happenings among them, because Necessity was king, but ever since the birth of the younger god, Love—the love of what is lovely—has showered every kind of blessing upon gods and men.

And so I say, Phaedrus, that Love, besides being in himself the loveliest and the best, is the author of those very virtues in all around him. And now I am stirred to speak in numbers, and to tell how it is he that brings

Peace upon earth, the breathless calm
That lulls the long-tormented deep,
Rest to the winds, and that sweet balm
And solace of our nature, sleep.

And it is he that banishes estrangement and ushers friendship in; it is he that unites us in such friendly gatherings as this—presiding at the table, at the dance, and at the altar, cultivating courtesy and weeding out brutality, lavish of kindliness and sparing of malevolence, affable and gracious, the wonder of the wise, the admiration of the gods, the despair of him that lacks, and the happiness of him that has, the father of delicacy, daintiness, elegance, and grace, of longing and desire, heedful of the good and heedless of the bad, in toil or terror, in drink or dialectic, our helmsman and helper, our pilot and preserver, the richest ornament of heaven and earth alike, and, to conclude, the noblest and the loveliest of leaders, whom every one of us must follow, raising our voices in harmony with the heavenly song of Love that charms both mortal and immortal hearts.

And there, my dear Phaedrus, he said, you have my speech.

Such is my offering to the god of love. I have done my best to be at once amusing and instructive.

Agathon took his seat, continued Aristodemus, amid a burst of applause, for we all felt that his youthful eloquence did honor to himself as well as to the god.

Then Socrates turned to Eryximachus and said, Well, Eryximachus, you laughed at my misgivings, but you see—they've been justified by the event. There's not much left for *me* to say after the wonderful speech we've just had from Agathon.

I admit, Eryximachus replied, that your prognosis was correct so far as Agathon's eloquence was concerned, but as to your own embarrassment, I'm not so sure.

My dear sir, protested Socrates, what chance have I or anyone of knowing what to say, after listening to such a flood of eloquence as that? The opening, I admit, was nothing out of the way, but when he came to his peroration, why, he held us all spellbound with the sheer beauty of his diction, while I, personally, was so mortified when I compared it with the best that I could ever hope to do, that for two pins I'd have tried to sneak away. Besides, his speech reminded me so strongly of that master of rhetoric, Gorgias, that I couldn't help thinking of Odysseus, and his fear that Medusa would rise from the lower world among the ghosts, and I was afraid that when Agathon got near the end he would arm his speech against mine with the Gorgon's head of Gorgias' eloquence, and strike me as dumb as a stone.

And then I saw what a fool I'd been to agree to take part in this eulogy of yours, and, what was worse, to claim a special knowledge of the subject, when, as it turned out, I had not the least idea how this or any other eulogy should be conducted. I had imagined in my innocence that one began by stating the facts about the matter in hand, and then proceeded to pick out the most attractive points and display them to the best advantage. And I flattered myself that my speech would be a great success, because I knew the facts. But the truth, it seems, is the last thing the successful eulogist cares about; on the contrary, what he does is simply to run through all the attributes of power and virtue, however irrelevant they may be, and the whole thing may be a pack of lies, for all it seems to matter.

I take it then that what we undertook was to flatter, rather than to praise, the god of love, and that's why you're all prepared to say the first thing about him that comes into your heads, and to claim that he either is, or is the cause of, everything that is loveliest and best. And of course the uninitiated are impressed by the beauty and grandeur of your encomiums; yet those who know will not be taken in so easily. Well then, I repeat, the whole thing was a misunderstanding, and it was only in my ignorance that I agreed to take part at all. I protest, with Euripides' Hippolytus, it was my lips that promised, not my soul, and that, gentlemen, is that. I won't have anything to do with your eulogy, and what is more, I couldn't if I tried. But I don't mind telling you the truth about Love, if you're interested; only, if I do, I must tell it in my own way, for I'm not going to make a fool of myself, at my age, trying to imitate the grand manner that sits so well on the rest of you. Now, Phaedrus, it's for you to say. Have you any use for a speaker who only cares whether his matter is correct and leaves his manner to take care of itself?

Whereupon Phaedrus and the others told him to go ahead and make whatever kind of speech he liked.

Very well, said he, but there's just one other thing. Has our chairman any objection to my asking Agathon a few simple questions? I want to make certain we're not at cross-purposes before I begin my speech.

Ask what you like, said Phaedrus. I don't mind.

Whereupon Socrates began, so far as Aristodemus could trust his memory, as follows.

I must say, my dear Agathon, that the remarks with which you prefaced your speech were very much to the point. You were quite right in saying that the first thing you had to do was to acquaint us with the nature of the god, and the second to tell us what he did. Yes, your introduction was admirable. But now that we've had the pleasure of hearing your magnificent description of Love, there's just one little point I'm not quite clear about. Tell me. Do you think it is the nature of Love to be the love of somebody, or of nobody? I don't mean, is he a mother's or a father's love? That would be a silly sort of question, but suppose I were to ask you whether a father, *as* a father, must be *somebody's* father, or not; surely the only reasonable answer would be that a father must be the father of a son or a daughter. Am I right?

Why, yes, said Agathon.

And could we say the same thing about a mother?

Yes.

Good. And now, if you don't mind answering just one or two more questions, I think you'll see what I'm driving at. Suppose I were to ask, what about a brother, *as* a brother? Must he be *somebody's* brother, or not?

Of course he must.

You mean, he must be the brother of a brother or a sister.

Precisely, said Agathon.

Well, then, Socrates went on, I want you to look at Love from the same point of view. Is he the love of something, or of nothing?

Of something, naturally.

And now, said Socrates, bearing in mind what Love is the love of, tell me this. Does he long for what he is in love with, or not?

Of course he longs for it.

And does he long for whatever it is he longs for, and is he in love with it, when he's got it, or when he hasn't?

When he hasn't got it, probably.

Then isn't it probable, said Socrates, or rather isn't it certain that everything longs for what it lacks, and that nothing longs for what it doesn't lack? I can't help thinking, Agathon, that that's about as certain as anything could be. Don't you think so?

Yes, I suppose it is.

Good. Now, tell me. Is it likely that a big man will want to be big, or a strong man to be strong?

Not if we were right just now.

Quite, for the simple reason that neither of them would be lacking in that particular respect.

Exactly.

For if, Socrates continued, the strong were to long for strength, and the swift for swiftness, and the healthy for health—for I suppose it *might* be suggested that in such cases as these people long for the very things they have, or are, already, and so I'm trying to imagine such a case, to make quite sure we're on the right track—people in their position, Agathon, if you stop to think about them, are bound here and now to have those very qualities, whether they want them or not; so why should they trouble to want them? And so, if we heard someone saying, "I'm healthy, and I want to be healthy; I'm rich, and I want to be rich; and in fact I want just what I've got," I think we should be justified in saying, "But, my dear sir, you've *got* wealth and health and strength already, and what you want is to go on having them, for at the moment you've got them whether you want them or not. Doesn't it look as if, when you say you want these things here and now, you really mean, what you've got now, you want to go on keeping?" Don't you think, my dear Agathon, that he'd be bound to agree?

Why, of course he would, said Agathon.

Well, then, continued Socrates, desiring to secure something to oneself forever may be described as loving something which is not yet to hand.

Certainly.

And therefore, whoever feels a want is wanting something which is not yet to hand, and the object of his love and of his desire is whatever he isn't, or whatever he hasn't got—that is to say, whatever he is lacking in.

Absolutely.

And now, said Socrates, are we agreed upon the following conclusions? One, that Love is always the love of something, and two, that that something is what he lacks.

Agreed, said Agathon.

So far, so good, said Socrates. And now, do you remember what you said were the objects of Love, in your speech just now? Perhaps I'd better jog your memory. I fancy it was something like this—that the actions of the gods were governed by the love of beauty—for of course there was no such thing as the love of ugliness. Wasn't that pretty much what you said?

It was, said Agathon.

No doubt you were right, too, said Socrates. And if that's so, doesn't it follow that Love is the love of beauty, and not of ugliness?

It does.

And haven't we agreed that Love is the love of something which he hasn't got, and consequently lacks?

Yes.

Then Love has no beauty, but is lacking in it?

Yes, that must follow.

Well then, would you suggest that something which lacked beauty and had no part in it was beautiful itself?

Certainly not.

And, that being so, can you still maintain that Love is beautiful?

To which Agathon could only reply, I begin to be afraid, my dear Socrates, that I didn't know what I was talking about.

Never mind, said Socrates, it was a lovely speech, but there's just one more point. I suppose you hold that the good is also beautiful?

I do.

Then, if Love is lacking in what is beautiful, and if the good and the beautiful are the same, he must also be lacking in what is good.

Just as you say, Socrates, he replied. I'm afraid you're quite unanswerable.

No, no, dear Agathon. It's the truth you find unanswerable, not Socrates. And now I'm going to leave you in peace, because I want to talk about some lessons I was given, once upon a time, by a Mantinean woman called Diotima—a woman who was deeply versed in this and many other fields of knowledge. It was she who brought about a ten years' postponement of the great plague of Athens on the occasion of a certain sacrifice, and it was she who taught me the philosophy of Love. And now I am going to try to connect her teaching—as well as I can without her help—with the conclusions that Agathon and I have just arrived at. Like him, I shall begin by stating who and what Love is, and go on to describe his functions, and I think the easiest way will be to adopt Diotima's own method of inquiry by question and answer. I'd been telling her pretty much what Agathon has just been telling me—how Love was a great god, and how he was the love of what is beautiful, and she used the same arguments on me that I've just brought to bear on Agathon to prove that, on my own showing, Love was neither beautiful nor good.

Whereupon, My dear Diotima, I asked, are you trying to make me believe that Love is bad and ugly?

Heaven forbid, she said. But do you really think that if a thing isn't beautiful it's therefore bound to be ugly?

Why, naturally.

And that what isn't learned must be ignorant? Have you never heard of something which comes between the two?

And what's that?

Don't you know, she asked, that holding an opinion which is in fact correct, without being able to give a reason for it, is neither true knowledge—how can it be knowledge without a reason?—nor ignorance—for how can we call it ignorance when it happens to be true? So may we not say that a correct opinion comes midway between knowledge and ignorance?

Yes, I admitted, that's perfectly true.

Very well, then, she went on, why must you insist that what isn't beautiful is ugly, and that what isn't good is bad? Now, coming back to Love, you've been forced to agree that he is neither good nor beautiful, but that's no reason for thinking that he must be bad and ugly. The fact is that he's between the two.

And yet, I said, it's generally agreed that he's a great god.

It all depends, she said, on what you mean by "generally."

Do you mean simply people that don't know anything about it, or do you include the people that do?

I meant everybody.

At which she laughed, and said, Then can you tell me, my dear Socrates, how people can agree that he's a great god when they deny that he's a god at all?

What people do you mean? I asked her.

You for one, and I for another.

What on earth do you mean by that?

Oh, it's simple enough, she answered. Tell me, wouldn't you say that all the gods were happy and beautiful? Or would you suggest that any of them were neither?

Good heavens, no! said I.

And don't you call people happy when they possess the beautiful and the good?

Why, of course.

And yet you agreed just now that Love lacks, and consequently longs for, those very qualities?

Yes, so I did.

Then, if he has no part in either goodness or beauty, how can he be a god?

I suppose he can't be, I admitted.

And now, she said, haven't I proved that you're one of the people who don't believe in the divinity of Love?

Yes, but what can he be, then? I asked her. A mortal?

Not by any means.

Well, what then?

What I told you before—halfway between mortal and immortal.

And what do you mean by that, Diotima?

A very powerful spirit, Socrates, and spirits, you know, are halfway between god and man.

What powers have they, then? I asked.

They are the envoys and interpreters that ply between heaven and earth, flying upward with our worship and our prayers, and descending with the heavenly answers and commandments, and since they are between the two estates they weld both sides together and merge them into one great whole. They form the medium of the prophetic arts, of the priestly rites of sacrifice, initiation, and incantation, of divination and of sorcery, for the divine will not mingle directly with the human, and it is only through the mediation of the spirit world that man can have any intercourse, whether waking or sleeping, with the gods. And the man who is versed in such matters is said to have spiritual powers, as opposed to the mechanical powers of the man who is expert in the more mundane arts. There are many spirits, and many kinds of spirits, too, and Love is one of them.

Then who were his parents? I asked.

I'll tell you, she said, though it's rather a long story. On the day of Aphrodite's birth the gods were making merry, and among them was Resource, the son of Craft. And when they had supped, Need came begging at the door because there was good cheer inside. Now, it happened that Resource, having drunk deeply of the heavenly nectar—for this was before the days of wine—wandered out into the garden of Zeus and sank into a heavy sleep, and Need, thinking that to get a child by Resource would mitigate her penury, lay down beside him and in time was brought to bed of Love. So Love became the follower and servant of Aphrodite because he was begotten on the same day that she was born, and further, he was born to love the beautiful since Aphrodite is beautiful herself.

Then again, as the son of Resource and Need, it has been his fate to be always needy; nor is he delicate and lovely as most of us believe, but harsh and arid, barefoot and homeless, sleeping on the naked earth, in doorways, or in the very streets beneath the stars of heaven, and always partaking of his mother's poverty. But, secondly, he brings his father's resourcefulness to his designs upon the beautiful and the good, for he is gallant, impetuous, and energetic, a mighty hunter, and a master of device and artifice—at once desirous and full of wisdom, a lifelong seeker after truth, an adept in sorcery, enchantment, and seduction.

He is neither mortal nor immortal, for in the space of a day he will be now, when all goes well with him, alive and blooming, and now dying, to be born again by virtue of his father's nature, while what he gains will always ebb away as fast. So Love is never altogether in or out of need, and stands, moreover, midway between ignorance and wisdom. You must understand that none of the gods are seekers after truth. They do not long for wisdom, because they are wise—and why should the wise be seeking the wisdom that is already theirs. Nor, for that matter, do the ignorant seek the truth or crave to be made wise. And indeed, what makes their cause so hopeless is that, having neither beauty, nor goodness, nor intelligence, they are satisfied with what they are, and do not long for the virtues they have never missed.

Then tell me, Diotima, I said, who are these seekers after truth, if they are neither the wise nor the ignorant?

Why, a schoolboy, she replied, could have told you that, after what I've just been saying. They are those that come between the two, and one of them is Love. For wisdom is concerned with the loveliest of things, and Love is the love of what is lovely. And so it follows that Love is a lover of wisdom, and, being such, he is placed between wisdom and ignorance—for which his parentage also is responsible, in that his father is full of wisdom and resource, while his mother is devoid of either.

Such, my dear Socrates, is the spirit of Love, and yet I'm not altogether surprised at your idea of him, which was, judging by what you said, that Love was the beloved rather than the lover. So naturally you thought of Love as utterly beautiful, for the beloved is, in fact, beautiful, perfect, delicate, and prosperous—very different from the lover, as I have described him.

Very well, dear lady, I replied, no doubt you're right. But in that case, what good can Love be to humanity?

That's just what I'm coming to, Socrates, she said. So much, then, for the nature and the origin of Love. You were right in thinking that he was the love of what is beautiful. But suppose someone were to say, Yes, my dear Socrates. Quite so, my dear

Diotima. But what do you mean by the love of what is beautiful? Or, to put the question more precisely, what is it that the lover of the beautiful is longing for?

He is longing to make the beautiful his own, I said.

Very well, she replied, but your answer leads to another question. What will he gain by making the beautiful his own?

This, as I had to admit, was more than I could answer on the spur of the moment.

Well then, she went on, suppose that, instead of the beautiful, you were being asked about the good. I put it to you, Socrates. What is it that the lover of the good is longing for?

To make the good his own.

Then what will he gain by making it his own?

I can make a better shot at answering that, I said. He'll gain happiness.

Right, said she, for the happy are happy inasmuch as they possess the good, and since there's no need for us to ask why men should want to be happy, I think your answer is conclusive.

Absolutely, I agreed.

This longing, then, she went on, this love—is it common to all mankind? What do you think, do we all long to make the good our own?

Yes, I said, as far as that goes we're all alike.

Well then, Socrates, if we say that everybody always loves the same thing, does that mean that everybody is in love? Or do we mean that some of us are in love, while some of us are not?

I was a little worried about that myself, I confessed.

Oh, it's nothing to worry about, she assured me. You see, what we've been doing is to give the name of Love to what is only one single aspect of it; we make just the same mistake, you know, with a lot of other names.

For instance. . . ?

For instance, poetry. You'll agree that there is more than one kind of poetry in the true sense of the word—that is to say, calling something into existence that was not there before, so that every kind of artistic creation is poetry, and every artist is a poet.

True.

But all the same, she said, we don't call them all poets, do we? We give various names to the various arts, and only call the one particular art that deals with music and meter by the name that should be given to them all. And that's the only art that we call poetry, while those who practice it are known as poets.

Quite.

And that's how it is with Love. For "Love, that renowned and all-beguiling power," includes every kind of longing for happiness and for the good. Yet those of us who are subject to this longing in the various fields of business, athletics, philosophy, and so on, are never said to be in love, and are never known as lovers, while the man who devotes himself to what is only one of Love's many activities is given the name that should apply to all the rest as well.

Yes, I said, I suppose you must be right.

I know it has been suggested, she continued, that lovers are people who are looking for their other halves, but as I see it, Socrates, Love never longs for either the half or the whole of anything except the good. For men will even have their hands and feet cut off if they are once convinced that those members are bad for them. Indeed I think we only prize our own belongings insofar as we say that the good belongs to us, and the bad to someone else, for what we love is the good and nothing but the good. Or do you disagree?

Good heavens, no! I said.

Then may we state categorically that men are lovers of the good?

Yes, I said, we may.

And shouldn't we add that they long for the good to be their own?

We should.

And not merely to be their own but to be their own forever?

Yes, that must follow.

In short, that Love longs for the good to be his own forever?

Yes, I said, that's absolutely true.

Very well, then. And that being so, what course will Love's followers pursue, and in what particular field will eagerness and exertion be known as Love? In fact, what is this activity? Can you tell me that, Socrates?

If I could, my dear Diotima, I retorted, I shouldn't be so much amazed at *your* grasp of the subject, and I shouldn't be coming to you to learn the answer to that very question.

Well, I'll tell you, then, she said. To love is to bring forth upon the beautiful, both in body and in soul.

I'm afraid that's too deep, I said, for my poor wits to fathom.

I'll try to speak more plainly, then. We are all of us prolific, Socrates, in body and in soul, and when we reach a certain age our nature urges us to procreation. Nor can we be quickened by ugliness, but only by the beautiful. Conception, we know, takes place when man and woman come together, but there's a divinity in human propagation, an immortal something in the midst of man's mortality which is incompatible with any kind of discord. And ugliness is at odds with the divine, while beauty is in perfect harmony. In propagation, then, Beauty is the goddess of both fate and travail, and so when procreancy draws near the beautiful it grows genial and blithe, and birth follows swiftly on conception. But when it meets with ugliness it is overcome with heaviness and gloom, and turning away it shrinks into itself and is not brought to bed, but still labors under its painful burden. And so, when the procreant is big with child, he is strangely stirred by the beautiful, because he knows that Beauty's tenant will bring his travail to an end. So you see, Socrates, that Love is not exactly a longing for the beautiful, as you suggested.

Well, what is it, then?

A longing not for the beautiful itself, but for the conception and generation that the beautiful effects.

Yes. No doubt you're right.

Of course I'm right, she said. And why all this longing for propagation? Because this is the one deathless and eternal element in our mortality. And since we have agreed that the lover longs for the good to be his own forever, it follows that we are bound to long for immortality as well as for the good—which is to say that Love is a longing for immortality.

So much I gathered, gentlemen, at one time and another from Diotima's dissertations upon Love.

And then one day she asked me, Well, Socrates, and what do you suppose is the cause of all this longing and all this love? Haven't you noticed what an extraordinary effect the breeding instinct has upon both animals and birds, and how obsessed they are with the desire, first to mate, and then to rear their litters and their broods, and how the weakest of them are ready to stand up to the strongest in defense of their young, and even die for them, and how they are content to bear the pinch of hunger and every kind of hardship, so long as they can rear their offspring?

With men, she went on, you might put it down to the power of reason, but how can you account for Love's having such remarkable effects upon the brutes? What do you say to that, Socrates?

Again I had to confess my ignorance.

Well, she said, I don't know how you can hope to master the philosophy of Love, if *that's* too much for you to understand.

But, my dear Diotima, I protested, as I said before, that's just why I'm asking you to teach me—because I realize how ignorant I am. And I'd be more than grateful if you'd enlighten me as to the cause not only of this, but of all the various effects of Love.

Well, she said, it's simple enough, so long as you bear in mind what we agreed was the object of Love. For here, too, the principle holds good that the mortal does all it can to put on immortality. And how can it do that except by breeding, and thus ensuring that there will always be a younger generation to take the place of the old?

Now, although we speak of an individual as being the same so long as he continues to exist in the same form, and therefore assume that a man is the same person in his dotage as in his infancy, yet, for all we call him the same, every bit of him is different, and every day he is becoming a new man, while the old man is ceasing to exist, as you can see from his hair, his flesh, his bones, his blood, and all the rest of his body. And not only his body, for the same thing happens to his soul. And neither his manners, nor his disposition, nor his thoughts, nor his desires, nor his pleasures, nor his sufferings, nor his fears are the same throughout his life, for some of them grow, while others disappear.

And the application of this principle to human knowledge is even more remarkable, for not only do some of the things we know increase, while some of them are lost, so that even in our knowledge we are not always the same, but the principle applies as well to every single branch of knowledge. When we say we are studying, we really mean that our knowledge is ebbing away. We forget, because our knowledge disappears, and we have to study so as to replace what we are losing, so that the state of our knowledge may seem, at any rate, to be the same as it was before.

This is how every mortal creature perpetuates itself. It cannot, like the divine, be still the same throughout eternity; it can only leave behind new life to fill the vacancy that is left in its species by obsolescence. This, my dear Socrates, is how the body and all else that is temporal partakes of the eternal; there is no other way. And so it is no wonder that every creature prizes its own issue, since the whole creation is inspired by this love, this passion for immortality.

Well, Diotima, I said, when she had done, that's a most impressive argument. I wonder if you're right.

Of course I am, she said with an air of authority that was almost professorial. Think of the ambitions of your fellow men, and though at first they may strike you as upsetting my argument, you'll see how right I am if you only bear in mind that men's great incentive is the love of glory, and that their one idea is, "To win eternal mention in the deathless roll of fame."

For the sake of fame they will dare greater dangers, even, than for their children; they are ready to spend their money like water and to wear their fingers to the bone, and, if it comes to that, to die.

Do you think, she went on, that Alcestis would have laid down her life to save Admetus, or that Achilles would have died for the love he bore Patroclus, or that Codrus, the Athenian king, would have sacrificed himself for the seed of his royal consort, if they had not hoped to win "the deathless name for valor," which, in fact, posterity has granted them? No, Socrates, no. Every one of us, no matter what he does, is longing for the endless fame, the incomparable glory that is theirs, and the nobler he is, the greater his ambition, because he is in love with the eternal.

Well then, she went on, those whose procreancy is of the body turn to woman as the object of their love, and raise a family, in the blessed hope that by doing so they will keep their memory green, "through time and through eternity." But those whose procreancy is of the spirit rather than of the flesh—and they are not unknown, Socrates—conceive and bear the things of the spirit. And what are they? you ask. Wisdom and all her sister virtues; it is the office of every poet to beget them, and of every artist whom we may call creative.

Now, by far the most important kind of wisdom, she went on, is that which governs the ordering of society, and which goes by the names of justice and moderation. And if any man is so closely allied to the divine as to be teeming with these virtues even in his youth, and if, when he comes to manhood, his first ambition is to be begetting, he too, you may be sure, will go about in search of the loveliness—and never of the ugliness—on which he may beget. And hence his procreant nature is attracted by a comely body rather than an ill-favored one, and if, besides, he happens on a soul which is at once beautiful, distinguished, and agreeable, he is charmed to find so welcome an alliance. It will be easy for him to talk of virtue to such a listener, and to discuss what human goodness is and how the virtuous should live—in short, to undertake the other's education.

And, as I believe, by constant association with so much beauty, and by thinking of his friend when he is present and when he is away, he will be delivered of the burden he has labored under all these years. And what is more, he and his friend will help each other rear the issue of their friendship—and so the bond between them will be more binding, and their communion even more complete, than that which comes of bringing children up, because they have created something lovelier and less mortal than human seed.

And I ask you, who would not prefer such fatherhood to merely human propagation, if he stopped to think of Homer, and Hesiod, and all the greatest of our poets? Who would not envy them their immortal progeny, their claim upon the admiration of posterity?

Or think of Lycurgus, she went on, and what offspring he left behind him in his laws, which proved to be the saviors of Sparta and, perhaps, the whole of Hellas. Or think of the fame of Solon, the father of Athenian law, and think of all the other names that are remembered in Grecian cities and in lands beyond the sea for the noble deeds they did before the eyes of all the world, and for all the diverse virtues that they fathered. And think of all the shrines that have been dedicated to them in memory of their immortal issue, and tell me if you can of *anyone* whose mortal children have brought him so much fame.

Well now, my dear Socrates, I have no doubt that even you might be initiated into these, the more elementary mysteries of Love. But I don't know whether you could apprehend the final revelation, for so far, you know, we are only at the bottom of the true scale of perfection.

Never mind, she went on, I will do all I can to help you understand, and you must strain every nerve to follow what I'm saying.

Well then, she began, the candidate for this initiation cannot, if his efforts are to be rewarded, begin too early to devote himself to the beauties of the body. First of all, if his preceptor instructs him as he should, he will fall in love with the beauty of one individual body, so that his passion may give life to noble discourse. Next he must consider how nearly related the beauty of any one body is to the beauty of any other, when he will see that if he is to devote himself to loveliness of form it will be absurd to deny that the beauty of each and every body is the same. Having reached this point, he must set himself to be the lover of every lovely body, and bring his passion for the one into due proportion by deeming it of little or of no importance.

Next he must grasp that the beauties of the body are as nothing to the beauties of the soul, so that wherever he meets with spiritual loveliness, even in the husk of an unlovely body, he will find it beautiful enough to fall in love with and to cherish—and beautiful enough to quicken in his heart a longing for such discourse as tends toward the building of a noble nature. And from this he will be led to contemplate the beauty of laws and institutions. And when he discovers how nearly every kind of beauty is akin to every other he will conclude that the beauty of the body is not, after all, of so great moment.

And next, his attention should be diverted from institutions to the sciences, so that he may know the beauty of every kind of knowledge. And thus, by scanning beauty's wide horizon, he will be saved from a slavish and illiberal devotion to the individual loveliness of a single boy, a single man, or a single institution. And, turning his eyes toward the open sea of beauty, he will find in such contemplation the seed of the most fruitful discourse and the loftiest thought, and reap a golden harvest of philosophy, until, confirmed and strengthened, he will come upon one single form of knowledge, the knowledge of the beauty I am about to speak of.

And here, she said, you must follow me as closely as you can.

Whoever has been initiated so far in the mysteries of Love and has viewed all these aspects of the beautiful in due succession, is at last drawing near the final revelation. And now, Socrates, there bursts upon him that wondrous vision which is the very soul of the beauty he has toiled so long for. It is an everlasting loveliness which neither comes nor goes, which neither flowers nor fades, for such beauty is the same on every hand, the same then as now, here as there, this way as that way, the same to every worshiper as it is to every other.

Nor will his vision of the beautiful take the form of a face, or of hands, or of anything that is of the flesh. It will be neither words, nor knowledge, nor a something that exists in something else, such as a living creature, or the earth, or the heavens, or anything that is—but subsisting of itself and by itself in an eternal oneness, while every lovely thing partakes of it in such sort that, however much the parts may wax and wane, it will be neither more nor less, but still the same inviolable whole.

And so, when his prescribed devotion to boyish beauties has carried our candidate so far that the universal beauty dawns upon his inward sight, he is almost within reach of the final revelation. And this is the way, the only way, he must approach, or be led toward, the sanctuary of Love. Starting from individual beauties, the quest for the universal beauty must find him ever mounting the heavenly ladder, stepping from rung to rung—that is, from one to two, and from two to *every* lovely body, from bodily beauty to the beauty of institutions, from institutions to learning, and from learning in general to the special lore that pertains to nothing but the beautiful itself—until at last he comes to know what beauty is.

And if, my dear Socrates, Diotima went on, man's life is ever worth the living, it is when he has attained this vision of the very soul of beauty. And once you have seen it, you will never be seduced again by the charm of gold, of dress, of comely boys, or lads just ripening to manhood; you will care nothing for the beauties that used to take your breath away and kindle such a longing in you, and many others like you, Socrates, to be always at the side of the beloved and feasting your eyes upon him, so that you would be content, if it were possible, to deny yourself the grosser necessities of meat and drink, so long as you were with him.

But if it were given to man to gaze on beauty's very self—unsullied, unalloyed, and freed from the mortal taint that haunts the frailer loveliness of flesh and blood—if, I say, it were given to man to see the heavenly beauty face to face, would you call his, she asked me, an unenviable life, whose eyes had been opened to the vision, and who had gazed upon it in true contemplation until it had become his own forever?

And remember, she said, that it is only when he discerns beauty itself through what makes it visible that a man will be quickened with the true, and not the seeming, virtue—for it is virtue's self that quickens him, not virtue's semblance. And when he has brought forth and reared this perfect virtue, he shall be called the friend of god, and if ever it is given to man to put on immortality, it shall be given to him.

This, Phaedrus—this, gentlemen—was the doctrine of Diotima. I was convinced, and in that conviction I try to bring others to the same creed, and to convince them that, if we are to make this gift our own, Love will help our mortal nature more than all the world. And this is why I say that every man of us should worship the god of love, and this is why I cultivate and worship all the elements of Love myself, and bid others do the same. And all my life I shall pay the power and the might of Love such homage as I can. So you may call this my eulogy of Love, Phaedrus, if you choose; if not, well, call it what you like.

Socrates took his seat amid applause from everyone but Aristophanes, who was just going to take up the reference Socrates had made to his own theories, when suddenly there came a knocking at the outer door, followed by the notes of a flute and the sound of festive brawling in the street.

Go and see who it is, said Agathon to the servants. If it's one of our particular friends you can ask him in, but if not, you'd better say the party's over and there's nothing left to drink.

Well, it wasn't long before they could hear Alcibiades shouting in the courtyard, evidently very drunk, and demanding where Agathon was, because he *must* see Agathon at once. So the flute girl and some of his other followers helped him stagger in, and there he stood in the doorway, with a mass of ribbons and an enormous wreath of ivy and violets sprouting on his head, and addressed the company.

Good evening, gentlemen, he said. I'm pretty well bottled already, so if you'd rather I didn't join the party, only say the word and I'll go away, as soon as I've hung this wreath on Agathon's head—which is what I really came for. I couldn't get along yesterday, so here I am tonight, with a bunch of ribbons on my head, all ready to take them off and put them on the head of the cleverest, the most attractive, and, I may say—well, anyway, I'm going to crown him. And now I suppose you're laughing at me, just because I'm drunk. Go on, have your laugh out, don't mind me. I'm not so drunk that I don't know what I'm saying, and you can't deny it's true. Well, what do you say, gentlemen? Can I come in on that footing? And shall we all have a drink together, or shan't we?

At that they all cheered and told him to come in and make himself at home, while Agathon gave him a more formal invitation. And while his people helped him in he started pulling off the ribbons, so that he could transfer them to Agathon's head as soon as he was near enough. As it happened, the wreath slipped over his eyes and he didn't notice Socrates, although he sat down on the same couch, between him and Agathon—for Socrates had made room for him as soon as he came in. So down he sat, with a "How d' you do!" to Agathon, and began to tie the ribbons round his head.

Then Agathon said to the servants, Here, take off Alcibiades' shoes, so that we can all three make ourselves comfortable.

Yes, do, said Alcibiades. But just a minute, who's the third?

And when he turned round and saw who it was, he leaped out of his seat and cried, Well I'll be damned! You again, Socrates! So that's what you're up to, is it?—The same old game of lying in wait and popping out at me when I least expect you. Well, what's in the wind tonight? And what do you mean by sitting *here,* and not by Aristophanes or one of these other humorists? Why make such a point of sitting next to the handsomest man in the room?

I say, Agathon, said Socrates, I'll have to ask you to protect me. You know, it's a dreadful thing to be in love with Alcibiades. It's been the same ever since I fell in love with him;

I've only got to look at anyone who's in the least attractive, or say a single word to him, and he flies into a fit of jealous fury, and calls me the most dreadful names, and behaves as if it was all he could do to keep his hands off me. So I hope you'll keep an eye on him, in case he tries to do me an injury. If you can get him to be friends, so much the better, but if you can't, and if he gets violent, you'll really have to protect me—for I should fear to think what lengths he might go to in his amorous transports.

Friends with *you*? said Alcibiades. Not on your life! I'll be getting my own back on you one of these days, but at the moment—Agathon, give me back some of those ribbons, will you? I want to crown Socrates' head as well—and a most extraordinary head it is. I don't want him to say I wreathed a garland for Agathon and none for him, when *his* words have been too much for all the world—and all his life too, Agathon, not just the other day, like yours.

So saying, he crowned Socrates' head with a bunch of ribbons, and took his seat again.

And now, gentlemen, he said, as he settled himself on the couch, can I be right in thinking that you're sober? I say, you know, we can't have this! Come on, drink up! You promised to have a drink with me. Now, I'll tell you, there's no one fit to take the chair at this meeting—until you've all got reasonably drunk—but me. Come on, Agathon, tell them to bring out something that's worth drinking out of.

No, never mind, he went on. Here, you, just bring me that wine cooler, will you?

He saw it would hold a couple of quarts or so. He made them fill it up, and took the first drink himself, after which he told them to fill it again for Socrates, and remarked to the others, But I shan't get any change out of *him*. It doesn't matter *how* much you make him drink, it never makes him drunk.

Meanwhile the servant had filled the wine cooler up for Socrates and he had his drink.

But here Eryximachus broke in, Is this the way to do things, Alcibiades? he asked. Is there to be no grace before we drink? Are we to pour the wine down our throats like a lot of thirsty savages?

Why, there's Eryximachus, said Alcibiades, the noblest, soberest father's soberest, noblest son, what? Hallo, Eryximachus!

Hallo yourself, said Eryximachus. Well, what do you say?

What do *you* say? retorted Alcibiades. We have to take *your* orders, you know. What's the tag?—"A good physician's more than all the world." So let's have your prescription.

Here it is, then, said Eryximachus. Before you came in we had arranged for each of us in turn, going round from left to right, to make the best speech he could in praise of Love. Well, we've all had our turn; so since you've had your drink without having made a speech I think it's only right that you should make it now. And then, when you've finished, you can tell Socrates to do whatever you like and he can do the same to the next man on his right, and so on all the way round.

That's a very good idea, Eryximachus, said Alcibiades. Only you know it's hardly fair to ask a man that's more than half cut already to compete with a lot of fellows who are practically sober. And another thing, my dear Eryximachus. You mustn't believe a word of what Socrates has just been telling you. Don't you see that it's just the other way round? It's him that can't keep his hands off *me* if he hears me say a good word for anyone—god or man—but him.

Oh, do be quiet, said Socrates.

You can't deny it, retorted Alcibiades. God knows I've never been able to praise anyone else in front of you.

Now there's a good idea, said Eryximachus. Why don't you give us a eulogy of Socrates?

Do you really mean that? asked Alcibiades. Do you think I ought to, Eryximachus? Shall I go for him, and let you all hear me get my own back?

Here, I say, protested Socrates. What are you up to now? Do you want to make me look a fool with this eulogy, or what?

I'm simply going to tell the truth—you won't mind that, will you?

Oh, of course, said Socrates, you may tell the truth; in fact I'll go so far as to say you must.

Then here goes, said Alcibiades. There's one thing, though. If I say a word that's not the solemn truth I want you to stop me right away and tell me I'm a liar—but I promise you it won't be my fault if I do. On the other hand, you mustn't be surprised if I tell them about you just as it comes into my head, and jump from one thing to another. You can't expect anyone that's as drunk as I am to give a clear and systematic account of all *your* eccentricities.

Well, gentlemen, I propose to begin my eulogy of Socrates with a simile. I expect he'll think I'm making fun of him, but, as it happens, I'm using this particular simile not because it's funny, but because it's true. What he reminds me of more than anything is one of those little sileni[1] that you see on the statuaries' stalls; you know the ones I mean—they're modeled with pipes or flutes in their hands, and when you open them down the middle there are little figures of the gods inside. And then again, he reminds me of Marsyas the satyr.

Now I don't think even you, Socrates, will have the face to deny that you *look* like them, but the resemblance goes deeper than that, as I'm going to show. You're quite as impudent as a satyr, aren't you? If you plead not guilty I can call witnesses to prove it. And aren't you a piper as well? I should think you were—and a far more wonderful piper than Marsyas, who had only to put his flute to his lips to bewitch mankind. It can still be done, too, by anyone who can play the tunes he used to play. Why, there wasn't a note of Olympus' melodies that he hadn't learned from Marsyas. And whoever plays them, from an absolute virtuoso to a twopenny-halfpenny flute girl, the tunes

1. [Sileni are representations of the satyr Silenus.]

will still have a magic power, and by virtue of their own divinity they will show which of us are fit subjects for divine initiation.

Now the only difference, Socrates, between you and Marsyas is that you can get just the same effect without any instrument at all—with nothing but a few simple words, not even poetry. Besides, when we listen to anyone else talking, however eloquent he is, we don't really care a damn what he says. But when we listen to you, or to someone else repeating what you've said, even if he puts it ever so badly, and never mind whether the person who's listening is man, woman, or child, we're absolutely staggered and bewitched. And speaking for myself, gentlemen, if I wasn't afraid you'd tell me I was completely bottled, I'd swear on oath what an extraordinary effect his words have had on me—and still do, if it comes to that. For the moment I hear him speak I am smitten with a kind of sacred rage, worse than any Corybant, and my heart jumps into my mouth and the tears start into my eyes—oh, and not only me, but lots of other men.

Yes, I've heard Pericles and all the other great orators, and very eloquent I thought they were, but they never affected me like that; they never turned my whole soul upside down and left me feeling as if I were the lowest of the low. But this latter-day Marsyas, here, has often left me in such a state of mind that I've felt I simply couldn't go on living the way I did—now, Socrates, you can't say that isn't true—and I'm convinced that if I were to listen to him at this very moment I'd feel just the same again. I simply couldn't help it. He makes me admit that while I'm spending my time on politics I am neglecting all the things that are crying for attention in myself. So I just refuse to listen to him—as if he were one of those Sirens, you know—and get out of earshot as quick as I can, for fear he keep me sitting listening till I'm positively senile.

And there's one thing I've never felt with anybody else—not the kind of thing you'd expect to find in me, either—and that is a sense of shame. Socrates is the only man in the world that can make me feel ashamed. Because there's no getting away from it, I know I ought to do the things he tells me to, and yet the moment I'm out of his sight I don't care what I do to keep in with the mob. So I dash off like a runaway slave, and keep out of his way as long as I can, and then next time I meet him I remember all that I had to admit the time before, and naturally I feel ashamed. There are times when I'd honestly be glad to hear that he was dead, and yet I know that if he did die I'd be more upset than ever—so I ask you, what is a man to do?

Well, that's what this satyr does for me, and plenty like me, with his pipings. And now let me show you how apt my comparison was in other ways, and what extraordinary powers he has got. Take my word for it, there's not one of you that really knows him. But now I've started on him, I'll show him up. Notice, for instance, how Socrates is attracted by good-looking people, and how he hangs around them, positively gaping with admiration. Then again, he loves to appear utterly uninformed and ignorant—isn't that like Silenus? Of course it is. Don't you see that it's just his outer casing, like those little figures I was telling you about? But believe me, friends and fellow drunks, you've only got to open him up and you'll find him so full of temperance and sobriety that you'll hardly believe your eyes. Because, you know, he doesn't really care a row of pins about good looks—on the contrary, you can't think how much he looks down on them—or money, or any of the honors that most people care about. He doesn't care a curse for anything of that kind, or for any of us either—yes, I'm telling you—and he spends his whole life playing his little game of irony, and laughing up his sleeve at all the world.

I don't know whether anybody else has ever opened him up when he's been being serious, and seen the little images inside, but I saw them once, and they looked so godlike, so golden, so beautiful, and so utterly amazing that there was nothing for it but to do exactly what he told me. I used to flatter myself that he was smitten with my youthful charms, and I thought this was an extraordinary piece of luck because I'd only got to be a bit accommodating and I'd hear everything he had to say—I tell you, I'd a pretty high opinion of my own attractions. Well, I thought it over, and then, instead of taking a servant with me as I always used to, I got rid of the man, and went to meet Socrates by myself. Remember, I'm bound to tell you the whole truth and nothing but the truth; so you'd all better listen very carefully, and Socrates must pull me up if I begin telling lies.

Well, gentlemen, as I was saying, I used to go and meet him, and then, when we were by ourselves, I quite expected to hear some of those sweet nothings that lovers whisper to their darlings when they get them alone—and I liked the idea of that. But not a bit of it! He'd go on talking just the same as usual till it was time for him to go, and then he said goodbye and went.

So then I suggested we should go along to the gymnasium and take a bit of exercise together, thinking that something was bound to happen there. And, would you believe it, we did our exercises together and wrestled with each other time and again, with not a soul in sight, and still I got no further. Well, I realized that there was nothing to be gained in *that* direction, but having put my hand to the plow I wasn't going to look back till I was absolutely certain how I stood; so I decided to make a frontal attack. I asked him to dinner, just as if I were the lover trying to seduce his beloved, instead of the other way round. It wasn't easy, either, to get him to accept, but in the end I managed to.

Well, the first time he came he thought he ought to go as soon as we'd finished dinner, and I was too shy to stop him. But next time, I contrived to keep him talking after dinner, and went on far into the night, and then, when he said he must be going, I told him it was much too late and pressed him to stay the night with me. So he turned in on the couch beside me—where he'd sat at dinner—and the two of us had the room to ourselves.

So far I've said nothing I need blush to repeat in any company, but you'd never have heard what I'm going to tell you now if there wasn't something in the proverb, "Drunkards and children tell the truth"—drunkards anyway. Besides, having once embarked on my eulogy of Socrates it wouldn't be fair not to tell you about the arrogant way he treated me. People say, you know, that when a man's been bitten by a snake he won't tell anybody what it feels like except a fellow sufferer, because no one else would sympathize with him if the pain drove him into making a fool of himself. Well, that's just how I feel, only I've been bitten by something much more poisonous than a snake; in fact, mine is the most painful kind of bite there is. I've been bitten in the heart, or the mind, or whatever you like to call it, by Socrates' philosophy, which clings like an adder to any young and gifted mind it can get hold of, and does exactly what it likes with it. And looking round me, gentlemen, I see Phaedrus, and Agathon, and Eryximachus, and Pausanias, and Aristodemus, and Aristophanes, and all the rest of them—to say nothing of Socrates himself—and every one of you has had his taste of this philosophical frenzy, this sacred rage; so I don't mind telling *you* about it because I know you'll make allowances for me—both for the way I behaved with Socrates and for what I'm saying now. But the servants must put their fingers in their ears, and so must anybody else who's liable to be at all profane or beastly.

Well then, gentlemen, when the lights were out and the servants had all gone, I made up my mind to stop beating about the bush and tell him what I thought point-blank.

So I nudged him and said, Are you asleep, Socrates?

No, I'm not, he said.

Then do you know what I think? I asked.

Well, what?

I think, I said, you're the only lover I've ever had who's been really worthy of me. Only you're too shy to talk about it. Well, this is how I look at it. I think it'd be just as absurd to refuse you *this* as anything else you wanted that belonged to me or any of my friends. If there's one thing I'm keen on it's to make the best of myself, and I think you're more likely to help me there than anybody else, and I'm sure I'd find it harder to justify myself to men of sense for refusing to accommodate a friend of that sort than to defend myself to the vulgar if I *had* been kind to him.

He heard me out, and then said with that ironical simplicity of his, My dear Alcibiades, I've no doubt there's a lot in what you say, if you're right in thinking that I have some kind of power that would make a better man of you, because in that case you must find me so extraordinarily beautiful that your own attractions must be quite eclipsed. And if you're trying to barter your own beauty for the beauty you have found in me, you're driving a very hard bargain, let me tell you. You're trying to exchange the semblance of beauty for the thing itself—like Diomede and Glaucus swapping bronze for gold. But you know, my dear fellow, you really must be careful. Suppose you're making a mistake, and I'm not worth anything at all. The mind's eye begins to see clearly when the outer eyes grow dim—and I fancy yours are still pretty keen.

To which I replied, Well, I've told you exactly how I feel about it, and now it's for you to settle what's best for us both.

That sounds reasonable enough, he said. We must think it over one of these days, and do whatever seems best for the two of us—about this and everything else.

Well, by this time I felt that I had shot my bolt, and I'd a pretty shrewd idea that I'd registered a hit. So I got up, and, without giving him a chance to say a word, I wrapped my own cloak round him—for this was in the winter—and, creeping under his shabby old mantle, I took him in my arms and lay there all night with this godlike and extraordinary man—you can't deny that, either, Socrates. And after *that* he had the insolence, the infernal arrogance, to laugh at my youthful beauty and jeer at the one thing I was really proud of, gentlemen of the jury—I say "jury" because that's what you're here for, to try the man Socrates on the charge of arrogance—and believe it, gentlemen, or believe it not, when I got up the next morning I had no more *slept* with Socrates, within the meaning of the act, than if he'd been my father or an elder brother.

You can guess what I felt like after *that*. I was torn between my natural humiliation and my admiration for his manliness and self-control, for this was strength of mind such as I had never hoped to meet. And so I couldn't take offense and cut myself off from his society, but neither was there any way I could think of to attract him. I knew very well that I'd no more chance of getting at him with money than I had of getting at Ajax with a spear, and the one thing I'd made sure would catch him had already failed. So I was at my wits' end, and went about in a state of such utter subjection to the man as was never seen before.

It was after all this, you must understand, that we were both sent on active service to Potidaea, where we messed together. Well, to begin with, he stood the hardships of the campaign far better than I did, or anyone else, for that matter. And if—and it's always liable to happen when there's fighting going on—we were cut off from our supplies, there was no one who put such a good face on it as he. But on the other hand, when there was plenty to eat he was the one man who really seemed to enjoy it, and though he didn't drink for choice, if we ever pressed him to he'd beat the lot of us. And, what's the most extraordinary thing of all, there's not a man living that's ever seen Socrates drunk. And I dare say he'll have a chance to show what he's made of before *this* party's over.

Then again, the way he got through that winter was most impressive, and the winters over there are pretty shocking. There was one time when the frost was harder than ever, and all the rest of us stayed inside, or if we did go out we wrapped ourselves up to the eyes and tied bits of felt and sheepskins over our shoes, but Socrates went out in the same old coat he'd always worn, and made less fuss about walking on the ice in his bare feet than we did in our shoes. So much so, that the men began to look at him with some suspicion and actually took his toughness as a personal insult to themselves.

Well, so much for that. And now I must tell you about another thing "our valiant hero dared and did" in the course of the same campaign. He started wrestling with some problem or other about sunrise one morning, and stood there lost in thought, and when the answer wouldn't come he still stood there thinking and refused to give it up. Time went on, and by about midday the troops noticed what was happening, and naturally they were rather surprised and began telling each other how Socrates had been standing there thinking ever since daybreak. And at last, toward nightfall, some of the Ionians brought out their bedding after supper—this was in the summer, of course—partly because it was cooler in the open air, and partly to see whether he was going to stay there all night. Well, there he stood till morning, and then at sunrise he said his prayers to the sun and went away.

And now I expect you'd like to hear what kind of a show he made when we went into action, and I certainly think you ought to know. They gave me a decoration after one engagement, and do you know, Socrates had saved my life, absolutely singlehanded. I'd been wounded and he refused to leave me, and he got me out of it, too, armor and all. And as you know, Socrates, I went straight to the general staff and told them *you* ought to have the decoration, and you can neither deny that nor blame me for doing it. But the authorities thought they'd rather give it to me, because of my family connections and so forth, and you were even keener than they were that I should have it instead of you.

And then, gentlemen, you should have seen him when we were in retreat from Delium. I happened to be in the cavalry, while he was serving with the line. Our people were falling back in great disorder and he was retreating with Laches when I happened to catch sight of them. I shouted to them not to be downhearted and promised to stand by them. And this time I'd a better chance of watching Socrates than I'd had at Potidaea—you see, being mounted, I wasn't quite so frightened. And I noticed for one thing how much cooler he was than Laches, and for another how—to borrow from a line of yours, Aristophanes—he was walking about with the same "lofty strut and sideways glance" that he goes about with here in Athens. His "sideways glance" was just as unconcerned whether he was looking at his own friends or at the enemy, and you could see from half a mile away that if you tackled *him* you'd get as good as you gave—with the result that he and Laches both got clean away. For you're generally pretty safe if that's the way you look when you're in action; it's the man whose one idea it is to get away that the other fellow goes for.

Well, there's a lot more to be said about Socrates, all very peculiar and all very much to his credit. No doubt there's just as much to be said about any of his little ways, but personally I think the most amazing thing about him is the fact that he is absolutely unique; there's no one like him, and I don't believe there ever was. You could point to some likeness to Achilles in Brasidas and the rest of them; you might compare Nestor and Antenor, and so on, with Pericles. There are plenty of such parallels in history, but you'll never find anyone like Socrates, or any ideas like his ideas, in our own times or in the past—unless, of course, you take a leaf out of my book and compare him, not with human beings, but with sileni and satyrs—and the same with his ideas.

Which reminds me of a point I missed at the beginning; I should have explained how his arguments, too, were exactly like those sileni that open down the middle. Anyone listening to Socrates for the first time would find his arguments simply laughable; he wraps them up in just the kind of expressions you'd expect of such an insufferable satyr. He talks about pack asses and blacksmiths and shoemakers and tanners, and he always seems to be saying the same old thing in just the same old way, so that anyone who wasn't used to his style and wasn't very quick on the uptake would naturally take it for the most utter nonsense. But if you open up his arguments, and really get into the skin of them, you'll find that they're the only arguments in the world that have any sense at all, and that nobody else's are so godlike, so rich in images of virtue, or so peculiarly, so entirely, pertinent to those inquiries that help the seeker on his way to the goal of true nobility.

And there, gentlemen, you have my eulogy of Socrates, with a few complaints thrown in about the unspeakable way he's treated me. I'm not the only one, either; there's Charmides, and Euthydemus, and ever so many more. He's made fools of them all, just as if he were the beloved, not the lover. Now, Agathon, I'm telling you this for your own good, so that you'll know what to look out for, and I hope you'll learn from our misfortunes, and not wait for your own to bring it home to you, like the poor fool in the adage.

As Alcibiades took his seat there was a good deal of laughter at his frankness—especially as he seemed to be still in love with Socrates. But the latter said, I don't believe you're as drunk as you make out, Alcibiades, or you'd never have given the argument such a subtle twist and obscured the real issue. What you were really after—though you only slipped it in casually toward the end—was to make trouble between me and Agathon, so that I as your lover, and he as your beloved, should both belong to you and nobody else. But you can't humbug me; I can see what you're getting at with all this satyr and silenus business. I only hope, Agathon, my dear, that he won't succeed, and I hope you'll be very careful not to let anybody come between us.

I'm inclined to think you're right, Socrates, said Agathon. Remember how he sat down in the middle so as to keep us apart. But—I'll come round and sit next to you, so that won't help him very much.

Yes, do, said Socrates. Come round the other side.

Oh, God! cried Alcibiades. Look what I have to put up with! He's determined to drive me off the field. All the same, Socrates, I think you might let Agathon sit in the middle.

Oh, no, said Socrates, that would never do. Now you've finished singing my praises, I've got to do the same by the next man on my right. So you see, if he sat next to you, he'd have to start eulogizing me before he'd had my eulogy of him. So be a good chap and let the boy alone; you mustn't grudge him the praise I'm going to give him, because I'm dying to start my eulogy.

Aha! cried Agathon. You don't catch me staying *here* much longer, Alcibiades. I shall certainly change places if it means a tribute from Socrates.

Oh, it's always the same, said Alcibiades bitterly. No one else gets a look in with the beauties when Socrates is there. Look how easily he trumped up an excuse for Agathon to sit beside him.

And then, all of a sudden, just as Agathon was getting up to go and sit by Socrates, a whole crowd of revelers came to the door, and finding it open, as someone was just going out, they marched straight in and joined the party. No sooner had they sat down than the whole place was in an uproar; decency and order went by the board, and everybody had to drink the most enormous quantities of wine. By this time Eryximachus and Phaedrus and some of the others were beginning to leave, so Aristodemus told me, while he himself fell off to sleep.

He slept on for some time, for this was in the winter and the nights were long, and when at last he woke it was near daybreak and the cocks were crowing. He noticed that all the others had either gone home or fallen asleep, except Agathon and Aristophanes and Socrates, who were still awake and drinking out of an enormous bowl which they kept passing round from left to right. Socrates was arguing with the others—not that Aristodemus could remember very much of what he said, for, besides having missed the beginning, he was still more than half asleep. But the gist of it was that Socrates was forcing them to admit that the same man might be capable of writing both comedy and tragedy—that the tragic poet might be a comedian as well.

But as he clinched the argument, which the other two were scarcely in a state to follow, they began to nod, and first Aristophanes fell off to sleep and then Agathon, as day was breaking. Whereupon Socrates tucked them up comfortably and went away, followed, of course, by Aristodemus. And after calling at the Lyceum for a bath, he spent the rest of the day as usual, and then, toward evening, made his way home to rest. ~

Interpretive Questions for Discussion

Why are human beings so confused about the nature of love, according to the *Symposium*?

1. Why does Plato present his dialogue on love as a symposium that considers the views of speakers other than Socrates?

2. Why is the story of the symposium retold by Apollodorus, a follower of Socrates who runs down others for wasting their lives "doing absolutely nothing"? (205)

3. Why do all of the speakers feel qualified and eager to speak on behalf of love? Why do all agree that love is misunderstood and defamed, and stands in need of a hymn of praise?

4. Why does Socrates complain that none of the previous speakers have spoken the truth about love, even though all have upheld its virtue and power for good?

5. Why does Pausanias focus on how the laws and attitudes of Athens are contradictory with regard to love? Why are the two kinds of love Pausanias describes—the earthly and the heavenly—both sexual? (214–217)

6. Are we meant to think that Socrates has difficulty reconciling true love with Pausanias' longing for boys—in which the "compliance" of the beloved is bought with the lover's "wealth" of wisdom and virtue? (219, 244)

7. Why does Aristophanes suggest that "mankind has never had any conception of the power of Love"? (224) Why does he portray love as a yearning to be merged into an "utter oneness"? (228)

8. Why does Socrates disparage Aristophanes' idea that lovers are searching for their other halves? (245–246)

9. Why do Aristophanes' globular beings have to fall from perfect happiness in order to become human?

10. Why do Socrates and Aristophanes agree that love is a longing lovers feel for "something to which they can neither of them put a name"? (228, 243, 245)

11. Does following the Socratic ideal of love involve a denial of nature?

12. Does Socrates agree with Pausanias that love can be a temptation to vice, or does he believe that the soul moved by love can do no wrong? (214–215)

Suggested textual analyses

Pages 215–217: beginning, "But I cannot help thinking, gentlemen," and ending, "shocked at the idea of yielding to a lover."

Pages 226–229: beginning, "Fortunately, however, Zeus felt so sorry for them," and ending, "upon the natures most congenial to our own."

Why does Diotima characterize the essence of love as a longing after wisdom?

1. Why does Socrates say that love is the one thing in the world he understands, although he complains of lacking wisdom? (208, 210)

2. If women are incapable of the virtue of a man, why does Socrates claim to have learned the nature of love from Diotima?

3. Why does Socrates downplay the physical in giving the true account of the nature of love?

4. Why do Socrates and Diotima use the "method of inquiry by question and answer" to teach about love? (240)

5. Why does Diotima teach that love is not a longing for the beautiful, "but for the conception and generation that the beautiful effects"? (246)

6. Is the vision of the "very soul of beauty" described by Diotima a divine revelation or the final achievement of reason? (251–253)

7. Is the earthly love of Pausanias a step on the heavenly ladder to Diotima's final vision?

8. Does Socratic love "bridge the gulf between one human being and another," or does it merely spur the lover on in the quest for an inhuman beauty? (227)

9. Why does Plato have Diotima portray love in the image of Socrates—as barefoot and "at once desirous and full of wisdom, a lifelong seeker after truth"? (242)

10. Is "discourse" the essence of all forms of love for Socrates? (251)

11. Is love for Socrates an intellectual or an emotional journey? Does Diotima's account of love become more impersonal and less emotional the further one progresses on the heavenly ladder?

12. Has Socrates achieved the final vision, or is he still climbing the heavenly ladder?

Suggested textual analyses

Pages 246–247: beginning, "I'll try to speak more plainly, then," and ending, "Love is a longing for immortality."

Pages 250–253: beginning, "Well then, she began," and ending, "if not, well, call it what you like."

Why does the *Symposium* conclude with the arrival of a drunken Alcibiades, who both loves Socrates and wishes him dead?

1. Why does Socrates have the power to turn Alcibiades' "whole soul upside down" and make him feel ashamed? (258)
2. Why is Socrates unable to impart his wisdom to Alcibiades and convert him?
3. Why does Socrates play his "little game of irony" when he squabbles with Alcibiades over Agathon? (254–255, 266–267)
4. Why does Alcibiades compare Socrates and his ideas to a hollow statue of Silenus with "little figures of the gods inside"? (257, 259, 265)
5. Is it arrogance or lack of self-love that keeps Alcibiades from ascending the heavenly ladder?
6. Why does Plato include the story of how Socrates refused to be seduced by Alcibiades? (261–263)
7. Why does Plato bring out not only Socrates' love of wisdom and beauty, but his courage, temperance, and ability to bear privations?
8. Does Socrates' philosophy enable him to enjoy life more fully than others?
9. Does Socrates purposely make a show of standing still for hours when considering a philosophical problem? Does he mean to irritate others by living life so simply? (207, 263–264)
10. Why does the *Symposium* end with an invasion by a crowd of revelers who join the party uninvited and create a drunken, indecent uproar in which Socrates is the only one left standing?
11. Why is the final discussion about whether the same person can write both comedy and tragedy?

12. Is Socrates successful in teaching others the way of love?

Suggested textual analysis
Pages 258–262: beginning, "Yes, I've heard Pericles," and ending, "than if he'd been my father or an elder brother."

For Further Reflection

1. Is a love relationship between equals more stable or less stable than one in which there is a dominant and a subordinate personality?
2. Can understanding Socrates' philosophy of love help us to love wisely?
3. Is love a search for truth, beauty, and wisdom? Is sexual attraction a part of this search?
4. Is love essentially an expression of our physical or biological natures, or is the ability to love an indication that we have a higher nature?
5. Are some people, by their natures, unable to climb the heavenly ladder?
6. Do you agree with Aristophanes that true lovers want to become one with the beloved?
7. Is love a longing for immortality?
8. Are human beings "lovers of the good" only, or can they also love the ugly and the destructive?
9. Does love lead the soul to the good and the true?
10. Should love be regulated by law, as Pausanias suggests?

Poetry

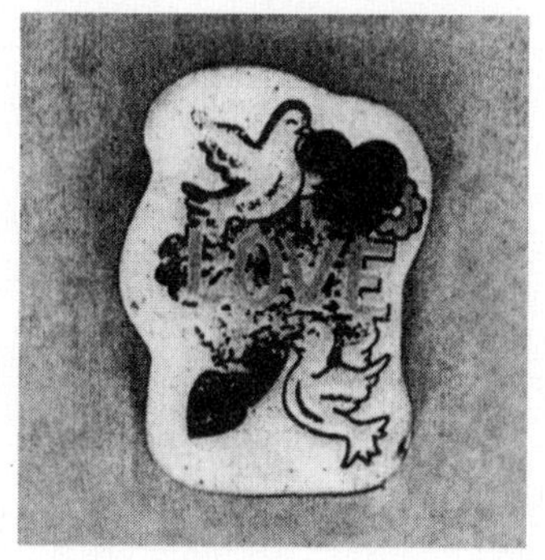

William Shakespeare

Sylvia Plath

Gregory Corso

Gwendolyn Brooks

WILLIAM SHAKESPEARE (1564–1616) wrote at least thirty-seven plays as well as numerous poems, including the sonnets. Born in Stratford-upon-Avon, Shakespeare pursued a successful career as an actor-playwright in London—his theater company became the King's Men under James I in 1603. He prospered financially and was able to buy one of the largest houses in Stratford, where he eventually retired.

~

SYLVIA PLATH (1932–1963), born in Boston, saw her first volume of poetry, *The Colossus,* published in 1960. Her most highly regarded collection, *Ariel,* was written during the last months of her life and published posthumously in 1965. Plath's only novel, *The Bell Jar,* originally published under a pseudonym in 1963, is a fictionalized account of the nervous breakdown Plath experienced when she was in college. Plath suffered severe bouts of depression throughout her adult life and committed suicide in 1963. She was married to the British poet Ted Hughes.

GREGORY CORSO (1930–), a native of New York, became a leading member of the beat movement in the 1950s. Raised in an orphanage and a series of foster homes, Corso went to prison for the first time at the age of twelve. His formal education ended at the sixth grade, but during a second term for theft at the age of seventeen, Corso was introduced to books by an older inmate, and he began to write poetry. Corso left prison in 1950 and soon struck up a friendship with the poet Allen Ginsberg, who further guided his education as a writer. Students at Harvard and Radcliffe gathered the money to publish Corso's first book, *The Vestal Lady on Brattle,* in 1955.

~

GWENDOLYN BROOKS (1917–) was born in Topeka, Kansas, and grew up in Chicago. Her first book of poetry, *A Street in Bronzeville,* was published in 1945. In 1950, Brooks became the first African American poet to be awarded the Pulitzer Prize. She succeeded Carl Sandburg as poet laureate of Illinois in 1968, and received the National Medal of Arts in 1995.

Sonnet 116

LET ME NOT to the marriage of true minds
Admit impediments. Love is not love
Which alters when it alteration finds,
Or bends with the remover to remove:
Oh, no! it is an ever-fixèd mark,
That looks on tempests and is never shaken;
It is the star to every wandering bark,
Whose worth's unknown, although his height be taken.[1]
Love's not Time's fool, though rosy lips and cheeks
Within his bending sickle's compass come;
Love alters not with his brief hours and weeks,
But bears it out even to the edge of doom.
If this be error and upon me proved,
I never writ, nor no man ever loved.

William Shakespeare

1. [*height be taken:* height above the horizon measured for purposes of navigation.]

The Applicant

FIRST, ARE YOU our sort of a person?
Do you wear
A glass eye, false teeth or a crutch,
A brace or a hook,
Rubber breasts or a rubber crotch,

Stitches to show something's missing? No, no? Then
How can we give you a thing?
Stop crying.
Open your hand.
Empty? Empty. Here is a hand

To fill it and willing
To bring teacups and roll away headaches
And do whatever you tell it.
Will you marry it?
It is guaranteed

To thumb shut your eyes at the end
And dissolve of sorrow.
We make new stock from the salt.
I notice you are stark naked.
How about this suit—

Black and stiff, but not a bad fit.
Will you marry it?
It is waterproof, shatterproof, proof
Against fire and bombs through the roof.
Believe me, they'll bury you in it.

Now your head, excuse me, is empty.
I have the ticket for that.
Come here, sweetie, out of the closet.
Well, what do you think of *that?*
Naked as paper to start

But in twenty-five years she'll be silver,
In fifty, gold.
A living doll, everywhere you look.
It can sew, it can cook,
It can talk, talk, talk.

It works, there is nothing wrong with it.
You have a hole, it's a poultice.
You have an eye, it's an image.
My boy, it's your last resort.
Will you marry it, marry it, marry it.

Sylvia Plath

Marriage

SHOULD I get married? Should I be good?
Astound the girl next door with my velvet suit and
faustus hood?
Don't take her to movies but to cemeteries
tell all about werewolf bathtubs and forked clarinets
then desire her and kiss her and all the preliminaries
and she going just so far and I understanding why
not getting angry saying You must feel! It's beautiful
to feel!
Instead take her in my arms lean against an old crooked
tombstone
and woo her the entire night the constellations in the sky—

When she introduces me to her parents,
back straightened, hair finally combed, strangled by a tie,
should I sit knees together on their 3rd degree sofa
and not ask Where's the bathroom?
How else to feel other than I am,
often thinking Flash Gordon soap—
O how terrible it must be for a young man
seated before a family and the family thinking
We never saw him before! He wants our Mary Lou!
After tea and homemade cookies they ask What do you do
for a living?

Should I tell them? Would they like me then?
Say All right get married, we're losing a daughter
but we're gaining a son—
And should I then ask Where's the bathroom?

O God, and the wedding! All her family and her friends
and only a handful of mine all scroungy and bearded
just wait to get at the drinks and food—
And the priest! he looking at me as if I masturbated
asking me Do you take this woman for your lawful
wedded wife?
And I trembling what to say say Pie Glue!
I kiss the bride all those corny men slapping me on
the back
She's all yours, boy! Ha-ha-ha!
And in their eyes you could see some obscene honeymoon
going on—
Then all that absurd rice and clanky cans and shoes
Niagara Falls! Hordes of us! Husbands! Wives! Flowers!
Chocolates!
All streaming into cozy hotels
All going to do the same thing tonight
The indifferent clerk he knowing what was going to
happen
The lobby zombies they knowing what
The whistling elevator man he knowing
The winking bellboy knowing
Everybody knowing! I'd be almost inclined not to do anything!
Stay up all night! Stare that hotel clerk in the eye!
Screaming: I deny honeymoon! I deny honeymoon!
running rampant into those almost climactic suites
yelling Radio belly! Cat shovel!
O I'd live in Niagara forever! in a dark cave beneath the Falls
I'd sit there the Mad Honeymooner
devising ways to break marriages, a sourge of bigamy
a saint of divorce—

But I should get married I should be good
How nice it'd be to come home to her
and sit by the fireplace and she in the kitchen
aproned young and lovely wanting my baby

and so happy about me she burns the roast beef
and comes crying to me and I get up from my big papa chair
saying Christmas teeth! Radiant brains! Apple deaf!
God what a husband I'd make! Yes, I should get married!
So much to do! like sneaking into Mr. Jones' house late at night
and cover his golf clubs with 1920 Norwegian books
Like hanging a picture of Rimbaud on the lawnmower
like pasting Tannu Tuva postage stamps all over the picket
   fence
like when Mrs. Kindhead comes to collect for the Community
   Chest
grab her and tell her There are unfavorable omens in the sky!
And when the mayor comes to get my vote tell him
When are you going to stop people killing whales!
And when the milkman comes leave him a note in the bottle
Penguin dust, bring me penguin dust, I want penguin dust—

Yet if I should get married and it's Connecticut and snow
and she gives birth to a child and I am sleepless, worn,
up for nights, head bowed against a quiet window, the past
   behind me,
finding myself in the most common of situations a trembling
   man
knowledged with responsibility not twig-smear nor Roman
   coin soup—
O what would that be like!
Surely I'd give it for a nipple a rubber Tacitus
For a rattle a bag of broken Bach records
Tack Della Francesca all over its crib
Sew the Greek alphabet on its bib
And build for its playpen a roofless Parthenon

No, I doubt I'd be that kind of father
not rural not snow no quiet window
but hot smelly tight New York City
seven flights up, roaches and rats in the walls

a fat Reichian wife screeching over potatoes Get a job!
And five nose running brats in love with Batman
And the neighbors all toothless and dry haired
like those hag masses of the 18th century
all wanting to come in and watch TV
The landlord wants his rent
Grocery store Blue Cross Gas & Electric Knights of Columbus
Impossible to lie back and dream Telephone snow,
  ghost parking—
No! I should not get married I should never get married!
But—imagine If I were married to a beautiful sophisticated
  woman
tall and pale wearing an elegant black dress and long
  black gloves
holding a cigarette holder in one hand and a highball in
  the other
and we lived high up in a penthouse with a huge window
from which we could see all of New York and even farther on
  clearer days
No, can't imagine myself married to that pleasant prison
  dream—

O but what about love? I forget love
not that I am incapable of love
it's just that I see love as odd as wearing shoes—
I never wanted to marry a girl who was like my mother
And Ingrid Bergman was always impossible
And there's maybe a girl now but she's already married
And I don't like men and—
but there's got to be somebody!
Because what if I'm 60 years old and not married,
all alone in a furnished room with pee stains on my underwear
and everybody else is married! All the universe married but me!

Ah, yet well I know that were a woman possible as I am
possible
then marriage would be possible—
Like SHE in her lonely alien gaud waiting her Egyptian lover[1]
so I wait—bereft of 2,000 years and the bath of life.

Gregory Corso

1. [In a science fiction novel by H. Rider Haggard, "She" gains eternal youth by bathing in a pillar of flame, and waits centuries for the return of her lover.]

To Be in Love

To be in love
Is to touch things with a lighter hand.

In yourself you stretch, you are well.

You look at things
Through his eyes.
A Cardinal is red.
A sky is blue.
Suddenly you know he knows too.
He is not there but
You know you are tasting together
The winter, or light spring weather.

His hand to take your hand is overmuch.
Too much to bear.

You cannot look in his eyes
Because your pulse must not say
What must not be said.

When he
Shuts a door—
Is not there—
Your arms are water.

And you are free
With a ghastly freedom.

You are the beautiful half
Of a golden hurt.

You remember and covet his mouth,
To touch, to whisper on.

Oh when to declare
Is certain Death!

Oh when to apprize
Is to mesmerize,

To see fall down, the Column of Gold,
Into the commonest ash.

Gwendolyn Brooks

Interpretive Questions for Discussion

In sonnet 116, why does the poet resolve not to admit impediments to love?

1. Why does the poet speak of love as "the marriage of true minds"?
2. Why does the poet not "admit" that tempests and "alteration" are impediments to love?
3. Why does the poet compare love to a star that guides a wandering ship? Why does he say the worth of love is "unknown"?
4. Why, according to the poem, would love not be love if it altered?
5. Why does the poet say that love is not "Time's fool," even though he acknowledges time's power over us?
6. Why does the poet close his lofty ode to love by proclaiming the absurd consequences of his being mistaken?
7. Why does the poet begin the poem with the words "let me" rather than "let us"?

In "The Applicant," why does the poet imagine marriage as a contract between a needy "applicant" and a "living doll"?

1. To whom is the applicant applying? Why is neither the man nor the woman given anything to say in the transaction?
2. Why must the applicant be an incomplete person in order to be given a wife? Why does he dissolve into tears under the speaker's questioning?
3. Why does the speaker describe the wife as a comforting hand, an "it" that is "guaranteed / To thumb shut your eyes at the end / And dissolve of sorrow"?
4. Why is the wedding suit described as if it were an impregnable suit of armor that will become the applicant's burial suit?
5. Why is the sweetie from the closet—"a living doll"—the "ticket" for an empty head?
6. Why do both the applicant and the prospective bride appear naked before the speaker?
7. Why is marriage the applicant's "last resort"?
8. According to the poem, does neither partner stand to gain from this marriage?

Why can't the man speaking in "Marriage" imagine marriage in any form that he can accept?

1. Why is the speaker both obsessed with and confused about marriage?
2. Why does the speaker imagine shocking the girl next door by dressing like Faust and taking her to cemeteries instead of to the movies?

3. Why does the fact that everyone would know what is going to happen on his honeymoon make the speaker want to "deny honeymoon" and become a "saint of divorce"?
4. Why does the speaker's vision of domestic bliss—his wife "in the kitchen / aproned young and lovely wanting my baby"—degenerate into nonsense such as asking the milkman for penguin dust?
5. Why does the speaker imagine finding himself as a parent "in the most common of situations a trembling man / knowledged with responsibility"? Why does he worry that as a parent he would be either too much of a pedant or too much of a bum?
6. Why does the speaker think of being married to a beautiful, sophisticated woman as a "pleasant prison dream"? Why can't he take this image seriously?
7. Why doesn't the speaker remember love until the end of the poem? Why does he see love "as odd as wearing shoes"?
8. Why does the speaker think marriage would be possible only if he could find "a woman possible as I am possible"? Why doesn't he portray this scenario as he has the others?

Why is the speaker in "To Be in Love" ultimately disappointed by love?

1. Why, according to the poem, is to be in love "to touch things with a lighter hand"?
2. Why does the speaker say that when you are in love you are well "in yourself"?
3. Why does the speaker say that being in love involves looking through "his" eyes at quite ordinary and simple things? Why is a simple caress "too much to bear"?

4. Why does the speaker have to hide her passion from her lover, even though "he knows too"? Why is it "certain Death" to "declare"?

5. Why, when her lover "shuts a door," does the speaker experience a "ghastly freedom" instead of merely a sense of loss? Why doesn't she experience his absence as "tasting together," as before?

6. Why does the speaker describe herself as "the beautiful half/Of a golden hurt"?

7. Are we meant to think that the love described in the poem has remained a secret from the beloved?

8. Is the poem suggesting that love is delicate and beautiful, or a deception whose reality is "the commonest ash"?

For Further Reflection

1. Does a marriage of true minds admit impediments?

2. Is it realistic to expect love to remain unaltered with the passage of time?

3. Are these poets too cynical or too idealistic about love and marriage?

4. Is the choice of marriage the choice of a whole way of life?

5. Is the reality of marriage obscured by the many popular images of married life and its attractions or dangers?

Questions for

To the Lighthouse

Virginia Woolf

VIRGINIA WOOLF (1882–1941), along with James Joyce and Marcel Proust, ushered in the modernist age in literature. With her husband, Leonard Woolf, and her sister, Vanessa Bell, Woolf played a central role in the Bloomsbury Group of writers, philosophers, and artists that included Lytton Strachey, John Maynard Keynes, Roger Fry, and E. M. Forster. In addition to her novels and numerous essays, Woolf kept a diary throughout her adult life and wrote thousands of letters, now published as *The Diary of Virginia Woolf* (5 vols.) and *The Letters of Virginia Woolf* (6 vols.). *To the Lighthouse,* published in 1927, is considered by many to be Woolf's masterpiece, simultaneously the most autobiographical of her novels and the most universal.

NOTE: All page references are from the Harcourt Brace & Company (Harvest) edition of *To the Lighthouse* (first printing 1989).

Interpretive Questions for Discussion

Why is Lily unable to achieve the intimacy she longs for with Mrs. Ramsay?

1. Why does Mrs. Ramsay both admire and condescend to Lily?

2. Why does Lily's love for the Ramsay family allow her to experience life as a whole, rather than as "little separate incidents"? (47)

3. Why does Lily think that the rapture Mr. Bankes feels when he watches Mrs. Ramsay reading to James is meant to be "spread over the world and become part of the human gain"? (47–48)

4. Why does Lily laugh hysterically at the thought of Mrs. Ramsay "presiding with immutable calm over the destinies which she completely failed to understand"? (50)

5. Why does Lily, sitting with her head in Mrs. Ramsay's lap late one night, imagine pressing through into the older woman's "secret chambers" of the "mind and heart"? Why is it "unity" more than knowledge that Lily desires? (50–51)

6. Of all Mrs. Ramsay's guests, why is only Augustus Carmichael immune to her civility and beauty? (40–42, 195)

7. Why does Lily conclude that Mrs. Ramsay, and people in general, are "sealed" and can only be known by buzzing around them like a bee around a hive? (51)

8. Why, when he looks at her painting, is Lily able to experience a sense of intimacy with Mr. Bankes that she is unable to achieve with Mrs. Ramsay? (52–54)

9. Why does Mrs. Ramsay feel freedom and peace only when she is alone? Why does she experience this as "losing personality" and a "triumph over life"? (62–63)

10. Why does Lily come to Mrs. Ramsay's aid at the dinner party by responding kindly to Charles Tansley? Why does Lily think that this act cost her a little of her self-respect? (92)

11. What is the "coherence in things," the "stability" that Mrs. Ramsay senses the moment she feels that everything is right at her dinner party? (104–105)

12. Why does Lily reject Mrs. Ramsay's view that "an unmarried woman has missed the best of life"? (49) Why does Lily choose not to marry Mr. Bankes, despite her love for him? (176)

Suggested textual analyses
Pages 45–54 ("The Window," Chapter IX)

Pages 96–111 (from "The Window," Chapter XVII): beginning, "Light the candles," and ending, "it had become, she knew, giving one last look at it over her shoulder, already the past."

Why does Mr. Ramsay need the sympathy of his wife in order to feel a part of life?

1. Why does Mrs. Ramsay revere her husband, a man whom Lily describes as "petty, selfish, vain, egotistical"—a spoiled tyrant, who "wears Mrs. Ramsay to death"? (24)

2. Why is the young James filled with anger and hate for his father when Mr. Ramsay intrudes upon him and Mrs. Ramsay with his demands for sympathy? (36–37)

3. Why are Mr. Ramsay's demands for sympathy compared to both a suckling infant and a rape—the sterile male plunging its "beak of brass" into Mrs. Ramsay's "delicious fecundity"? (37–38)

4. Why does Mrs. Ramsay dislike, "even for a second, to feel finer than her husband"? Why does she not let herself put this dissatisfaction into words? (39)

5. Why does Mrs. Ramsay believe herself happiest when carrying a baby in her arms? Why does she think that the world could condemn her—"say she was tyrannical, domineering, masterful"—but she wouldn't mind if she could always have a baby? (58)

6. Why are we told that Mrs. Ramsay has a more pessimistic view of life than Mr. Ramsay? Why is she more in tune with the sorrows and terrors of life than her husband, the metaphysician? (59–60, 70)

7. Why does Mrs. Ramsay have a presentiment of death as she merges with the Lighthouse beam? (63)

8. Why does Mrs. Ramsay feel that the whole effort of bringing together the people at the dinner party rests on her? Why does a part of her wish that she could give up the effort and, like a sunken ship, whirl round and round to rest on the floor of the sea? (83–84)

9. Why does Mr. Ramsay like to exaggerate his wife's simplicity and her lack of book learning? (121)

10. Why isn't Mrs. Ramsay able to tell her husband, in words, that she loves him? Why does she experience a sense of triumph when she communicates her love to him without saying the words he longs to hear? (123–124)

11. Why does Lily go to such lengths to avoid Mr. Ramsay's demands and "imperious need"? (147) Why does she feel accused of being an "ill-tempered, dried-up old maid" when she refuses to give Mr. Ramsay the sympathy he wants? (151)

12. Why does Lily's praise of Mr. Ramsay's beautiful boots cause his self-pity to dissipate? Why does Lily finally feel genuine sympathy for Mr. Ramsay while he talks about his boots and demonstrates how to tie them? (153–154)

Suggested textual analyses

Pages 36–40 ("The Window," Chapter VII)

Pages 117–124 ("The Window," Chapter XIX)

Pages 145–156 ("The Lighthouse," Chapters I and II)

Why does the trip to the Lighthouse help resolve everyone's feelings about the death of Mrs. Ramsay?

1. Why does chaos reign in the Ramsay family after Mrs. Ramsay dies? Why are they "a house full of unrelated passions"? (148–149)
2. Why does Mr. Ramsay insist that only James and Cam—his two youngest children—accompany him to the Lighthouse ten years after the first trip was aborted?
3. Why do James and Cam have a silent pact never to give in to Mr. Ramsay's tyranny? Why is Cam more wavering in her commitment to the pact than James? (163–165)
4. Why do Cam and James think their father is going to the Lighthouse "in memory of dead people"? Why don't they want to honor their mother in this way? (165)
5. Why does Mr. Ramsay end up comforting himself through his daydream of how women would soothe him and sympathize with him? (166)
6. Why does Lily Briscoe watch the boat's progress to the Lighthouse?

7. Why does James insist that his childhood image of the Lighthouse—"a silvery, misty-looking tower with a yellow eye"—is just as "true" as the stark and straight tower he sees ten years later? (186) Why does the true look of the Lighthouse satisfy James and confirm "some obscure feeling of his about his own character"? (203)

8. Why does James enter into his father's imaginings, saying, "We are driving before a gale—we must sink," half-aloud, exactly as his father said it? (203)

9. Why does Cam feel "this is right, this is it" when she thinks about being protected by her father? Why does she tell herself her father's own heroic imaginary story, "but knowing at the same time what was the truth"? (205)

10. Why does Mr. Ramsay compliment James on his piloting of the boat to the Lighthouse? Why is James "so pleased" that he is "not going to let anybody share a grain of his pleasure"? (206)

11. Why, at the moment that his two children would give him anything he asked, is Mr. Ramsay silent, asking and saying nothing? (207)

12. Why has Lily's effort of looking at the Lighthouse and thinking of Mr. Ramsay landing there "stretched her body and mind to the utmost"? When the boat finally lands, why does Lily feel that she has at last given Mr. Ramsay "whatever she had wanted to give him"? (208)

Suggested textual analyses

Pages 162–170 ("The Lighthouse," Chapter IV)

Pages 182–188 ("The Lighthouse," Chapter VIII)

Pages 202–207 ("The Lighthouse," Chapter XII)

Why is Lily finally able to finish her painting?

1. Why, in her painting of Mrs. Ramsay and James, does Lily make no attempt at likeness, focusing instead on "the relations of masses, of lights and shadows"? Why does she strive for "unity"? (52–53)

2. Early in the dinner party, why does Lily become inspired to avoid an "awkward space" in her painting by moving a tree further into the middle? (84) Why does this thought occupy her throughout the dinner? (92–93, 102)

3. Why has Lily's unfinished picture "been knocking about in her mind" for 10 years? (147) Why, upon her return to the house, does she remember the dinner party and how "it had flashed upon her that she would move the tree to the middle, and need never marry anybody"? (176)

4. Why is Lily so disturbed by Mr. Ramsay's "insatiable hunger for sympathy" that she cannot paint until he and the children leave for the Lighthouse? Why does she think of him as bearing down on her, bringing ruin and chaos every time he approaches her? (148, 150–151)

5. Why is Lily's act of creation described in much the same way as Mr. Ramsay's solitary quest for truth? Why are her doubts about the importance or quality of her paintings so similar to Mr. Ramsay's concerns about his work? (158–159; cf. 33–35)

6. As she works on her painting, why does Lily begin thinking about Mrs. Ramsay and how she "resolved everything into simplicity"? As she recalls Mrs. Ramsay's ability to transform strife into unity, why does Lily reflect that these moments of friendship "stayed in the mind affecting one almost like a work of art"? (160)

7. Why does Lily consider Mrs. Ramsay's wish to make life stand still a way of answering "what is the meaning of life"? Why does Lily say she owes her "revelation" to Mrs. Ramsay? (161)

8. After thinking she does not mourn Mrs. Ramsay, why does Lily suddenly, physically, feel her heart wrung by her memory? Why does she experience Mrs. Ramsay's absence as a "centre of complete emptiness" in the garden and house, and as a "hollowness" in her body? (178–180)

9. Why does Lily feel that if she and Mr. Carmichael together demanded an explanation for why life is so short and inexplicable, then Mrs. Ramsay would return? (178–180)

10. In order to finish her painting, why must Lily realize that she—like Mrs. Ramsay—is a lover "whose gift it was to choose out the elements of things and place them together . . . giving them a wholeness not theirs in life"? (192–193; cf. 161)

11. Why must Lily "start afresh" on her painting and rely on inspiration, rather than concentrate on its design? (193) Why is her painting finished when she draws "a line there, in the centre"? (209)

12. Why does Lily feel that it no longer matters whether her painting is hung in an attic or destroyed? What does Lily mean when she thinks, "I have had my vision"? (208–209)

Suggested textual analyses

Pages 156–162 ("The Lighthouse," Chapter III)

Pages 191–202 ("The Lighthouse," Chapter XI)

Pages 208–209 ("The Lighthouse," Chapter XIII)

For Further Reflection

1. Are we better or worse off with the disappearance of the Mrs. Ramsays of the world who sacrifice themselves for the sake of others?

2. Why is it so difficult to balance the mutuality of marriage with the autonomy necessary for intellectual or artistic achievement?

3. Is it still true that most men strive for knowledge and most women strive for intimacy?

4. Why do married people want everyone else to be married?

5. Is a capacity for empathy like Mrs. Ramsay's more a phenomenon of gender or of individual personality?

Questions for

LOLITA

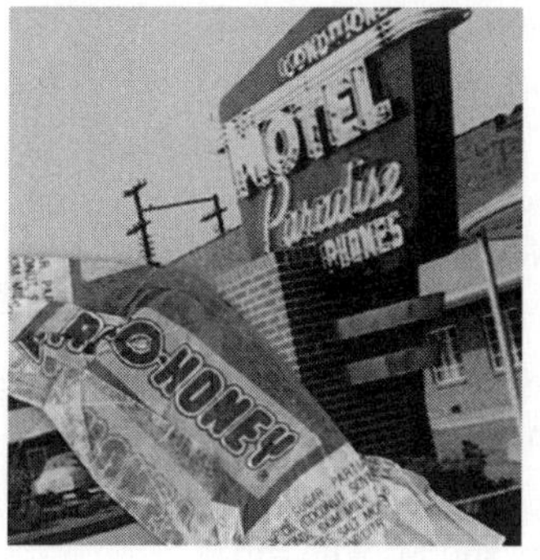

Vladimir Nabokov

VLADIMIR NABOKOV (1899–1977) was born in St. Petersburg into an aristocratic Russian family. Best known for his novels, Nabokov was also a poet, essayist, dramatist, English teacher, literary critic, and entomologist specializing in butterflies. He received a degree in French and Russian literature from Trinity College, Cambridge, in 1922. He then spent the next eighteen years residing in Germany and France, where he pursued his writing, mainly in Russian. During this period, Nabokov published his first eight novels and earned his living by giving lessons in tennis, Russian, and French. In 1940 he moved to the United States and began writing in English while teaching English literature. Although the publication of *Lolita* brought Nabokov wealth, he and his wife still preferred to live in a series of houses they rented from other professors on sabbatical leave: Nabokov's greatest assets were, in his own words, the "unreal estate" of memory and art.

NOTE: All page references are from the Vintage International edition of *Lolita* (first printing 1989).

Interpretive Questions for Discussion

Why does Humbert, an intellectual European gentleman, choose vulgar, ignorant, and conventional Lolita as the great love of his life?

1. Why does Humbert claim at the beginning of his confession that "in a certain magic and fateful way Lolita began with Annabel," his adolescent Riviera love? (14)

2. If, as Humbert claims, he is able to break Annabel's "spell" with Lolita, why is his sexual relationship with her so compulsive? (161, 164–165)

3. Why does Humbert say that he was not concerned with "so-called 'sex' at all," but rather with the greater endeavor of fixing "once for all the perilous magic of nymphets"? (134)

4. Why does Humbert so abhor grown-up women, or even the " 'college girl'—that horror of horrors"? (65, 72)

5. Why does the "bland American Charlotte" frighten Humbert in a way that his first wife, Valeria, never did? (83)

6. What does Humbert mean when he says that what drives him insane is the mixture in Lolita of "tender dreamy childishness and a kind of eerie vulgarity . . . the exquisite stainless tenderness seeping through the musk and the mud, through the dirt and the death"? (44)

7. Why do we learn that Humbert's mother died in a freak accident when he was three, and that nothing of her remains in his memory except "a pocket of warmth in the darkest past"? (10)

8. Why does Humbert say that Lolita had "*already* proved to be something quite different from innocent Annabel" and that there was "nymphean evil breathing through every pore of the fey child"? (124–125)

9. Why does Humbert dream that "Our Glass Lake" is glazed over with a sheet of emerald ice and that a pockmarked Eskimo is trying in vain to break it with a pickaxe? Why does Humbert say that Dr. Blanche Schwarzmann would have paid a sack of schillings for such a "libidream"? (54)

10. If Lolita has already been "utterly and hopelessly depraved" by American mores, why does Humbert feel a "horror" that he can't shake off after having intercourse with Lolita for the first time? (133, 135)

11. Why does Humbert praise Lolita's innocence and grace in language that echoes his extolling of the "heart-rendingly beautiful" American wilds with their "quality of wide-eyed, unsung, innocent surrender"? (168; cf. 232–233)

12. Why does Humbert say that his long journey across America with Lolita had "only defiled with a sinuous trial of slime the lovely, trustful, dreamy, enormous country"? (175–176)

Suggested textual analyses

Pages 38–45 (from Part I, Chapters 10 and 11): beginning, "Reluctantly I followed her downstairs again;" and ending, "and over everything else there is—Lolita."

Pages 166–176 (Part II, Chapter 3)

Why does Humbert say that what he had madly possessed was not Lolita but his "own creation, another, fanciful Lolita . . . having no will, no consciousness—indeed, no life of her own"?

1. Why does Humbert introduce the erotic lap episode as if it were a scene from a play or a segment of film—laying out its main character, time, place, and props? Why does Humbert assert that if his readers participate in the erotic scene he is about to "replay," they will see for themselves how "chaste" the whole event is? (57)

2. Just prior to climaxing during the lap scene, why does Humbert envision Lolita as "safely solipsized"? Why does he feel "above the tribulations of ridicule, beyond the possibilities of retribution"? (60)

3. Why does Humbert instruct his readers to take down the remark "the artist in me has been given the upper hand over the gentleman," and soon after declare, "But I am no poet. I am only a very conscientious recorder"? (71–72)

4. Why does Humbert claim that there are "nymphets"—certain girl-children between the ages of nine and fourteen—who put men of "infinite melancholy" under their spell? (16–17)

5. Why does Lolita "seduce" Humbert when she wakes up to find him in bed with her at the Enchanted Hunters? (132–133)

6. Why does contemplating Lolita's physical grace and beauty when she plays tennis give Humbert the delirious feeling of "teetering on the very brink of unearthly order and splendor"? (230) Is Humbert's appreciation and pursuit of such rapture intended to justify his obsessive love for Lolita?

7. Why does Humbert say that Lolita's tennis was the highest point to which he could imagine a young person "bringing the art of make-believe"? Why does he add that for Lolita, however, it was probably "the very geometry of basic reality"? (231)

8. What does Humbert mean when he says that "the very attraction immaturity has for me lies not so much in the limpidity of pure young forbidden fairy child beauty as in the security of a situation where infinite perfections fill the gap between the little given and the great promised"? (264)

9. Why does Humbert prefer the "mental hygiene of noninterference" when he is confronted with Lolita's unspoken pain at the loss of her mother? (287) Why do both Lolita and Humbert become strangely embarrassed whenever Humbert tries to discuss anything genuine? (284)

10. Why does Humbert find a cure for his second bout of insanity in the sport of duping psychiatrists with invented dreams and fake "primal scenes"? (34–35)

11. Why does Humbert say that the only remedy for the misery of his guilt is the "very local palliative of articulate art"? Why does he quote the lines "The moral sense in mortals is the duty / We have to pay on mortal sense of beauty"? (283)

12. Why does Humbert say that "sex is but the ancilla of art"? (259)

Suggested textual analyses

Pages 57–63 (from Part I, Chapters 13 and 14): beginning, "The Sunday after the Saturday," and ending, "to protect the purity of that twelve-year-old child."

Pages 229–234 (from Part II, Chapter 20): beginning, "By permitting Lolita to study acting," and ending, "An inquisitive butterfly passed, dipping, between us."

Why does Humbert kill Quilty, even though he realizes that while Quilty had broken Lolita's heart, he had broken her life?

1. Why does Humbert think it "intolerable bliss" to have Quilty trapped "after those years of repentance and rage"? (295)
2. Why does the author have Quilty write a play—*The Enchanted Hunters*—with the "profound message . . . that mirage and reality merge in love"? (201)
3. Why does the author put Humbert back on the road with Lolita, involved in an elaborate cat-and-mouse game with priapic Quilty? Why does the author have Humbert, a lover of games, become enmeshed in Quilty's "demoniacal game," his "cryptogrammic paper chase"? (249–250)
4. Why does the author have Lolita fall in love with Quilty? Why does Lolita tell Humbert that Quilty is the only man she has ever been crazy about? (272)
5. Why does Humbert need Lolita to tell him that it was Quilty she ran away with—something he had known "without knowing it, all along"? (272)
6. Why does Humbert think of Quilty as his brother and note that the "tone of his brain" had affinities with his own? (249) Why does the author make Quilty almost impotent, as opposed to the sexually voracious Humbert? (298)
7. Why is Humbert's account of Quilty's murder a mixture of horror and burlesque?
8. Why does Humbert compose a poem that begins "Because you took advantage of a sinner" and make his victim read it aloud? Why does Quilty pause during his reading to give a critique of the poem's merit? (299–300)
9. Why do Quilty and Humbert seem to merge ("I rolled over him. We rolled over me. They rolled over him. We rolled over us.") during their fight for the gun? (299)

10. Why does the author make it necessary for Humbert to shoot and wound Quilty multiple times in order to kill him? Why does Humbert think that his bullets, far from killing Quilty, were injecting "spurts of energy into the poor fellow"? (303)

11. After assuring himself that Quilty is dead, why does Humbert say that "a burden even weightier than the one I had hoped to get rid of was with me, upon me, over me"? (304)

12. Why does Humbert think of the murder as "the end of the ingenious play staged for me by Quilty"? (305)

Suggested textual analysis
Pages 293–305 (Part II, Chapter 35)

Does Humbert transcend the destructive nature of his love for Lolita, or does he remain solipsistic to the end?

1. What does Humbert mean when he says that he had "broken" something within Lolita? Why does the author have Humbert undercut this realization by immediately adding that if Lolita *had* become a "girl champion," he could have been her "gray, humble, hushed husband-coach, old Humbert"? (232)

2. How are we meant to respond to Humbert's claim that there is "no other bliss on earth comparable to that of fondling a nymphet," that it was "a paradise whose skies were the color of hell-flames—but still a paradise"? (166)

3. Why is Humbert suddenly struck by the thought that he does not know a thing about Lolita's mind when he overhears her say, "You know, what's so dreadful about dying is that you are completely on your own"? (284)

4. Is Humbert's moving description of Lolita's despair and helplessness, her efforts to keep some part of herself inviolable, an act of self-mortification or self-pity? (283–284)

5. Are we meant to think of Humbert's passionate admission of his immorality in having inflicted his "foul lust" upon Lolita, thus depriving her of her childhood, as entirely authentic? (283)

6. Why is the story told so that Humbert is captured by the authorities when he is driving on the wrong side of the road? Why does he say that he purposely disregarded the traffic rules "not by way of protest, not as a symbol . . . but merely as a novel experience"? (306)

7. Does Humbert redeem himself when he declares that he loved "*this* Lolita, pale and polluted, and big with another's child, but still gray-eyed, still sooty-lashed, . . . still Carmencita, still mine"? (278)

8. While waiting to surrender himself to the police, why does Humbert recall the time that he listened to the melody of children at play, and knew that "the hopelessly poignant thing was not Lolita's absence from my side, but the absence of her voice from that concord"? (307–308)

9. Why are we told that Lolita (Mrs. "Richard F. Schiller") died giving birth to a stillborn girl? Why does the author embed this information in the fictional foreword by John Ray, Jr., Ph.D.? (4)

10. Is the foreword correct in stating that *Lolita* is a "tragic tale tending unswervingly to . . . a moral apotheosis"? (5)

11. Given the chance, would Humbert take possession of Lolita all over again, or would he leave her free to live out the remainder of her childhood unencumbered by his lust and love? (308–309)

12. Why does Humbert end his confession with the recognition that the "refuge of art" is the only immortality he and Lolita may share? (309)

Suggested textual analysis
Pages 277–287 (from Part II, Chapters 29–32): beginning, "There was not much else to tell," and ending, "was the best I could offer the waif."

For Further Reflection

1. While not pornographic, can *Lolita* justifiably be regarded as an "obscene" book?
2. Is Humbert pitiable or contemptible?
3. Does *Lolita* have a moral purpose in addition to an artistic one?
4. Is Humbert correct in linking evil and passionate love?
5. Does *Lolita* offer insight into the nature of love, or only portray the mind of a sick personality?

A C K N O W L E D G M E N T S

All possible care has been taken to trace ownership and secure permission for each selection in this anthology. The Great Books Foundation wishes to thank the following authors, publishers, and representatives for permission to reprint copyrighted material.

The Spinoza of Market Street, from THE SPINOZA OF MARKET STREET, by Isaac Bashevis Singer. Translated by Martha Glicklich and Cecil Hemley. Copyright 1961, 1989 by Isaac Bashevis Singer. Reprinted by permission of Farrar, Straus & Giroux, Inc.

Either/Or, from EITHER/OR, by Søren Kierkegaard. Translated by Walter Lowrie, David F. Swenson, and Lillian Marvin Swenson. Copyright 1944, 1959, 1987 by Princeton University Press. Reprinted by permission of Princeton University Press.

Emöke, from THE BASS SAXOPHONE, by Josef Škvorecký. Copyright 1977 by Josef Škvorecký. Reprinted by permission of Alfred A. Knopf, Inc.

Caporushes and *Tom-Tit-Tot,* from ENGLISH FAIRY TALES, by Flora Annie Steel. Copyright 1918 by Macmillan Publishing Company; renewed 1946 by Mabel H. Webster. Reprinted by permission of Simon & Schuster.

Patriotism, from DEATH IN MIDSUMMER AND OTHER STORIES, by Yukio Mishima. Translated by Geoffrey W. Sargent. Copyright 1966 by New Directions Publishing Corporation. Reprinted by permission of New Directions Publishing Corporation.

Cover and book design: William Seabright and Associates